**W9-DBG-881**

Praise for
SWISS WATCHING

A FINANCIAL TIMES *BOOK OF THE YEAR*

"We all know that Switzerland gave us the world cuckoo clocks, triangular chocolate and penknives, but how about the Toilet Duck, Velcro and LSD? Europe's 'landlocked island' is a great subject for a cultural anthropologist and Bewes, manager of an English language bookshop in Bern, is a perfect guide."

Financial Times

"A journalist who now lives in Switzerland, Bewes is a well-qualified guide to a country that, although familiar, requires expertise to understand... Bewes reveals how Switzerland is riddled with contradictions... Informative and entertaining."

★ ★ ★ ★

Harry Ritchie, *Mail on Sunday*

"Bewes has an engagingly light and comic touch. The narrative moves between subjects as diverse as graffiti and recycling with ease, and as the book is divided into sections, it's easy to dip in and out of. This isn't a read to change your life, but it will make you smile and perhaps think a little more deeply about cultural stereotypes."

Clover Stroud, *Sunday Telegraph*

"It's a real page turner, a treasure trove. Absolutely jam-packed with fascinating facts that really got me thinking."

Margaret Oertig-Davidson, author of *Beyond Chocolate*

"This book is excellently researched and reads wonderfully well. As well as being packed with material, it contains a heart-warming sense of irony... [It] is in a league of its own."

Jürg Müller, *Swiss Review*

"Everything you wanted to know about Switzerland. Not just a travel book, *Swiss Watching* is a no-stone-left-unturned exploration of what makes (and has made) this enigmatic country tick."

Peter Kerr, author of *Snowball Oranges*

"Diccon Bewes has written the ideal book for Swiss national day. As an Englishman he has the necessary ironic distance, but he knows the object of his enquiry, perhaps better than many a Swiss patriot... Diccon Bewes' background as a travel writer gives the book a special flair: the author's observations are insightful, with a sure eye for comic or exotic detail, and described with typically English humour."

Artur K. Vogel, *Der Bund*

"He is one of those Anglo-Saxon authors who describe foreign countries with a mix of loving irony and a well-trained eye for eccentricity."

Ralph Poehner, *Die Zeit*

"With Swiss Watching Diccon Bewes has achieved a book that holds surprising insights about the Swiss, and not just for foreigners."

Jonathan Spirig, *Berner Zeitung*

"A fascinating book, teeming with facts and figures, and anecdotes which even the Swiss don't know. A journalist, anthropologist and satirist, Diccon Bewes gives us a book that is serious without being academic and funny without ever falling into caricature."

Michel Guillaume, *L'Hebdo*

SWISS WATCHING

Happy travels with Cosa

with best wishes

Diccon

For Gregor

SWISS WATCHING

INSIDE THE LAND OF MILK AND MONEY

DICCON BEWES

THIRD EDITION

NICHOLAS BREALEY
PUBLISHING

London • Boston

This third edition first published in
Great Britain in 2018 by Nicholas Brealey Publishing
An imprint of John Murray Press
An Hachette UK Company

First edition published in 2010 by Nicholas Brealey Publishing

5

A CIP catalogue record for this title is
available from the British Library

ISBN 978-1-473-67741-8
Ebook ISBN UK 978-1-857-88991-8
Ebook ISBN US 978-1-473-64494-6

Printed and bound by Clays Ltd, Elcograf S.p.A.

Nicholas Brealey policy is to use papers that are natural,
renewable and recyclable products and made from wood grown
in sustainable forests. The logging and manufacturing processes
are expected to conform to the environmental
regulations of the country of origin.

Nicholas Brealey Publishing
John Murray Press
Carmelite House
50 Victoria Embankment
London EC4Y 0DZ
Tel: 020 3122 6000

Nicholas Brealey Publishing
Hachette Book Group
Market Place Center, 53 State Street
Boston, MA 02109, USA
Tel: (617) 263 1834

www.nicholasbrealey.com
www.dicconbewes.com

CONTENTS

Ten: Climb every mountain

238

How trains and tourism go hand in hand

Eleven: Seeking Heidi

264

How one little girl is a national icon

List of Maps

A WORD ABOUT NAMES

In a quadrilingual country, there's bound to be some confusion over place names. For example, the city called Geneva in English is known as Genève, Genf, Ginevra and Genevra in the different languages of Switzerland. Luckily, Geneva is an extreme case of multilingualism; other places in Switzerland make do with two or three variations rather than five.

Unlike countless examples in Italy, most Swiss cities escaped the English habit of anglicising the names. In general the British preferred French to German, so it's Neuchâtel not Neuenburg (and certainly never Newcastle), Valais not Wallis, and Lucerne not Luzern. I have stuck to that rule throughout the book, except where the German version has always been used, such as Zug, or where it's become old-fashioned to use French for somewhere in the German-speaking part of Switzerland.

The Swiss tourist board and most English guidebooks now use the German spellings for Bern and Basel, possibly because it's the majority language in both cities. Similarly, Aargau, Thurgau, Graubünden and St Gallen have replaced the hopelessly antiquated Argovia, Thurgovia, Grisons and Saint Gall, all of which are rarely seen in modern publications. It's not a Bombay/Mumbai bout of political correctness, more trying to make it easier for everyone to understand where they are. In English, the most daring thing we do now is leave the umlaut off Zürich; not that any British ear would hear the difference anyway.

For other official names, such as the houses of parliament, I have generally given only the German version, as it's the one used most often. For the German words in the book there are usually French and Italian equivalents, which I have omitted to list, but that doesn't mean they don't exist.

STYLISH PEOPLE

Basel

JURA

Watches

Bern

Holey
Cheese

Chocolate

ROMANDIE

Lausame

ALP

Geneva

MATTERHORN

E 'BIG CANTON'
ks
Zurich
ne
William Tell
Heidi
HERE BE AUSTRIANS
DB
GOTTHARD PASS
GRAUBÜNDEN
Romansh
TICINO
Lugano
N
UD PEOPLE

AUTHOR'S NOTE

Every book has to begin somewhere, but this book had more than one beginning, each of them needed to reach the end.

Its first beginning was getting a job at *Holiday Which?* magazine. They took a chance on me and helped me become a travel writer. Everything that has gone into this book I learned there; without that, these pages would be blank.

Its second beginning was when I met Gregor and became a regular on easyJet flights between London and Switzerland. A long-distance relationship did nothing to improve my bank balance or my dislike of airports, but it gave me the chance to fall in love with another country.

Its third beginning was endless illness and my doctor telling me to leave work, leave London, get some fresh air and get better. Goodbye Britain, hello Switzerland! No lakeside sanatorium or exclusive clinic for me; instead I moved to Bern and never looked back.

Its fourth beginning was after arriving in Switzerland. Armed with both free time and a railcard, I explored the parts I'd never even heard of before. And I began to realise there was more to the country than I'd thought. An awful lot more.

Its last beginning was in a writers' workshop in Geneva. I wrote down a sentence that had been swimming around in my head, and it became a paragraph. Months later the paragraph had turned into a chapter, which secured me an agent, who found me a publisher, who signed me up to write a whole book. So I guess this all began with a girl named Heidi and a man called Ronald.

Now, here's the real beginning.

INTRODUCTION

Close your eyes and tell me the first word you associate with Switzerland. Chances are you'll say cheese. Or chocolate. Or mountains. Or banking, cuckoo clocks, skiing, watches, the Red Cross, snow or Toblerone. Those were the top ten answers when I asked 100 non-Swiss people to do just that, and every single person said something. No don't knows or passes. What was clear is that everyone has something in mind when they think of Switzerland. This small mountainous country at the centre of Europe has captured a place in the imaginations of millions of people.

It's not as if the Swiss themselves are so famous. Let's do that test again, but this time try to name a famous Swiss person. Much harder, isn't it? Of the same 100 people, a quarter couldn't think of a single celebrity from Switzerland; they obviously weren't tennis fans. How odd it is that the Alpine republic has managed to make its products famous the world over but hasn't produced many well-known citizens. Are the Swiss so busy making things and being inventive that they have no time to be famous? Or do they just stay out of the limelight? It seems that while we all have our preconceptions of what Switzerland is like, we don't know much about the people who live there.

Then again, what do we know about the real Switzerland, the enigmatic one behind those clichéd images? The truth might surprise you. Its clean and polite reputation hides a country where graffiti and cigarette ends are commonplace, where queueing is an alien concept, and where recycling is forbidden on Sundays. As for the Swiss themselves, they can be conservative (and yes, even dull), but they have an unexpectedly liberal attitude to drug use and assisted suicide, and are amazingly creative when it comes to technology and

1

innovation. In fact, the Swiss are a nation of contradictions held together by a capacity and the desire to overcome them. How else could they conquer their mountains, repel their enemies and survive for over seven centuries?

This book won't tell you where to eat in Zurich, what to see in Lausanne or how to use the trains. What it will do is take you behind the scenes and beyond the stereotypes on a journey into the heart of Switzerland and the minds of its sometimes quirky people. I'll show you how the breathtaking scenery helped shape a nation not just a tour itinerary, and why tradition is as important as technology. We'll see that the Swiss have more power than their politicians, but can't speak to one other in the same language. You'll meet some famous Swiss people, even if two are fictional, as well as discover what makes the rest of them tick.

But we'll begin with the basics: what has made the Switzerland we know today. The first five chapters show how the country is the product of its geography, history, religion, politics and wealth. Then we move on to what Switzerland has created. A journey around and across the country reveals the real Switzerland behind the Red Cross, watches, cheese, chocolate, trains and Heidi.

By the end, you'll be able to go behind the stereotypes and will have a complete insight into the Swiss identity, and you'll possibly know more about the Swiss and their country than the Swiss do themselves.

ONE

THE LANDLOCKED ISLAND

Switzerland is a country with nine names, and that's not including the English one at the start of this sentence. While it's logical for somewhere with four national languages to have four names, two very Swiss traits make this more complicated: their love of formality and their need for consensus. The former means that there are two levels of politeness in Swiss society, with people using either first or last names; so of course the country also has its own equivalents of formal and informal names. The latter resulted in the ninth, the name that's reduced to the letters CH on the back of Swiss cars.

Let's start, just as the Swiss would, with formal introductions. The Swiss love nothing more than the formality of surnames. People can live in the same building or work together for years and never get past using them. This is changing slowly with the younger generations, but even they often still write and say their last name first and first name last; a quick look on Facebook or a Swiss credit card will show that. Or a phone call. Ring a German-speaking Swiss person[1] and the phone will be answered with one word: a surname, possibly in case you've forgotten who you're calling. But it's not just the names, it's the pronouns that go with them. Whereas English now only has one word for you,[2] German, French and Italian have two levels of formality. With strangers and people older or more important, you stick to surnames and use the formal *Sie, vous* or *lei* to mean 'you'; with family, close friends and children, you can switch to first names and the more familiar *du, tu* or *tu*.

It's the same with the country itself. Any country worth its salt has to have a formal name, and since in Switzerland salt is worth a lot (it's a state-controlled monopoly so there's no free market, only two producers and it's subject to tax[3]), the country has four. In German, the language of the majority,[4] it is *Schweizerische Eidgenossenschaft*, which is as hard to translate as it is to say. The closest in English is Swiss Confederation, the phraseology also used by French, Italian and Romansh, the other three national languages: *Confédération suisse, Confederazione svizzera* and *confederaziun svizra*. In reality *Eidgenossenschaft* means something more like 'the brotherhood of men who stood in a field and swore an oath of eternal cooperation and friendship'; confederation is a lot simpler. *Eidgenosse* is still used by the German-speaking population to refer to the real Swiss, the ones from the original heart of the country.

These formal names are all a bit of a mouthful, so it's no surprise that the Swiss use a much more informal version in everyday life: *Schweiz, Suisse, Svizzera* and *Svizra*, all of which are the equivalent of being on first-name terms. However, with eight different names floating around, half of them far too long to be used in Eurovision Song Contests or football matches, it's no wonder that the Swiss decided to have one official one – not just to make things easier but to have a name acceptable to all the national languages, so that no one could argue that one was being favoured over another. Finding a solution acceptable to all is the Swiss way of doing things, and is perhaps the biggest reason they have managed to overcome their historic divisions. It's all about consensus, but the challenge was reaching one. The solution? Use a long-dead language.

Drive along almost any motorway in Europe and you'll soon see a car with a CH sticker on the back. If you watched too many episodes of *It's a Knockout* or take part in too many pub quizzes, you might know that CH is the international registration code for Switzerland (not just for cars but also for the internet domain suffix .ch). But what if you were asked what those two letters actually stand for? You mentally glide over a map of Europe, searching for a logical answer. There's a flicker of hope when you realise that the codes are abbreviations of a country's name in its own language or in English, so D is for Deutschland and E for España, but FIN is for Finland and GR for Greece. Nevertheless, CH doesn't fit into either; it's in a class of its own.

The answer is not cheese or chocolate, though you'd be surprised how many people could believe that, but *Confœderatio Helvetica*, Switzerland's ninth, and official, name. There can't be many modern countries that have a Latin name, but then again there aren't many countries like Switzerland. The name is derived from the Helvetii, one of the local pre-Roman tribes, and the literal English translation is the Helvetic Confederation. But for a country that prides itself on accuracy – and not just in its train timetables – it's ironic that its official name is technically incorrect.

Until a rather civil civil war in 1847, Switzerland was indeed a confederation, or a loose alliance of autonomous states who more or less cooperated with each other. It was barely a country, in the modern sense of the word, but was definitely more than the sum of its parts. The new state created in 1848 was a federation in everything but name. Despite having a shiny new federal government, the Swiss decided to keep their old title. It might have been inaccurate but it made them feel better about the new-fangled structure, which seemed so centralised and therefore very un-Swiss. And, more significantly for the Swiss, using the old name gives them an unbroken link to their past, something which is fundamental to every Swiss person.

Ask a Swiss man where his *Heimatort*, or place of origin, is and he won't necessarily tell you where he was born but where his ancestors came from, probably a little village halfway up a mountain. It may well be that no one in his family has lived there for generations, but it is this, not the place of birth, that is written in a Swiss passport. In Switzerland knowing where you came from is as important as knowing where you're going to, and that applies as much to the country as its people.

If the paradox of having an official name that doesn't reflect the actual country seems odd, to the Swiss it's normal, because Switzerland itself is a paradox. For this is a country that shouldn't really exist. It defies nature, both Mother and human, with borders that make no geographic, linguistic, religious or political sense.

AT THE HEART OF EUROPE

European countries, unlike many American states, tend not to have straight-line boundaries that march across the map without bothering about complications like rivers and mountains. But even by European standards, Switzerland is a decidedly odd shape. Its borders wiggle all over the place, following rivers then leaping them to create bulges on the other bank, or zigzagging over lakes so that a simple boat trip has you crossing and re-crossing the lines. Essentially, the country looks like a horribly misshapen jigsaw piece, uncomfortably locked into its neighbours. And at times, it can seem like the missing piece, the last one needed to complete the puzzle; one look at a modern map of Europe and you'll notice a Switzerland-shaped hole in the middle of the European Union.

Nevertheless, look at that same map another way and Switzerland changes from a hole in the heart of the continent to an island in the middle of a vast sea of deep blue. It is surrounded on every side by the EU, with Austria, France, Germany and Italy[5] all flying the blue flag dotted with gold stars. This mountainous country isn't huge (at 41,285 square kilometres,[6] it's roughly twice the size of either Wales or New Jersey), but it would be Europe's fourth largest island[7] – and easily its most unusual, not least because it has no coastline. Welcome to the landlocked island!

For most of its history Switzerland has been an anomaly at the centre of Europe, an Alpine republic encircled by monarchies and empires, dictators and generals. Occasionally the tide of history has washed across its borders, bringing Europe's conflicts and ideas into the farthest mountain valleys, but Switzerland has always managed to restore its island status, one it still relishes today. The Swiss have long recognised that their country is often as isolated as any dot of land in the middle of the open sea, and have used their location to their advantage. While historically this was achieved by controlling trade routes or making the most of being surrounded by great powers, the Swiss are still doing it today. For an example, we can look at duty-free.

A duty-free shop is not normally the place to discover how a nation sees itself. In among the stacks of Toblerone, Smirnoff, Chanel and Marlboro you might find a few over-priced 'authentic' souvenirs or delicacies, but such shops are rather like Hiltons or Starbucks: you could be anywhere in the world. At Swiss duty-free shops there was, and periodically still is, a poster that said as much about Swiss business sense as it did about the national mentality. It appeared after duty-free shopping was abolished within the EU[8] and showed Switzerland as a palm-covered island in a sea of very blue water. No matter that, even duty-free, the cigarettes, perfume and alcohol were probably still more expensive than in a supermarket in Milan, Munich or Manchester. The message was clear: this was the last place for tax-free shopping in Europe, the last-chance saloon for anyone gasping for a drop of Johnnie Walker Red Label.

The poster revealed how well the Swiss can grasp an opportunity to capitalise on their position at the heart of Europe, and in the not-so-distant past there have been less charitable examples. Business opportunities aside, the poster also shows how the Swiss see their own country. Eurosceptics might prefer to view Switzerland as a welcome oasis of sanity in the desert of pan-European unity, but the Swiss themselves are more likely to see it as a desert island, albeit one with mountains and glaciers instead of palm trees and ice creams (though they can be found together in Switzerland as well).

Desert islands, both real and imagined, need three basic characteristics to live up to their name: sand, sea and solitude. They offer an escape from the outside world, where you can lie back and let the day slip by to the sound of gently lapping waves, or even a few favourite records. Or perhaps they are a last hope of survival for castaways washed ashore in tattered clothes, with only dates for company. Either way, such islands don't normally have the world's most used train system, one of the highest levels of computer ownership and (arguably) best chocolate. Then again, this is a desert island like no other, not least because it's 200 kilometres from the nearest stretch of seaside.

Although Switzerland may not physically have the three requirements of a desert island, it has long acted as one. It has been both a retreat from the outside world, for those who can afford it, and a lifeboat in a storm, for those who won't rock that boat too much. In fact, the Swiss Family Robinson didn't need to be shipwrecked to find their desert island; they could have just stayed at home. The island status is a mental, not physical one, with inhabitants choosing to isolate themselves from the outside world and, until recently, very often from each other.

The Swiss are very much a product of their geography. Separated by mountains, the valley communities developed in semi-isolation, as shown by the many distinct dialects and customs still in evidence today. It was a case of local things for local people, helping your neighbours, being wary of foreigners and trying not to be different. Some Swiss, particularly those on the right, see that as a lost ideal; for others it's an outdated view that belongs in the past. The funny thing is, they don't always realise that today it's largely true for Switzerland as a whole, though in a much watered-down form. But keeping yourself to yourself, either as an individual or as a community, is very Swiss – and it's all down to the Swiss being a bunch of coconuts.

LIFE'S A PEACH, OR A COCONUT

The German psychologist Kurt Lewin developed an interesting fruity analogy to explain the cultural differences between societies. Fittingly enough for desert islanders, the Swiss are coconuts. This doesn't mean that they are all small, brown and hairy, though some might be, but that they make a clear distinction between public and private spheres of their lives. Breaking through a coconut's outer shell isn't easy, just as it can be hard to get onto first-name terms with Swiss people, or even to get to know them at all. For the Swiss it's clear that most people belong in this outer shell, where surnames are used and private details are not shared. The inner part is reserved for closest friends and family, who use first names and whose relationships last a lifetime; in the case of friendships, this often dates from meeting at primary school or in the Scouts. This private sphere often includes the home, which is rarely opened up to strangers, rendering a Swiss home more fortress than castle. All this can make the Swiss seem cold and distant, but what to outsiders appears unfriendly is actually them respecting personal space and taking time to get to know someone.

9

In contrast to those cautious coconuts, societies in the English-speaking world are all peaches. In the soft, fleshy outer part every stranger is a potential friend, first names are more readily used, the home is more open to all and everything is a lot more relaxed. And since friends can come and go throughout your life, the much smaller inner core is essentially your immediate family, the ones you can't choose or lose. Perhaps the peach works best for Americans, whereas the British are possibly more like pineapples, a little prickly at first, though easier to get past than a coconut shell. Then comes the large, softer part where work colleagues, neighbours, friends and acquaintances all mix without much formality. Last, the family makes up the firmer centre.

While the coconut analogy clearly can't work for everyone, as a general picture it's quite accurate. The Swiss are polite and friendly, but not exactly forthcoming with newcomers, and they certainly like to bunch together. Break through that shell and it's a different story – a Swiss friend is for life, not just for Facebook. But the Swiss and the British are probably more alike than either realise. Both societies are ruled by unspoken etiquette and red tape, and outsiders might find it hard to make friends or become fully integrated. Added to that, both share a reluctance to commit to European federalism, have a common distrust of the Germans and want to keep their own currency.

Of course there are differences too. For example, there is no state religion in Switzerland and there is never likely to be, as the country is evenly split between Catholics and Protestants. And Switzerland is a republic, one of the world's oldest, but Britain a monarchy, though both countries are similarly made up of disparate parts held together by a common will. The fact is that many Swiss are Anglophiles and Brits have always come to Switzerland, with the Swiss tourist industry practically being created just for the English. And, after all, pineapple and coconut together make a great piña colada.

If the Swiss can be seen as coconuts, then Switzerland itself is much like its people, only bigger. On this scale it's the mountains that act as the shell, protecting its inhabitants and stopping outsiders from getting too close. To the rest of the world these mountains are the face of Switzerland, which isn't too surprising given how much they dominate the landscape. It might have to share the Alps with all of its neighbours, but with 48 peaks over 4000 metres, Switzerland can justifiably be called the Roof of Europe. Almost two-thirds of the country is taken up by the Alps, with the Jura range in the northwest making up another 10 per cent of the surface area. And in this land of countless mountains, one stands out: the Matterhorn.

CONQUERING THE MOUNTAINS

There are no world-famous Swiss monuments or buildings: no Taj Mahal or Eiffel Tower or Opera House. Instead there are mountains, and possibly two of the best known in Europe. With its forbidding North Face the Eiger gets more starring roles in books and films, but it's the Matterhorn that is the real Swiss icon. This singular, triangular wonder with a slightly crooked peak is known around the world, though not always at home. None of the 16 candidates for the 2009 Miss Switzerland title could put a name to the photo of the Matterhorn;[9] apparently, competing for that crown really is only about looks. For most other Swiss, however, the Matterhorn is an instantly recognisable symbol of their country, even if they do have to share it with Italy. The mountain lies not in the middle of Switzerland but in the middle of nowhere, down on the Swiss–Italian border. That means that getting there is no picnic: from Zurich, for example, it takes three trains, each smaller and slower than the last, to make the trip up the ever-narrower valleys to Zermatt and beyond. But it's worth it. For one simple reason – the view.

The Matterhorn literally stands out from the crowd. Not because of its size, though at 4478 metres it's more than a pimple, but because it sits in solitary isolation, uncluttered by neighbouring peaks. That's why it looks so majestic, because you can see the whole mountain from bottom to top. And that's exactly where one Englishman went. In 1865 Edward Whymper led the team that scaled the Matterhorn for the first time, though four of them died in the process. Most visitors today are happy to stick with the view from the train or from the end of the line at Gornergrat. From there the panorama includes the Matterhorn, the mighty Gorner Glacier and snowy Dufour Peak,[10] Switzerland's highest. Looking at all that it's hard to believe that, as the crow flies, it's about 70 kilometres to Switzerland's lowest point at Lake Maggiore[11]; that's equivalent to having a height difference of over 4400 metres between Leeds and Sheffield, or Washington DC and Baltimore. Such extremes so close together show how compact Switzerland really is, but also the possible obstacles to even the shortest journey. Then again, the Swiss were never ones to let a few mountains stand in their way.

If there's one date that proves the Swiss commitment to conquering their landscape, it's 25 June 1930. That marks an event that, in the scheme of Swiss transport history, isn't so momentous. It wasn't the opening of the Gotthard Tunnel or the completion of Europe's first mountain railway; it was the inaugural journey of the Glacier Express from Zermatt to St Moritz.[12] The joining of two upmarket ski resorts may not seem like much until you look at the map: the two are at opposite ends of the country and separated by rather a lot of mountain. It's almost as if someone just decided to join the

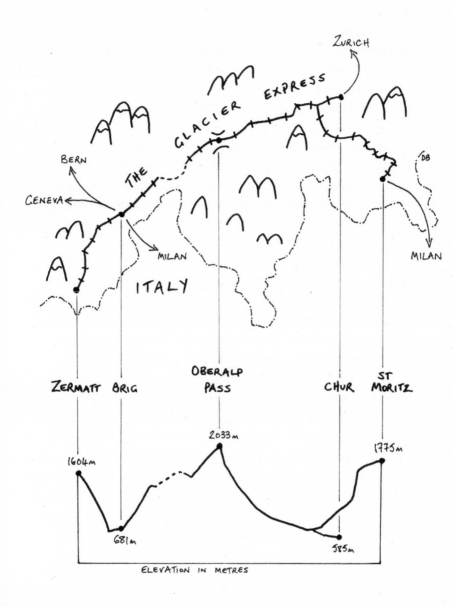

ZURICH

THE GLACIER EXPRESS

BERN

GENEVA

MILAN

ITALY

MILAN

DB

ZERMATT BRIG

OBERALP
PASS

CHUR

ST
MORITZ

2033m

1775m

1604m

681m

585m

ELEVATION IN METRES

13

dots in spite of what was in between. With two altitude changes to overcome, each of 1400 metres, the line resembles a long roller-coaster, though not in speed. It is possibly the world's slowest express train – glacial is a good adjective – but that slow pace, and the glass-roofed panorama cars, means that it's a great ride for seeing the Alps.

The thing about the Glacier Express is not its 291 bridges or 91 tunnels,[13] or even the fact that it runs all year round despite the snow. It's that nowhere along its route is particularly big enough to warrant building such a line. The two largest towns, Brig and Chur, are connected to the rail network by mainline routes, meaning that the Express serves a few villages along the way, as well as tourists wanting the experience. And that's the crucial part. Regular trains run along the same route, stopping at every hamlet, but it's the tourist trains which make the line feasible. In high season you have to reserve well in advance to get a seat, and there's no standing allowed (not that you'd want to for 7½ hours).

From the base of the Matterhorn at Zermatt the train chugs down to the Rhone valley, which is flat enough for it to practically race along to Brig. Then it's up and over the Oberalp Pass – cue splendid craggy peaks softened by lush green meadows, or in winter a white wonderland – before dropping again to the Rhine gorge. It's rather amazing that two of Europe's largest rivers have their sources so close together, with each flowing in a different direction: the Rhine northwards to the North Sea, the Rhone west- then southwards to the Mediterranean. Not forgetting that just over another mountain the Inn begins its eastward journey to the Black Sea, making a triple watershed at the heart of the continent. Include the 1500 or so lakes, Europe's largest waterfalls and a few glaciers, and it's easy to see how Switzerland accounts for 6 per cent of the fresh water in Europe.[14] No wonder over half of the country's electricity comes from hydroelectric stations.[15]

It's perhaps only on the last part of this epic train ride that you really notice the engineering involved. To manage the climb from Chur up to glitzy St Moritz, the line has to curl round on itself repeatedly, going up through loop tunnels blasted in the rock. To cross the ravines it uses towering arched viaducts sitting on stone stilts, and bridges that seem to hang on thin air. All quite enough to give you sweaty hands if you look down at the tumbling waters below.

The Glacier Express shows that for the Swiss the mountains are a challenge rather than a barrier, there to be tunnelled under and driven over. They are also a playground, to be walked up and skied down, as much as a defence against the outside world. They are, in essence, the Swiss equivalent of the sea, the soul of the country and the reason it is the way it is, beautiful and inviting yet defensive and unwelcoming. And, like the sea for any island, they affect the weather. The big difference is that while the Swiss love their mountains, the weather rarely gets a look in.

WHEN THE WIND BLOWS

Ask any Swiss person about the weather and... In fact, don't ask a Swiss person about the weather. It's not something they publicly talk about as willingly as other nations, particularly the British. That's partly to do with the Swiss dislike of small talk, but also because for them it's a pointless conversation. Here's a typical British–Swiss chat about the weather:

Brit, coming in from outside: 'Brrr, it's so cold out today.'
Swiss: 'It's winter.'

Whereas the opening line could be a cue for an exchange about the weather, purely as a way of breaking the ice or making conversation, the Swiss sees it as a statement of fact, and not a very bright one at that: it's winter, therefore it's cold, therefore there's nothing left to talk about. Never mind that last week it was still T-shirt weather, or that the forecast is for 30 centimetres of snow by the weekend, or that it's not nearly as bad as last year (any or all of which could be a natural response in British small talk). This Swiss habit of being direct and stating the facts can give the impression they are either rude or uninterested in you, when in fact they are neither; well, most of them anyway. They're just not used to others wanting to talk about trivia or divulge personal information, particularly with strangers. For a Swiss person, standing beside someone watching the rain in silence is more comfortable than talking about it. The ironic thing is that Swiss weather actually is worth talking about.

Living in the shadow of Europe's highest mountains means that the weather can be both remarkably static and extremely changeable. Systems can sit over Switzerland for days, roasting or freezing its inhabitants, but then something shifts and temperatures change twenty degrees overnight. With all those the mountains and no sea nearby to cool the summer and warm the winter, Swiss weather can reach both extremes: its coldest and hottest recorded temperatures, −41.8°C and 41.5°C respectively,[16] are figures more readily associated with Siberia and Libya.

There is one weather feature that the Swiss love to claim as their own and will happily chat about: the *Föhn*, pronounced roughly like Inspector Clouseau saying 'phone'. Mention that and you won't be able to get a word in for the next few minutes. Whereas its cold counterpart, the *Bise*, blasts chilly air down from the north, the *Föhn* is a wind that comes from the south over the Alps. It generally brings warm, dry air, hence its name; *Föhn* is German for hairdryer, though who knows which came first. But this can be quite some hairdryer, with wind speeds regularly over 100 kilometres an hour[17] and dramatic temperature changes. It's not unusual for it to be 25°C where the *Föhn* is blowing and 6°C a few valleys away.

Perhaps it's this atmospheric disturbance that makes the *Föhn* an ill wind for the Swiss, blamed for causing migraines, suicides and generally unsettling everyone. More likely it's just an extrapolation of the Swiss hatred of draughts in any shape or form. What to you and me is a breath of fresh air to many Swiss is the cause of every illness known to man. Most houses are hermetically sealed to avoid draughts creeping in; no need for sausage-dog draught excluders or heavy curtains in Swiss homes. Despite that, for a few minutes each day windows are thrown open to let out the stale air; apparently that's not a draught, that's healthy. As for opening a train window on anything less than the hottest day of the century, forget it.

It's late July, the sky is blue, the thermometer is nudging 30°C and the sun is streaming in through the train windows. With the carriage feeling like a mobile sauna, you're dripping and your neighbours are turning beetroot; there's no choice but to open a window. You barely manage more than three gulps of mountain air before a Swiss woman comes over and suggests in no uncertain terms that you shut it. She even pulls her scarf tighter round her neck for added effect, though not tight enough for your liking. It seems the draught is annoying her, even though she is sitting four rows in front; must be a mighty strong draught to go against the motion of the train and whoosh across half the carriage. Everyone is watching with bated breath, possibly because of the lack of air, so you compromise and semi-close the window, earning periodic hard stares from the draught lady for the rest of the journey.

Of course Swiss newspapers and television have weather forecasts, usually in the form of a simplified map. And that in itself is enlightening. One look at a Swiss weather map and you can instantly see how the Swiss view their own country, at least in geographic terms.

NORTH AND SOUTH

A typical Swiss weather map is reduced to two halves, north and south, which doesn't mean either side of the Alps. In Swiss shorthand, north means the bit where all the people live and south is where they all go on holiday; that is, the mountains. The latter might be the soul of the country, but modern Switzerland's beating heart is to be found elsewhere, in the flatter foothills known as the Swiss Plateau. With so much wild open space you might not think of Switzerland as crowded, but the inhabited bit is, because everything – people, houses, factories, farms, transport – has to fit into the narrow arc of land between the Alps and Jura mountains. The Plateau stretches from Geneva, across Romandie[18] (the French-speaking part) to Bern, then past Zurich and on to Lake Constance. It hosts all the major cities and two-thirds of Switzerland's 8.4 million people, making it one of the most heavily populated areas in Europe, with 518 people per square kilometre.[19] That's quite a lot more densely populated than South East England[20] and marginally more than the Netherlands.[21] Strangely enough it doesn't feel that overcrowded, possibly because many people live in flats rather than houses, so urban areas are less sprawling. But the fact that most Swiss are squished together might help explain why they keep a little distance; when living space is in short supply, private space is even more important, something to be cherished and protected.

The Swiss Plateau is high but not flat. It's actually an undulating landscape of hills, rivers, lakes and valleys, all of which in many, flatter countries would present enough natural obstacles to hinder the building of an effective transport system. In Switzerland they had bigger problems in the shape of the Alps, but they conquered those as well with roads and railways that are the envy of the world. Ever since the opening of the Gotthard Pass in the thirteenth century, Switzerland has sat at the crossroads of Europe. And it still does. A high-speed corridor of intercity trains and motorways running through the Plateau intersects with the crucial transalpine routes tunnelling under the mountains. It may not be a member, yet, but ironically enough Switzerland is at the heart of the EU's transport network. And all because of those mountains, which are the real north–south divide in Europe.

This Swiss concept of north and south is easy to grasp until you bring in the idea of up and down. For many English speakers up is synonymous with north, and down with south; you go up to Scotland or Canada and down to Devon or Florida. For the Swiss it's about gradient not direction, making up short for uphill or upstream, which is logical for a mountainous country. So the Bernese talk about going down (north) to Basel but up (south) to Interlaken. With most of the country lying in or north of the Alps, the only part that is truly down south is Ticino, the Italian-speaking region; no wonder its residents feel cut off and sidelined from the rest of the country. But Ticino is positively integrated compared to Graubünden, the largest, least densely populated and most isolated canton. Sitting high in the eastern Alps, it is neither north nor south but has a place central to the Swiss view of their country.

Unless you like skiing in posh St Moritz or Klosters, or attend the World Economic Forum in Davos, you probably haven't heard of Graubünden. Whereas most foreign tourists head for the mountains of central Switzerland, many Swiss go east for their holidays, to the wilderness (relatively speaking) of the Engadine and Switzerland's only National Park. Nevertheless, as beautiful as it is, Graubünden is more interesting for linguistic reasons, because it's the only trilingual canton, thanks to a living descendant of Latin: Romansh. Only about 40,000 people use Romansh as a first language,[22] but even then it manages five different dialects and one authorised written version, Rumantsch Grischun. Since a referendum in 1938 it has been classed as a national language, though this being Switzerland, where nothing is uncomplicated, Romansh isn't always an official language.

In a typically Swiss hair-splitting definition, it is only an official language when officialdom has to communicate with Romansh speakers. Federal laws and other official acts don't have to be in Romansh, and outside Graubünden you rarely see or hear it. At a national level, twice as many people use English as their mother tongue as Romansh,[23] but it does at least have a modern seal of linguistic approval – since 2007 Romansh speakers have been able to *tschertgar cun* Google and use Microsoft Office in their own language.[24]

Graubünden is, in many ways, like a mini-Switzerland, with its different languages (but German spoken by the large majority) and a clear but cordial religious divide. Until it consented to become part of Switzerland,[25] Graubünden was once as fiercely independent as the whole country is today, and many of its inhabitants still call themselves *Bündner* before saying they're Swiss. Then again, it is a fairly common Swiss trait to put canton before country. It doesn't matter that your canton has fewer inhabitants than spectators at a Second Division football match, it's your home canton and therefore a source of immense pride. So what exactly is this most Swiss of creations?

MEETING THE CANTONS

The 26 Swiss cantons[26] are the size of British counties but have the power of American states. Each has its own constitution, laws, parliament, courts and flag; it also sets its own taxes, issues car number plates, and has its own police force and education system. In true federal style, the canton is both the basic building block of the country and a balance against the centre having too much power. And for the Swiss, the canton is emotionally as important as the country, if not more so. Of course, this being Switzerland, nothing is that clear-cut or easy to understand.

Six of the 26 are actually half-cantons, not because of their size (some cantons are smaller than these halves) but in political terms. The half-cantons are legally equal to the cantons, having the same powers in almost all aspects of daily life, such as taxation, except when it comes to representation. Then the half-cantons truly are half, in terms of seats in parliament and voting rights in a referendum. The Swiss political system is so different from any other that such fine distinctions are essential. For the six halves to become whole would require a constitutional earthquake and upset the delicate national balance that is the bedrock of Swiss government, not to mention go against centuries of history; if anything is more important than politics in Switzerland, it's history.

For example, the two halves of Appenzell, Innerrhoden and Ausserrhoden, fell out over religion back in the days when such things mattered. While the Aussers turned Protestant, the inner six parishes around the town of Appenzell itself remained Catholic, making a split inevitable. It was all fairly amicable, with both sides voting on the matter, and the six together became Appenzell Innerrhoden. It's the smallest member of the Swiss federal system, with only 16,000 inhabitants. Compare that to the 1.5 million people who live in Canton Zurich and the disparity is clear, just as it is between vast Texas and tiny Rhode Island. Appenzell wasn't the only one unable to stay together. Basel also suffered irreconcilable internal differences over reforms, this time of a political nature, and split into Basel-Stadt and Basel-Land. Each is more populous than quite a few whole cantons, but the historical hangover means that they remain halves.

Ten cantons have a distinct name, such as Ticino or Vaud, but the rest are named after the main town, making it necessary to distinguish between the two. Just as in England there's a big difference between Derby and Derbyshire, so in Switzerland Bern is not the same as Canton Bern. At least the Swiss are logical about it. Haven't you ever wondered what happened to the English towns of Berk, Wilt and Shrop? Their shires remain though the towns are long gone.

The cantons are so independently minded that it can sometimes seem as if there isn't one Switzerland but 26 mini ones, all going in roughly the same direction but each doing their own thing. This is such a part of Swiss life that they have a word for it, *Kantönligeist*. The polite translation is that each canton has its own identity, culture and history; the more realistic is that each is as bloody-minded as its neighbour. And, as cantonal differences are fiercely defended, they're unlikely to disappear any time soon. But it is exactly those differences that make Switzerland a uniquely fascinating place, sometimes making it feel like a country in name only.

Switzerland as an entity, both physical and emotional, is still a relatively new concept, even for some Swiss. The same goes for its capital city.

A TALE OF FIVE CITIES

For centuries the cantons were bound together by pacts but grew independently, rather like the Italian city-states. That's why Switzerland never had one big capital, *à la* Paris or London, but a group of more or less equal cities. Even in today's united country, each of the five large cities has its role: Bern, site of the federal government, is the political centre; Basel, thanks to the pharmaceutical companies, the industrial one; Lausanne, home of the Supreme Court, the legal; Geneva, HQ for the United Nations, the international; and Zurich, the biggest of the five, the economic. It's as if London were to be dissected and dropped off around Britain. Even then, each part would be far larger than Zurich, whose population is only 415,000. Take a walk along the pedestrianised, cobbled streets in the centre of Zurich and it doesn't feel like a big city at all. Londoners and New Yorkers would say that it isn't, but for the Swiss it's a veritable metropolis. Or at least that's how it's marketed by its inhabitants, who like nothing more than to look down on everyone else.

Just as with the cantons, there's a palpable sense of rivalry between the main Swiss cities, and not only on the football pitch. Zurich, as the economic powerhouse, sees itself as superior to the rest, who in turn view its inhabitants as brash and arrogant, with mouths as big as their heads. In contrast, the Bernese, with their rolling dialect and almost country-bumpkin ways, are dismissed as slow, quiet and rather old-fashioned. As for Basel, it's famous for its carnival but remains a mystery to most other Swiss, as if being so close to the border makes it somehow odd. And no one likes its football team; even the Bernese would rather have Zurich win than Basel. All three cities are German speaking, so tend to forget about French-speaking Geneva and Lausanne. Perhaps it's also because neither seems truly Swiss. Geneva is too international, and almost too French, while Lausanne is the closest thing Switzerland has to an alternative culture. That might not be much by other countries' standards, but for the serious (German-speaking) Swiss it's verging on racy.

One thing that all five, and almost every other Swiss town, have in common is that they survived the last century or so untroubled by minor annoyances like world wars, meaning that they have an intact medieval city at their heart. True, around them is usually a body of modern buildings, many of them carbuncles, along with the industry and transport needed by a western society, but compared with many modern urban spaces, Swiss ones are a delight. At first glance, the cities that pass by the train or tram window could be anywhere in Mitteleuropa. They're definitely not British – there are far too few brick buildings and not nearly enough litter – and nor are they Mediterranean – the stone apartment buildings are too solemn and the traffic too well behaved for that. But somehow they don't seem as dour as some German or as pompous as some French cities, almost as if the *Föhn* brings a whiff of something exotic over the Alps that infuses itself into the very fabric of the buildings.

Maybe this mix of northern solidity and southern vibrancy is why Swiss cities are so often rated among the best places in the world to live, though it might have more to do with cleanliness and transport. They may be expensive, even by Swiss standards, but Zurich and Geneva regularly make the top ten of the world's most liveable cities.[27] True, with populations well under half a million they don't have the problems faced by Berlin or Chicago, but even if they did, knowing the Swiss a way would be found to solve them.

Switzerland became a country in spite of its geographical divisions, but it also became the country it is today because of those divisions. The mountains at its heart are the reason it grew up as a collection of distinct communities, and the reason those communities survived and prospered. As we'll see in the next few chapters, this very localised geography has influenced and shaped Swiss history and politics over the centuries. The landscape, and especially the weather, also meant that the Swiss always had to be careful with everything. Surviving the winter took planning and prudence, while compensating for the lack of natural resources needed inventiveness and attention to detail – all pretty much traits the Swiss still show.

Cut off by the mountains, Switzerland has acted like an island for much of its history, living in splendid isolation from the world around it. Or at least thinking it did. However, just as Britain discovered at the start of the twentieth century, so Switzerland realised at the beginning of the twenty-first: no land is an island. Surrounded by the EU and confronted with a global market, the Swiss are slowly, and sometimes reluctantly, building bridges to the outside world. But in their hearts, and minds, they will always be a landlocked island.

SWISS WATCHING TIP NO 1: MEETING AND GREETING

A drinks party, or *Apéro*, is one of the best places to get to know the Swiss — not because they need some wine before they can relax, but because this all-purpose Swiss form of socialising is held at every possible occasion. Organising a leaving do for a colleague? Throw an *Apéro*. Want something less elaborate than a sit-down dinner? Have a stand-up *Apéro*. It can be merely a glass of something alcoholic with some nibbles, but most stretch to finger food, be that savoury tartlets or little cups of pumpkin soup. Supermarkets sell platters of cheese or meat, caterers offer themed menus and posh hotels conjure up gourmet titbits. All because the *Apéro* is a big deal in Switzerland. And once you're at one, a very Swiss custom makes the introductions simple, as long as you know the rules.

Social disgrace is quite easily achieved in Switzerland within minutes of arriving at an *Apéro*. The moment you walk into the room is the moment of truth. It's not about dress codes, because the Swiss rarely have those, or about being late, where a simple apology is enough. It's all about saying hello. At any gathering in Switzerland, every guest's first duty is to go round and greet everyone. Faced with a crowd of people, most of them strangers, you might be tempted to lurk in a corner until you spot someone you know, or wait for your host to make the introductions. Bad idea. What you should do before anything else, and that includes getting a drink, is introduce yourself to everyone, regardless of how long it takes.

Going up to people with an open hand and your name at the ready feels so forward, so American. And so un-Swiss. But it's not a question of being pushy, rather a question of politeness. How rude it would be to stand in a room with someone whose name you did not know. You may never speak to Stefan or Frau Weber again for the rest of the evening, but at least you did the right thing and introduced yourself. This custom is the real reason most Swiss people are punctual. If you arrive first then you can stand around chatting or drinking and so make all the newcomers do the hard work with the introductions. This may feel like being in the receiving line at a wedding reception, but it's better than arriving last. Do that and you face a long wait, and lots of handshakes, before you can relax and have a drink.

While this might all sound rather odd for a nation renowned for its reserve, for the Swiss it's normal. And if you think that all the pressure is on the guests, think again. As a host of anything other than a sit-down dinner, you have to provide food that can be eaten easily and quickly; after all, guests need one hand for a glass and the other free for shaking. If both hands are full, there'd be no handshakes and Swiss society would collapse. Not much pressure, then. Maybe multiple greetings aren't so bad after all.

Nineteen handshakes, nineteen hellos and nineteen name exchanges may sound exhausting, but to help speed things along there is a method in the madness. Just as there are various words for hello – *Grüezi* is the Swiss German norm – there are different levels of hello. The most basic is with complete strangers: a handshake, a name exchange, with optional smile, before moving on. With people you've met before, it's perfectly acceptable to linger a moment or two for a few niceties. But both of you know it would be unseemly to chat too long until you have met everyone else, so you part company. With friends, the handshake is supplemented by three cheek kisses (right–left–right) and a 'How are you?', safe in the knowledge that once your hellos are done, you can return for a proper conversation. It's all second nature to the Swiss, who have been doing this since they were old enough to walk and talk, but for unknowing foreigners it takes some getting used to.

If all that wasn't hard enough, there's also knowing how formal to be. As mentioned above, German has two words for you: *Sie* and *du*. Well, it actually has three, but we'll ignore the third one for now. If others introduce themselves as Herr or Frau So-and-So, then it's *Sie*; first names from the start means it's safe to use *du*. Saying *du* instead of *Sie* is unpardonably rude, but luckily for German learners the *Sie* form of the verb is the simplest so it's easy to be very polite.

At some point you might be offered (or be moved to offer) *Duzis*, or changing from *Sie* to *du*, a clear sign that your friendship has progressed by becoming less formal. After that, you must never use *Sie* again with that person, as that might infer a cooling of the friendship. All of this also applies in French and Italian, just with *vous/tu* and *lei/tu* replacing German *Sie/du*. Simple, isn't it?

Forgetting the rules is more trouble than it's worth. Once, when offering an old lady my seat on a tram, I undid my good deed by inadvertently using *du*. Not only did she remain standing, she proceeded to castigate me for being so forward and impolite. Then again, I have undoubtedly offended countless people by saying *Sie* even though we had agreed to *Duzis*.

If and when you have more than one Swiss German friend, you then need *ihr*, the third form of you and the plural of *du*. Perhaps that's why it's hard to make friends in Switzerland; sticking to the formal *Sie* (which can be singular or plural) is so much easier.

When it comes to chatting, the Swiss art of small talk is simple as it can be very small. Many Swiss people would prefer to sit in silence than chatter about traffic, or holidays or celebrity gossip. And they will certainly never ask, or expect to be asked, anything too personal such as marital status, religious views or the price of their house. Private and public lives are kept very separate, and anyone who freely mixes the two is regarded with suspicion. Polite yes, friendly usually, but sharing their life story in the first few hours (or even months) of meeting – never. As for breaking the ice with a joke, please don't. Jokes are something to share with friends and family, not for strangers or business meetings. Swiss humour does exist, honestly it does, but like sex and money, it's something best kept in the privacy of the home.

Having stumbled through all that, you still have to master the farewells. Leaving a party is, in effect, the same process as arriving but in reverse. You go round, shaking hands as you say goodbye but – and it's a big but – using the person's name. After all, you know the name of everyone there. Trying to remember which name goes with which face feels like a Mensa memory test, so the trick is to wait until someone else starts to leave. As they go round you follow a step or two behind, carefully listening to each name. Then you come along with 'Goodbye Herr Schmidt' and 'See you next time, Petra' and get a gold star for remembering everyone's name. This leaving process gives a whole new meaning to 'saying your goodbyes', with the emphasis on the plural, and can take anything up to half an hour. Nevertheless, merely thanking the hosts and then saying goodbye to the whole gathering is a big no-no; you might as well have 'socially inept' stamped on your forehead. I am still trying to scrub mine clean.

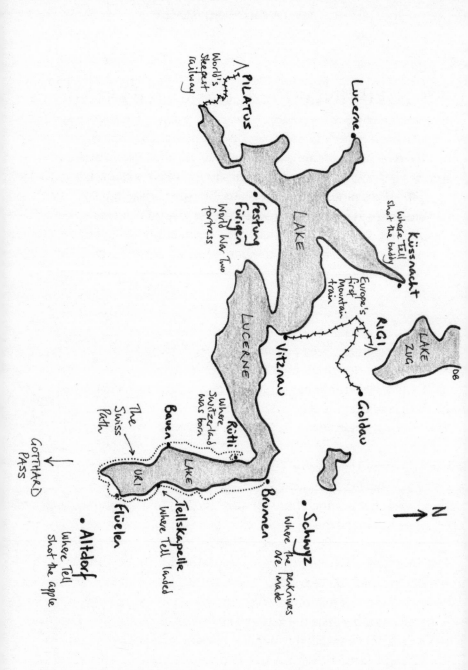

PILATUS
World's steepest railway

Lucerne

Küssnacht
where Tell shot the baddy

Festung Fürigen
World War Two fortress

LAKE

Europe's first Mountain train

RIGI

LAKE ZUG

LUCERNE

Vitznau

Goldau

Where Switzerland was born
Rütli

The Swiss Path

Bauen

LAKE

Brunnen

Schwyz
Where the penknives are made

URI

Tellskapelle
where Tell landed

Flüelen

GOTTHARD PASS

Altdorf
Where Tell shot the apple

N

TWO

STEPPING BACK THROUGH TIME

When it came to commemorating its 700th birthday, Switzerland chose a uniquely Swiss way of doing it: inaugurating a footpath. But the Swiss Path isn't any old path; it's one that involves every single person in the country. In 1991, in honour of the momentous anniversary, it was decided to create a 35-kilometre trail around a lake.[1] In a country criss-crossed with well-beaten tracks, what makes this one stand out is that every 5 millimetres represents one person. Every one of the then seven million inhabitants of Switzerland became a 5-millimetre stretch of path.[2] How precise is that! In a way it's a fittingly Swiss memorial, combining as it does two great national passions: walking and attention to detail. No other country could come up with such a project, let alone execute it so well.

But there's more. To show the 26 different cantons, each has its own section of the path, the length of which is determined by that canton's population in 1991. Smaller cantons like Schaffhausen get a few metres, while populous ones like Zurich get a huge chunk of lake shore. Stone plaques along the path mark the boundaries between the cantonal sections, which are placed in the order of joining the Confederation. Thus this 35-kilometre path symbolises both seven million people and 700 years of history, with each 5 millimetres representing not just one person but also about one hour of the past. And because the cantons appear in chronological order, it is in effect a walk through the history of the country. It's like taking a stroll down Switzerland's memory lane, and the apt starting point for the Swiss Path is the place where Switzerland was born.

31

IN THE BEGINNING

It all began when three men took a vow in a meadow. Not the most dramatic beginning for a country but one which rather suits the modern Switzerland: low key and peaceful, without any bloodshed, beheadings or bullets. The meadow in question, called Rütli, sits above Lake Uri in central Switzerland and is still only accessible by boat or on foot. It isn't at all clear why they had their little oath-swearing ceremony there and not somewhere easier to reach like a town hall or someone's house. In fact, not much of what took place on that day, 1 August 1291, is clear. The number of participants, the location, the oath and the date have all been questioned, but however misty the real history is, this act of allegiance is generally taken to denote the birth of Switzerland. And since 1891, Switzerland has celebrated its birthday with a national holiday on 1 August,[3] one of the few non-religious holidays observed by everybody. Nevertheless, that's not the best day to visit Rütli as it's when the Swiss President goes to make a speech, along with, in recent years, far-right nationalists trying to muscle in on the proceedings. Far better to go on a sunny day in June and enjoy the scenery as much as the history.

Look at a Swiss map and you might well not spot Lake Uri because it's really just the final leg of Lake Lucerne, and that you might also miss because locally it's known as *Vierwaldstättersee*. That's a bit of a mouthful even for a German speaker, although luckily the hardest thing most English visitors have to get their tongue around is an ice cream. We don't bother with 'Lake of the Four Forest Cantons', its literal translation, but take the easier option instead, which is just as logical given what sits at the northern end.

Lucerne is possibly Switzerland's prettiest city and definitely one of its most visited. The cobbled streets and squares seethe with camera-clickers and selfie-snappers, all peering up at the muralled buildings. It's just as bad around the city's most famous landmark, the Chapel Bridge, a covered wooden affair originally built in the fourteenth century. It's a fair bet that few of the massed photo takers realise that this bridge is a replica of the original, most of which burnt down in 1993. New it may be but it is very photogenic, with the imposing stone Water Tower to one side and the not-so-distant hulk of Mount Pilatus brooding in the background. Right across from this picture-perfect spot is the city dock, where a handsome paddle steamer is waiting to go south to Rütli. With a long blast of the horn and a loud hiss of steam, it sets off across the clear blue water.

There can be few more elegant ways to travel than in a gleaming white steamboat, its two large red paddle wheels slicing their way through the water, its wooden decks shimmering in the sun. It feels like the setting for an Agatha Christie novel or a Merchant Ivory film and I half expect Maggie Smith to appear, parasol in hand. From out on the water it's hard to tell that this is Switzerland's second largest lake (after Lake Neuchâtel), simply because its true size is disguised by all the kinks and fingers, bulges and bottlenecks that make up its weird shape. It actually feels rather small, especially further south where the cliffs and hills get steeper and higher, crowding in right down to the water so there's barely any room for habitation.

We progress at a stately, almost languid, pace, zigzagging to stop at villages on both shores, so that it's over two hours before we round the final promontory into Lake Uri. Not that anyone notices; it's not as if there's a canal, or a border or a change in water colour. It is essentially all the same lake, but don't mention that to the good citizens of Canton Uri; they're very possessive about their lake. Only three other passengers disembark; Switzerland's *Heimatort* clearly isn't a top attraction for most tourists, or indeed for many Swiss people.

There's no sign of a meadow; no sign of much at all apart from a lot of rocks, trees and water. The only way off the boat dock is via wooden steps to a switchback path that threads its way up the hillside. Ten minutes later I am standing in Rütli; and I'm rather underwhelmed. It is merely a long, misshapen patch of grass, and a sloping, lumpy one at that, although it is very bucolic, complete with grazing cows and protruding rocks. The only sign that it has national significance is a towering flagpole sporting a giant Swiss flag. If this were in America, it would have been made into a National Park and have a visitor centre, souvenir shop and café all on site; then again, you can't get here by car, so maybe not. In Britain, it would be fenced off to protect the hallowed turf, but you'd be charged to look at it as you listen to an audio guide before buying a commemorative tea towel on your way out. So, on second thoughts, it's rather nice that the Swiss haven't made a big deal of it, meaning that, flagpole apart, it probably hasn't changed much in the past 700-odd years. Certainly, the splendid lake-and-mountain view is timeless. Maybe that's why those three men met here and not down the pub; as well as swearing an oath of mutual support against the Austrians, they wanted a nice day out in the countryside.

Ask most Swiss people who stood in the meadow that day and few will be able to name one let alone all three. It's not as if their faces have been carved into a mountain or put on the banknotes; that wouldn't be very Swiss at all. But neither are there any towns named after them nor many statues in their honour; they are the forgotten founding fathers. So before their names are lost for ever, here they are: Walter Fürst from Canton Uri, Werner Stauffacher from Canton Schwyz and Arnold von Melchtal from Canton Unterwalden. These three men, the original *Eidgenosse*, stood in the August sunshine, placed their left hands together, one on top of the other, raised their right hands above their heads in a sort of elevated scout's honour salute, and swore to help each other through thick and thin, in peace and war, for ever and ever, Amen. Even today, Swiss politicians are sworn in using the same raised, three-fingered salute – clench the two smallest fingers to your palm and stick out the other two with your thumb – and the words *Ich schwöre* or I swear. If most of what actually happened at Rütli is unsubstantiated, what is incontrovertible is that a pact was signed in August 1291 by the first three cantons, and that historic document now sits in its own museum in Schwyz; clearly an essential stop on this magical history tour.

To do the whole 35-kilometre path in one go would take about 15 hours of solid walking, not forgetting that a height difference of 350 metres is involved not once but four times. For many Swiss that's a stroll in the woods, but for normal people it realistically means doing a few sections, dipping in and out of both the cantons and the history on the way. Not forgetting being prepared with sensible shoes and a bottle of water. I leave Rütli and head for the first stone marker.

ON THE TIME TRAIL

Until about 1220 no one took much notice of the remote valleys and villages in what is now Switzerland. Then the route over the St Gotthard Pass opened, and everyone wanted to muscle in on the lucrative trade with the Mediterranean. To do that meant controlling the farmers, whose valleys had sole access to the northern approach to the pass, and they eventually sought protection from the Holy Roman Emperor himself. The communities of Uri and Schwyz were granted imperial freedom, meaning that the Emperor was their only boss, not some local lord or jumped-up duke, although this semi-autonomy wasn't enough of a guarantee. Enter the Austrians as the bad guys in the form of the Habsburg monarchy, who sent in the bailiffs and threw their weight around to get what they wanted. All that did was push the Swiss closer together, culminating in the Rütli pact, one of many around at that time but the only one to have survived in written form.

As none has a particularly large population, between them the first three cantons manage roughly 1 kilometre of path, but it's a steady uphill climb, as it probably was for them too. The one big event in that kilometre's time frame was a Swiss victory against the Austrians in 1315 at the David-and-Goliath battle of Morgarten. Losing there might have crushed Switzerland at birth, but victory encouraged Lucerne to unite with its lakeside neighbours. Then the big cheese at the time, the city of Zurich, joined the Swiss party, and suddenly a large chunk of territory belonged to the nascent confederation. And a lot of people. Lucerne and Zurich account for over 7 kilometres of path; what a pity it couldn't have stayed a club for small cantons for a bit longer. It doesn't help that not a lot happened in those early decades, so no great historical moments to relive during the two-hour walk. Instead I contemplate how many people I am walking on.

Each of my size 42 feet is 26 centimetres long, which means that every step I take is equivalent to 52 people. I feel like a giant, especially when I then consider that if I were to lie down on the path, which would clearly be a rather strange thing to do, I would be lying on 366 people. For those of you bad at maths, that makes me 1.83 metres tall (or six feet, but this is complicated enough in metric so no more conversions). I could start measuring various body parts in terms of numbers of 5-millimetre people, but I'll make do with one. I've never had anyone under my thumb before – now I can have six people all at the same time. Such power. This is a good walk for self-confidence. Maybe that's the secret meaning of this path. It's nothing to do with anniversaries and precision, but all about not feeling small in a big world. Very appropriate for the Swiss. Or alternatively, it could merely be about enjoying the scenery, which is spectacular from this level, with grandstand views across the squintingly bright turquoise lake to craggy mountains. Trust Zurich to nab the most scenic bit of the path. Not that there's a bad bit, with the sections in the woods exuding their own sense of tranquillity and proximity to nature. It helps that, being a weekday and early in the summer, there aren't many other walkers out today, just the odd few to exchange a nod and a *Grüezi* with. Come on a summer weekend and it'd be like rush hour, given how much the Swiss like a good walk.

WHERE BOOTS ARE MADE FOR HIKING

Walking and hiking are a Swiss national obsession. As soon as they can toddle Swiss children are taken on a walk, and it's fairly common to see a gaggle of eightysomethings setting off for a hike, with the only walking sticks in sight being the sporty ones to help you up and down hillier slopes. At lower altitudes the walking happens all year long, but higher up it has to wait for the spring, unless you want to strap on some snowshoes. When the melting starts, the snow line slowly climbs up the slopes and the hikers are not far behind. Come peak season, from June to September, the popular paths are busier than Oxford Street at Christmas. As are the trains to the mountains; catch a 7 a.m. train to Interlaken on a sunny Sunday in July and it'll be standing room only, with almost everyone wearing hiking boots and carrying sticks.

It's enough to make me feel tired seeing them all dressed up with somewhere to go, although it's great news for the mountain resorts, who get two bites at the tourist cherry, skiing and hiking, with visitor numbers split pretty evenly between the two. The sports shops love it as well. A sure sign that winter is over is when their displays change, with boots going from giant ski ones to sturdy hiking numbers, and jackets shrinking from big and puffy to high-tech lightweight.

Walking is definitely big business in Switzerland. More to the point, these marching masses are well catered for with 65,451 kilometres of *Wanderwege*, or walking paths[4] (or *sentiers*, if you're walking in the French-speaking part, though they're not as keen on walking as the Swiss Germans). This network of paths is almost as extensive as the national road system[5] and the paths are just as well signposted, with little yellow indicators showing how long a walk it is to various places. When going up (or down) a mountain these can be very useful, especially as they're usually quite accurate, and these signs really are everywhere in Switzerland: in the city centres, on a windswept ridge, in the tiniest of hamlets and on many a road to nowhere. Of course, paths reach the parts that roads can't – the mountains, with over a third of Swiss footpaths classified as mountain ones, meaning they are harder as well as higher.

Fitness freaks and Sunday walkers, those on day-trips and hiking holidays, locals and tourists. The hills are alive every summer with those wanting to enjoy the magnificent views and the sense of solitude, assuming half the world isn't up there too. But for many, the point is to be a hiker not a walker. For the Swiss, the difference is rather like that between a traveller and a tourist. One is serious, the other not, in the same way that trainers and a kagoule make you a walker, boots and sticks make you a hiker. If it takes less than three hours, involves negligible height differences (under 400 metres), doesn't include at least one mountain view and has any part that is asphalted, then sorry but it's just a walk, even if you are a panting wreck by the end of it. In Switzerland, boots are made for hiking.

And for some hardy souls, boots are all they wear. Naked hiking is alarmingly popular, even in winter, though luckily I have yet to meet anyone who likes to let the sun kiss his whole body while out walking. Public nudity is not a trauma in Switzerland. Many Swiss bathing areas have FKK (*Freikörperkultur* or free body culture; that is, nudist) sections, and wellness centres usually require guests to strip off in the saunas and steam rooms. No one cares, except if you aren't naked, but when it's busy it can be like sitting cheek to cheek. It's still not quite on the German scale, where you never know when the next naked person might appear. Have a picnic in the wrong part of Munich's English Garden and you'll never eat another Scotch egg. Thankfully, everyone on the Swiss Path is fully dressed.

SKIPPING THROUGH THE MIDDLE AGES

Down at the lakeside village of Bauen it seems a good idea to cut out two million people (or more exactly their share of path) by catching a ride for the 20-minute trip to the other shore. This second boat fast-forwards me through another hundred years, during which the Swiss defeated the Austrians again. This rivalry continues today, albeit more peacefully, most noticeably in sporting terms; no winter is complete without comparing how well Austrian and Swiss skiers did in various competitions. It's like England and Germany at football all over again, though at least the Swiss win more often than the English.

In the Winter Olympics, the overall medals tally[6] is Austria 232, Switzerland 153, which cuts deep into the Swiss psyche. Then again, Switzerland actually has done far better in the

Summer Olympics, thanks to shooting, riding, rowing and cycling. And no Swiss history book is complete without noting their victory in the 1386 Battle of Sempach against Austria. It might mean nothing to most Europeans, but it's still commemorated every year by the Swiss. This was their Agincourt. The victory pretty much secured their independence within the Habsburg Empire and their reputation as soldiers to be reckoned with. In those days, Switzerland was not the goody-two-shoes of Europe but was as militaristic as anyone – invading neighbours, grabbing land, fighting wars and taking spoils were all totally acceptable. And this fearsome war machine would now play a major role in European history.

It is 1476, and one of the richest and biggest powers is Burgundy, under its duke, Charles the Bold. He rules over a large part of western Europe, from Holland and Belgium through northern France and Alsace down towards Geneva. With France and England having spent the previous hundred years fighting each other to a standstill, and Germany and Italy divided into piecemeal states, the way is clear for Burgundy to rule the roost. However, for Charles it all comes unstuck when he picks a fight with the Swiss, who now number eight cantons. Twice in that year, in March at Grandson (which is a real place despite the odd name, pronounced the French way to rhyme roughly with *chanson*) and in June at Murten, the Burgundians are resoundingly defeated and never truly recover. But Charles isn't a quitter and tries again six months later, though he should have stayed at home. He dies on the battlefield at Nancy, killed by Swiss soldiers, and Burgundy disappears, absorbed by France, which goes on to dominate European affairs for the next few centuries.

The boat docks at Flüelen, a busy little spot at the head of Lake Uri and about halfway along the Swiss Path; at least it's halfway in terms of distance travelled rather than time covered. At this point on the path the now-powerful Confederation has

13 cantons, plus various subject territories, and that's how it stayed for the next three centuries. But while the map of Switzerland remained stable, its history did not. Three crucial events changed the country fundamentally, so much so that all three still affect it today. A perfect time for a well-earned pause, with a late lunch and a quick skip through 300 years.

HOW THE WHOLE NEUTRALITY THING STARTED

There comes a time in every country's history when it over-stretches itself and suffers a humiliating defeat, and Switzerland is no exception. Where Britain had its Suez and America its Vietnam, Switzerland had its Marignano. After trouncing the Burgundians, the Swiss flashed their military prowess around, defeating those Austrians yet again and then taking Milan from the French. In 1515 the French hit back, near the small village of Marignano in northern Italy, and the unthinkable happened: the seemingly invincible Swiss troops were bloodily crushed. It wasn't the defeat itself that was momentous, but the way the Swiss responded. Unlike other would-be powers, they didn't just go off and invade someone else, as the British did after losing the American colonies. Neither did they fight on while their world slowly disintegrated, as the Romans did for a couple of centuries. Instead they made peace with the French, gave them back Milan, and decided not to fight any more. This wasn't quite Swiss neutrality as we know it (that had to wait until formal recognition from the powers-that-be in the nineteenth century) and it took a while for all the Swiss to stop fighting completely; for example, the Bernese couldn't resist conquering Vaud in 1536, but essentially Marignano marks the last shots of Swiss expansion and the first shoots of Swiss neutrality.

Of course, some things are more important than not fighting, such as making money. And if all your strapping young men are not off killing an enemy, they may end up fighting among themselves. The perfect answer was to hire them out to whoever wanted an army, so killing two birds with one stone, though hopefully not many of your men. Why fight a war if you can get paid to fight someone else's? Manpower was thus one of the earliest Swiss exports, with a 'Made in Switzerland' seal of approval. And these weren't individual volunteers, they were whole battalions hired out by the cantons themselves, complete with officers.

Swiss troops proceeded to fight and die for almost every European power, and they even fought each other when rented out to opposing sides. Their most famous moment was perhaps their futile defence of the Tuileries Palace during the French Revolution when over 600 died, a massacre commemorated today by the forlorn Lion Monument in Lucerne. Mercenary armies were abolished by the Swiss in the mid-nineteenth century, but one remnant remains: the Pope's Swiss Guard. Since 1506 this elite troop has guarded the Pontiff, not always successfully, and stood still for millions of tourists' pictures. New recruits have to be Swiss, of course, but also male, single, aged 19 to 30, in good health and have an 'irreproachable reputation'.[7] Protestants need not apply. As for those jaunty stripey uniforms, Michelangelo apparently had little to do with them; contrary to popular belief, they were designed in the early twentieth century using the Medici colours.[8]

The Swiss had barely got used to their new-fangled neutrality when along came the next big idea – the Reformation, which arrived in Zurich in 1519. Mirroring what happened in the rest of Europe, the country split down the middle, as did Canton Appenzell. This Catholic–Protestant rift still divides Switzerland today, and is such a fundamental part of the culture that it gets the next chapter all to itself.

After those two upheavals the Swiss had a relatively quiet time, staying out of everyone's way. Until Napoleon.

BONEY SHAKES THINGS UP

Despite being surrounded by bigger, stronger countries, Switzerland has only been conquered once in its history, a feat that is still the source of some pride. When France came calling in 1798, there was short-lived resistance and the old Confederation was soon swept away. Up to that point, and in spite of linguistic and religious differences, the Swiss and the French had enjoyed good relations since their little altercation at Marignano. Not bad going, considering the French have been at war with someone for most of their history. While the French occupiers weren't exactly welcomed with open arms, it's fair to say that a few Swiss were glad to see them, at first anyway. Switzerland then wasn't the über-democracy we know today. The old Confederation was essentially a loose collection of 13 mini-states, some still with aristocratic governments and feudal systems. Alongside them were over 70 territories, most of which are now part of what we call Switzerland. These ranged from independent allies, such as the powerful cities of Geneva and St Gallen, through subject dependencies, for instance Ticino, to mere protectorates, like the tiny republic of Gersau, population 2000. The first thing the French did was to abolish the lot and create the Helvetic Republic, a unitary state with a central government. Switzerland as a nation-state was born.

Even with Napoleon in charge, things didn't work out as planned. No one liked the new government and its accumulation of power, but even less popular was being forced to host (and feed) an occupying army. Things got even worse when those pesky Austrians and their Russian friends invaded to try to oust the French. Being a battleground for the Great Powers did not suit the Swiss at all, proving to them it was right to stay out of such affairs. Switzerland's first great experiment in central government lasted a mere five years before collapsing from internal squabbling and external power play. Seeing sense, Napoleon abolished the Helvetic Republic and created a new, improved version of the old Confederation.

As the nation's only conqueror Napoleon has a special place in Swiss history, even if it's one they don't like to celebrate, and his influence can still be seen today. Six cantons owe their existence to his changes, as does the concept of being a Swiss citizen rather than a cantonal one. His republic may have been an example of how not to rule, but he did at least give every Swiss man the same rights (women had to wait a while longer to be considered equal with men under Swiss law), abolishing both feudalism and subjected territories. And in Bern there's a physical reminder of his army's presence: the street signs in the city centre are still in five different colours, a system used to help illiterate French troops find their quarters. In some streets signs are green on one side, yellow on the other; a little historical anomaly that modern tourists barely notice as they take photos.

One other by-product of Napoleon's intervention was the creation of a Swiss national flag. Until then each canton flew its own flag both at home and in battle. Napoleon brought in a tricolour, a rather ugly green, red and yellow affair that vanished as quickly as the republic it represented. However, the lack of national cohesion in the face of invasion prompted General Dufour (he of the highest peak in Switzerland) to promote the value of one flag for the army. This new flag was square, like its cantonal cousins, and red with a white cross at its centre. As an army flag it saw action only once (in 1847, see below) before being adopted as the national flag. Nevertheless, as this is Switzerland, there was a heated debate over the exact shape of the cross until a federal decree in 1889 defined the arms as being of equal length but one sixth longer than they are wide.[9] It took another 118 years to decide exactly what shade of red should be used (Pantone 485, in case you're interested). The Swiss flag is still square, one of only two national flags to be that shape; the other being that of the Vatican City, home of the Swiss Guard. Coincidence? I think not.

THE NAME'S TELL, WILLIAM TELL

The next few kilometres of path cover the six cantons Napoleon created, all of which joined *en masse* in 1803, rather like the European Union's big expansion in 2005. This rebirth of the Confederation coincided with the reappearance of a Swiss folk hero: William Tell. Thanks to a play written by a German and then a catchy piece of music composed by an Italian, Mr Tell became a household name across Europe. These days he'd probably be designated a terrorist and incarcerated without trial, but back in the early nineteenth century Romanticism was all the rage and so Tell became a hero in the mould of Robin Hood. For the Swiss he'd always been that, but his legend becoming an international phenomenon dovetailed neatly with a bit of nation building. The trouble is no one really knows if he existed, although to dismiss the story as fiction is tantamount to treason for Swiss nationalists. Seeing as William was a native of these parts, this seems an appropriate moment to tell his story.

Every legend has its baddy and in this one he's an Austrian (what else?) called Hermann Gessler. As the new Habsburg bailiff in Altdorf, the capital of Canton Uri, Gessler puts his hat on a pole in the main square, demanding that everyone bow to it when they pass. Our hero, who is in town with his son Walter, wanders past without so much as a nod to the hat, and is promptly arrested. Gessler gives Tell a challenge to win his freedom: shoot an apple from Walter's head. Needless to say, Tell is a crossbow whizz and the apple is shot clean away. An unimpressed Gessler asks Tell why he has a second arrow ready. When Tell tells him it was for him, in case it was Walter's head and not the apple that was split by the first arrow, Gessler's less than happy and has Tell dragged off to prison in Küssnacht, on the other side of Lake Lucerne. Luckily, a storm whips up as they cross the lake by boat and Tell leaps to safety as they near the shore. Then he legs it to Küssnacht, ambushes Gessler in a dark alley and fires the arrow into his heart. Tell is a hero, the baddy is dead and the Swiss are inspired to fight for their freedom from those dastardly Austrians.

In Altdorf's main square, the site of the apple-shooting incident, there now stands a huge statue of Tell, who's portrayed all beardy and barrel-chested, a giant of a man more like Little John than Robin Hood. Every summer Schiller's play is produced in an open-air theatre in Interlaken, a town which has nothing to do with the Tell legend but is full of tourists willing to watch a rollicking affair with local actors, galloping horses, a cast of hundreds (if you include all the cows) and Rossini's rousingly bouncy tune to wrap things up, and not a lone ranger in sight. Schiller casts Tell right in the heart of the events leading up to Rütli, which means that at least Fürst, Stauffacher and Melchtal all get a role. But they still take a backseat to Tell as the father of the nation; a poll in 2004 showed that 60 per cent of Swiss people believed he actually lived.[10]

Incidentally, the play was once banned by Hitler[11] even though Schiller was an upstanding eighteenth-century German (he also wrote the poem 'Ode to Joy', which Beethoven used in his Ninth Symphony). Perhaps Hitler didn't like its message of standing up to tyranny and oppression. Either that or he objected to the choice of bad guys; he was Austrian, after all.

A NEW BEGINNING

On the south side of the lake the path is most definitely a walk not a hike, not least because a large section of it is asphalted. But it is as interesting as any rocky mountain path because it's a surviving part of the historic *Axenstrasse*, a road blasted through the rock in 1865. Walking through the narrow, deserted tunnels and galleries is rather spooky, like being in one of those films where the hero wakes up and everyone else has vanished. The modern road is half buried in the hillside, though unfortunately not buried enough and I have to walk alongside it for a stretch.

It's a relief to get back into the woods – maybe the hikers have a point – for the next stretch of path to the Tell Chapel, built on the spot where our hero supposedly leapt ashore from Gessler's boat. At the top of the many steps down to the water's edge is a rather incongruous sight: Switzerland's largest carillon, with 37 bells in total. For the first ten minutes of every hour it plays a selection of 20 tunes, including the 'William Tell Overture', naturally, and more bizarrely 'Auld Lang Syne'. This metal tower of bells was donated by the Swiss chocolate industry, though the connection isn't immediately clear, nor why it's out here in the middle of nowhere. Still, it leaves me humming Rossini all the way down to the chapel and the next boat.

Taking this easy way to reach the end of the path neatly bypasses a whole chunk of time. After the 1815 Congress of Vienna established Switzerland's borders and guaranteed its neutrality, not a lot changed on the map front. No cantons came or went, meaning that the Swiss Path doesn't exactly represent the rest of the nineteenth century and most of the twentieth. Although the Swiss map might not have changed in that period the country certainly did, most notably in 1848 when it was completely reinvented. With revolutions rippling through most of Europe in that year, it's not too surprising that Switzerland succumbed as well. The big difference is that the Swiss revolution was a political one, with no shots fired or blood shed. Both of those had occurred the previous year during Switzerland's last armed conflict, a mini-war that lasted less than a month. It was the final round of the religious struggle that had divided Switzerland since the Reformation, but the reconciliation between Catholic and Protestant was remarkably quick, and has remained intact almost ever since. And that is all down to the reinvention of the country.

Out went the confederation of self-governing cantons, in came a brand new system. Under the Federal Constitution, a central government and parliament were created in the newly designated federal city, aka Bern. Cantons had their powers reduced, but remained sovereign in all areas where their sovereignty was not restrained by the Constitution, so acting as a balance to the centre. Switzerland was now a federal state with control divided between the three branches of government: executive, legislative and judicial. This new state brought order to the chaos, giving the Swiss what they have wanted ever since: proper rules and regulations. A common market was created by abolishing internal tariffs, a single currency was established, and citizens had the freedom to move to any canton. All rather like what happened within the whole of Europe a century or so later, showing that the Swiss were well ahead of the rest of us.

The new constitution was a pragmatic, peaceful solution to an intractable problem, and that became the typically Swiss way of resolving conflict. Ever since, communication and compromise have defined the Swiss attitude in almost every sphere of life. From government and politics through business and finance to local communities and clubs, finding a consensus is the accepted way forward. Carefully deliberated conclusions are so much more Swiss than instant action. Hardly any decision is taken without weighing up every argument, possibility, ramification and viewpoint, so that the outcome is acceptable to everyone, or at least the majority. This all-inclusive approach is fair and worthy, but also tediously slow and cumbersome, even back in the nineteenth century.

To the outside world in those days, this new politics meant very little; it was during the height of European imperialism after all. Everyone else was far too busy carving out empires, racing arms, converting the natives and plundering colonies to notice a nation built on consensus. However, the events of one year would change all that and make the world look at Switzerland in a fresh light.

MR COOK AND THE CROSS

As years go, 1863 was a notable one in world history. Clearly not on a par with 1492 or 1945, but certainly more interesting than, say, 1329 or 1754. For a start, roller skates, the fire extinguisher, the Football Association and the world's first underground railway (in London) all saw the light of day. As did the name Mark Twain (as a pseudonym of the then 28-year-old Samuel Clemens). A certain spa in Vergèze in southern France also got an imperial decree declaring that its water was of the natural mineral variety; a few decades later the name was changed to Perrier.[12] So much for the good news. In the US it was mostly bad, as the Civil War reached its apocalyptic peak at Gettysburg. As busy as he was, President Lincoln found the time to make three historic pronouncements: the Emancipation Proclamation, the Gettysburg Address and fixing Thanksgiving Day to the last Thursday of November. Americans have been remembering all three ever since.

For the Swiss 1863 was a momentous year, though they may not have realised it at the time – and possibly still don't. In that year not only was the Red Cross founded in Geneva, but a certain Mr Thomas Cook conducted the first package tour of Switzerland. And so the modern image of the country was created: a champion of neutrality and fair play, as well as a pretty, peaceful place to go on holiday. The Swiss have been cashing in on that ever since. As an early tourist, you could admire the scenery, buy a pocket watch and be comforted to know that if war broke out, Switzerland wouldn't take sides. You couldn't, however, taste some milk chocolate or take a mountain train, as neither invention, both Swiss, would appear until the following decade. Those two very modern delights helped fuel a boom in Swiss tourism (and the Swiss economy) right up until the world collapsed in 1914.

THE END OF TIME

While the Swiss Path can be seen as a 35-kilometre-long microcosm of the country and its history, the twentieth century hardly features because Switzerland remained uninvolved. For Swiss men this meant business as usual; for Swiss women it meant being left on the sidelines. No boys off fighting meant no jobs for the girls back home, so no impetus for reform. Despite the whirlwinds of change that ripped through Europe, Switzerland survived untouched by being in the eye of the hurricane and letting the storms blow themselves out elsewhere. Only once, when surrounded by the Axis powers in 1940, was the Swiss position threatened, although Nazi

Germany baulked at the prospect of facing an army of sharp-shooters and guerrilla warfare in the mountains – or that's how the typical Swiss version of the story goes. Switzerland's survival has become almost as mythical as Britain's in the same conflict, with both countries guilty of viewing the war with heroes-tinted spectacles. In later chapters we'll look in more depth at Swiss attitudes to war and peace, particularly in relation to the Second World War.

When change finally came, it came from within. Almost every European country has its domestic discontents: Germany had its Baader-Meinhof gang, Italy its Red Brigade, Britain the IRA and Switzerland Les Béliers. These separatists wanted Jura, then part of Canton Bern, to be a separate canton, but this being Switzerland there were no car bombs or assassinations. The battle was fought with the ballot box not with bullets, though it was sometimes accompanied by riots and petrol bombs. It took a while, and a few referenda, but in 1979 Jura finally became the newest canton.[13] That means its 70,000 inhabitants make up the last section of Swiss Path before it ends in Brunnen, the town at the junction of Lakes Lucerne and Uri. The boat docks and connects seamlessly with a bus for the 10-minute ride to Schwyz, my final stop.

Considering it gave its name to the whole country, Schwyz is an understated town. Its most prominent building is the painted *Rathaus*, or town hall, which has nothing to with rats or some Pied Piper legend, but is as simple as *Rat* meaning council in German. This one is decorated with murals telling the story of early Switzerland, including that victory at nearby Morgarten. Another piece of the story is housed nearby, the last resting place of Switzerland's birth certificate. The Rütli charter sits in a large flag-lined hall, which is maybe why it seems so small – a pocket handkerchief of a document compared to the beach towel that is the American Declaration of Independence. The yellowed parchment is covered with exceedingly neat and dense Gothic script, making it look like something from a Tolkien novel, and two wax seals hang like chunky tassels from the bottom; sadly, the third, that of Schwyz itself, is missing. It looks far too small and delicate to have survived the boat trip back from Rütli, let alone started a country.

This history tour has now come full circle: having begun in a field where an oath was taken, the time trail has ended with the charter that vow produced.

The past isn't another country, it is what makes any country the way it is today. Even the briefest look back in time helps us to understand the present, and that is as true for Switzerland as any nation. Over 700 years after three men (allegedly) met in a field above a lake, it's still easy to see the result of that pact. For sure there have been changes, for better or worse, but that initial union of three free communities is still at the core of modern Switzerland. Thanks to conflict and compromise it is now a more perfect union than in 1291, while it has shown that success isn't dependent on size or might. Against all the odds, this small country at Europe's heart has survived where greater empires and other republics have fallen. Not bad going for a collection of farmers and mountain herders. It helped that they controlled the crossroads of Europe, the mountain passes that other countries wanted but, more importantly, didn't want anyone else to have. The Great Powers have been content to let the Swiss hold the ring, to the benefit of everyone involved. And a common enemy, be that the Habsburgs, Napoleon, the Nazis or Brussels, has consistently kept the Swiss focused on the benefits of remaining united. There's nothing like an external threat to keep internal divisions at bay.

The Swiss don't wear their history on their sleeves. There are few statues of past heroes, few monuments for forgotten battles and few memorials to the dead. That's not to say that history is ignored, more that the focus is on other parts of the past: traditions are defended, customs are cherished and buildings are restored, all with a passion that outsiders don't expect from the Swiss. They are proud of their history, even if they are prone to ignore the less savoury or more uncomfortable bits. Then again, what country doesn't?

It could be argued that this isn't living in the real world, where the past isn't romantic and the present can be just as bloody. The truth is that the Swiss haven't been living in the real world for some time, haven't been part of the recent history that has helped shaped their country. Being neutral isn't always easy, but it's often a lot easier than taking sides. Perhaps the Swiss have been sitting on the fence so long that they have forgotten what it's like to have to make a choice, and then live (or die) with the consequences. Their history might have made them complacent, even arrogant, about their position in the world, but it has also given that world a model of how a country can succeed through consensus, despite having the same fault lines as any other. If there had been more Switzerlands in the past, maybe the world today would be a better place.

SWISS WATCHING TIP NO 2: THE RED SHOE BRIGADE

If you want to look like a local, then wear a pair of red shoes. It may sound daft, but I have never seen so many red shoes as in Switzerland. Men, women, old, young, posh, scruffy, town and country – everyone seems to have a pair. It's hard to walk down the street for more than a few minutes without seeing red. It seems to be a bit of a national fetish, though having asked many Swiss people about it, none of them seems to have noticed. But I have.

The first time was on a shady bench in the elongated square in the heart of Bern, roughly marking the position of the old city walls. After a few minutes, it dawned on me that every tenth person or so was wearing red footwear. Boots, sandals, trainers and high heels. Suede, canvas, plastic and patent. Every possible shape, size and shade of scarlet. Ever since then, red shoe spotting has become a favourite pastime while out shopping, walking or sightseeing. No matter where you are in Switzerland, summer or winter, it never takes long to see a pair. On one occasion, standing in Bern station waiting for a train, I counted so many it felt like there was a red shoe convention going on that no one had told me about. Now, you might think that anyone who decides to count red shoes can't be normal, but I'm convinced I have stumbled across an interesting cultural phenomenon. Back in Britain, I tried the same experiment. Dismal. A busy day in Edinburgh and only eight pairs. A morning shopping at Gunwharf Quays in Portsmouth and a pathetic three pairs. I can see more than that in Bern just popping out to buy some milk. Even ten minutes sitting on a bench in Oxford Street and not a single pair.

So what's with all the red shoes in Switzerland? I have various theories, of varying degrees of plausibility:

❖ Theory No 1: The Swiss are very patriotic. The national colours are red and white, and as the latter isn't a practical colour for footwear, that only leaves red. Certainly, Switzerland is a patriotic nation. Apart from in the US, I have never seen so many national flags on display as a matter of course. They hang from balconies, flutter on car aerials, stand guard over allotments and adorn building sites. On high days and holidays buses and trams have little flags on the front, while come Swiss National Day (1 August) the whole place is a sea of white crosses on red flags. But reason enough to wear red? Maybe not.

✚ Theory No 2: The Swiss are friends of Dorothy. It feels traitorous, almost blasphemous, to say that in the land of Heidi, but maybe subconsciously they want to wear ruby-red slippers, even the men. Trouble is *The Wizard of Oz* doesn't have the same cult following in Switzerland, largely because it isn't on television every Christmas. I know people who have never seen it! Imagine.

✚ Theory No 3: The Swiss don't know how to accessorise. Almost half the red shoe wearers I see are either wearing nothing else in that colour or, heaven forbid, wearing things that positively clash with it. I'm not suggesting they all have to be perfectly coordinated all the time, but do they not look in a mirror before they leave the house? There's a limit to what goes with red footwear.

✚ Theory No 4: The Swiss are colour blind. This would mean, however, that they all think they're wearing green shoes, and I'm not sure which is worse.

✚ Theory No 5: The Swiss are all devout Catholics. Until the funeral of John Paul II (in Switzerland it was shown on 19 channels in six different languages), I hadn't realised that the Pope wore red shoes. Apparently that's his traditional footwear. But only 37 per cent of Swiss are Catholic, and I'm sure that a fair few non-Catholics sport the occasional scarlet slipper. I wonder if they know about the Pope's red shoe fetish.

Time to ask Jane, an English friend who has lived here far longer than me and so might have a better insight into the Swiss shoe psyche. Being a woman might also give her inside knowledge that I am not party to. After some thought, she came up with Theory No 6: The

Swiss need to rebel. In a society that's big on conformity there aren't many ways to be different without drawing too much approbation. Ditching the boring brown/black/grey shoes in favour of red is one way of showing you have a mind of your own, and is certainly more socially acceptable, though less daring, than punk hair or a tongue stud. Discreet non-conformity is a very Swiss concept.

Perhaps all the theories are wrong (sorry Jane) and it is merely a case of national taste, rather like the French wearing white socks with anything, or Brits of a certain age believing that highly patterned jumpers are stylish, or Germans thinking the mullet is still the best hairstyle around. At least the red shoe brigade in Switzerland is far less offensive on the eye and might one day be out of step with fashion. Red shoes could well disappear from Swiss feet, unlike Americans wearing socks and sandals, an abomination that sadly continues to stand the test (and taste) of time.

THREE

IN THE LAND OF COCKS
AND CROSSES

Imagine it's *Who Wants to Be a Millionaire?*, the opening round. Nine other contestants in the circle. Your finger hovering over the buttons. The challenge: put these religious holidays in the correct order that they appear during the year.

A: Pentecost   C: Corpus Christi
B: Feast of the Assumption   D: Good Friday

Could you get it right? Most people would struggle, unless they are churchgoers or live in a Catholic country. In an effort to become all inclusive, countries like Britain have made public holidays non-religious, apart from Easter and Christmas, and some would argue that even they have lost their original significance. It's a state of ignorance aided by the state itself. But in Switzerland most public holidays are still religious ones, with their traditional names and meanings. It's not that the Swiss aren't politically correct, though that is somewhat the case, but more that religion has an influence, more noticeably outside the main cities.

There is no national state religion in Switzerland, but cantons are nominally Protestant or Catholic, though some are much more mixed than others. This amicable separation is taken for granted by the locals, even though it took three centuries of bloodshed before the Swiss came up with a solution that lasted.

By the way, you might like to know the correct answer: D, A, C, B. The easy one is Good Friday, the day Jesus was crucified, followed seven weeks later by Pentecost, also known as Whitsun, when the 11 remaining Apostles received the Holy Spirit. Ten days after that is Corpus Christi, which celebrates the Eucharist rather than a specific event, and finally comes the Feast of the Assumption on 15 August, when Mary went up to heaven. Not all are celebrated everywhere in Switzerland, but which ones you get depends on where you live.

Since the Reformation Switzerland has been split between Protestant and Catholic, a conflict that used to be all about war and martyrs; today the biggest argument is about who gets more public holidays. As with everything else, the Swiss holiday calendar is the product of years of negotiation and consensus building.

HOLIDAYS AND HOLY DAYS

Visit a Protestant city like Bern on 8 December, and it's likely that the streets will be packed and the Christmas market full. That's not because it's a few weeks before the big event but because that date is a Catholic holiday, celebrating the Immaculate Conception. In my Anglican ignorance, I thought that meant something to do with Mary getting pregnant. Admittedly, it would have meant a miraculous pregnancy of only 17 days, barely enough time to have morning sickness let alone get to Bethlehem on a donkey. But when God's the father, anything is possible. However, it's not Jesus who was being conceived, but Mary herself. This is a holiday to celebrate Anna's impending motherhood; what made it immaculate isn't too clear. Maybe it was just very tidy, with no spillage, or perhaps Anna was Swiss – everything's immaculate here so surely the conceptions are too. What is certain is that Swiss holidays mean the shops are shut. In this case, the Catholic ones.

Canton Bern is rather like Elizabethan England, a Protestant island in a sea of Catholics, with almost all the surrounding cantons closed on Catholic holidays. And when the Catholics have a holiday, they go shopping in the nearest Protestant canton. Mary is conceived, go shopping. Mary ascends to heaven, go shopping. Mary had a little lamb... or maybe not. When it comes to public holidays, it pays to live in a Catholic canton, no matter what you believe. It may sound clichéd but Protestants work more, though possibly only because they have to.

Let's look at the two half-cantons of Appenzell which, having voted on the matter first, split over the Reformation back in 1597. Live in Ausserrhoden, the Protestant half, and you get four fewer public holidays than your Catholic cousins over the border. As a hard-working Protestant you only get eight days and miss out on celebrating the aforementioned Immaculate Conception as well as Corpus Christi, the Feast of the Assumption, and All Saints' Day on 1 November. Great news if you own a business catering for all those Catholic day-trippers; tough if you work in an office. It's a wonder the Aussers put up with it. Can you imagine folks in Norfolk agreeing to work four days more than those in Suffolk? I don't think so.

However, the best canton to live in is Ticino, the Italian-speaking one south of the Alps, and not just for the food. The rest of Switzerland may cast aspersions on the Ticinese work ethic, or lack thereof, but it's surely no coincidence that this is the canton with more public holidays than any other. In addition to the seven recognised nationally, the Ticinese get another eight to enjoy. That's fifteen in total.[1] They have the same four extra days as those fellow good Catholics in Appenzell Innerrhoden, but they also need to celebrate Epiphany, St Joseph's Day, Labour Day and the day of St Peter and St Paul, the canton's patron saints.

The interesting holiday is Good Friday, which (unlike Christmas Day) isn't universally observed. In a typically Swiss compromise, for Protestant cantons it's the trade-off for having fewer holidays overall. Some Catholic cantons, such as Fribourg, observe Good Friday along with all their Protestant neighbours, but for others, such as Valais, this is unthinkable as it would mean celebrating the crucifixion of Christ. And for once, Ticino is in the workers' camp. Just as well or the Ticinese would rack up another day off. It's a similar case of compromise for observing St Berchtold's Day, which is largely a Protestant holiday; not because they think he was anything special but because his feast day is on 2 January. Those canny Protestants may work more, but they still managed to create a longer holiday by tacking an extra day off on to an existing one; clever or what? Nevertheless, the holiday calendar isn't the only reminder of a past religious divide.

BELLS, SMELLS, COCKS AND CROSSES

Most tourists rarely notice the difference between Catholic and Protestant cantons; it's not as if the former all eat fish on Fridays or the latter are all workaholics. It's only when you're in a Catholic city like Lucerne on one of its extra holidays, when everything is shut, that you might realise something odd is going on.

Visit almost any Swiss town or village and there's one quick way to tell if the church is Protestant or Catholic: look up and see what's on top of the spire or tower. Usually a cockerel means it's a Protestant church, a cross means it's Catholic. That's it. Almost 500 years of religious strife reduced to cocks and crosses, which is at least better than bullets and bombs. Of course, going inside a church gives the game away instantly. On the whole, Swiss Protestants are in the less-is-more camp when it comes to interior décor. Their churches are so bare as to make English ones look fussily over-decorated. Few have any fripperies such as paintings, choir stalls, ornate lecterns or even an altar. It's all about singing and praying, and not being distracted by stucco cherubs, ceiling murals, or bells and smells. For that, you need to go to a Catholic church, preferably a big one.

In the heart of Canton Schwyz is a huge plaza in front of an even huger monastery. This is Einsiedeln, about as Catholic as it gets. A gaggle of nuns and a black-cassocked priest hurry across the cobbles, an ornate fountain has a gilded Madonna as its centrepiece, souvenir stalls are piled high with rosaries, crucifixes and Jesus-and-Mary knick-knacks. This is definitely not in Protestant country. In fact, I'm beginning to wonder if it's still in Switzerland; it feels more like Spain or Italy. The monastery's twin-towered entrance is monumentally impressive but only until you step inside; then it's hard to remember what the outside even looks like. Welcome to a world designed by a wedding cake artist on acid. It is breathtaking, though not necessarily in a good way.

The white walls are encrusted with flowery pink stucco, curling its way round pillars and paintings. Throw in a pulpit fit for a Pope, golden capitals and angels popping up all over the shop and you have a Protestant's nightmare. It's probably going to give me bad dreams. Beyond the eye-bulging Baroque interior, this is a working Benedictine monastery, with about a hundred monks in residence and six services daily. The most memorable is Vesper, every afternoon at 4.30, when the monks sing Salve Regina. It's goose-bumpingly good, but all it brings to mind is the same line sung by Whoopi Goldberg and her nuns in the film *Sister Act*. A very different black woman is the main attraction for the pilgrims who flood in all year round: a Madonna holding a baby Jesus, both swathed in sumptuous robes, both their faces originally stained black by decades of smoke from candles and lamps.

For all its overt Catholicness, Einsiedeln is only an hour from Zurich, the cradle of Swiss Protestantism. Two towns, two beliefs, two worlds apart. Only 40 kilometres separates two of Switzerland's greatest religious landmarks, the Grossmünster in Zurich and the monastery in Einsiedeln, but the gulf between them is huge. Together they illustrate how different Protestant and Catholic still are, in terms of style if nothing else. One is Queen Mary, all severe and proper with the merest hint of tasteful decoration, and the other Princess Diana, full of exuberance and colour to attract an adoring audience. But what is most Swiss is that the two live together in peace. Then again, the church in Switzerland is a very different beast.

A DEMOCRATIC CHURCH

The most notable thing about Einsiedeln is not the ostentatious décor or the quarter of a million pilgrims who come every year, but that it is an autonomous entity within the Catholic Church. It doesn't belong to a Swiss diocese but reports directly to His Holiness himself, down there in Rome. It's a hangover from long ago, but there are fewer than a dozen other such examples in the world. For Swiss Catholics, however, it might not seem strange, as their branch of Catholicism has its own rules. There's no archdiocese in Switzerland, meaning that, like Einsiedeln, all six dioceses are directly beneath the Pope in the Catholic hierarchy. Not only that, but Swiss bishops are chosen in consultation with the people rather than by orders from Rome. The Catholic Church being influenced by a secular democracy? How very Swiss.

It's not just the Catholics in Switzerland who have their

own way of doing things; the Protestants manage it as well. The Swiss Protestant Church doesn't exist as a single body, the way the Anglican Church does in England. Known as the Federation of Swiss Protestant Churches, it is in effect an alliance of cantonal churches, all independent from each other. Some are still essentially state churches, others not; some liberal in tone, others stricter; some French speaking, most German. In essence it is a mirror of Switzerland itself, all very egalitarian with no one dominant authority.

The fact that both Catholics and Protestants have a more democratic way of running their affairs is perhaps the biggest reason religion has ceased to be the issue it is elsewhere in the world. For anyone who grew up during the conflict in Northern Ireland, it's rather astounding to see that the Catholic–Protestant divide in Switzerland, while still there, no longer really matters. That wasn't always the case. It took the Swiss a while, and some bloodshed, to sacrifice religious dogma in favour of national interest. The trouble all began with one man. No, not that one 2000 years ago, but a Swiss man a little more recently.

THE THIRD MAN

The Grossmünster in Zurich is not, despite its name (literally meaning 'great minster'), Switzerland's largest or most splendid cathedral; it's too small and plain for that. Neither is it the Swiss equivalent of Canterbury Cathedral, as Swiss Protestants are not organised hierarchically. However, the Grossmünster can be considered the mother church of Swiss Protestantism, as it was here that the Swiss Reformation was born in 1519. And the father – one Ulrich, or Huldrych, depending on what you read, Zwingli – was present at the birth.

Zwingli is the forgotten third man of the Reformation; Martin Luther and Jean Calvin get all the press. Around the world you can find Lutheran and Calvinist churches, but Zwinglian ones are hard to come by. I stumbled across one in rural Wisconsin, which isn't too surprising given that the nearby town of New Glarus was founded by settlers from old Glarus, and they clearly brought their Zwinglian beliefs with them. Instead of being remembered as one of the martyrs of Protestantism, or even a great Swiss man, he is merely a foot-note in its history. In Zurich, his adopted home town, his statue is hard to find, almost lost behind bushy pine trees on the riverside. That might have more to do with the Swiss reluctance to glorify the dead by erecting monuments in their honour. Swiss cities are relatively statue free, unlike their European counterparts, which are littered with stone or metal likenesses of past heroes. This is undoubtedly helped by the fact that the country hasn't had any monarchs and emperors, or notable generals and presidents, to revere for ever. But it's also a typical example of Swiss modesty and unwillingness to show off.

Born near Appenzell in eastern Switzerland, Zwingli left the country backwater for the wider world. He studied in Basel and Vienna, perfected his Latin and Greek, and traded ideas with the great humanist Erasmus. His self-imposed retreat in Einsiedeln monastery ended when he was elected to the post of priest at the Grossmünster. On 1 January 1519, his 35th birthday, he broke all the rules in his first sermon by read-ing out the Gospel of St Matthew. More daring was being party to eating sausages on a Sunday in Lent, though it was not the sausages themselves that were the problem, rather the timing. Today, it would be hard to find a non-vegetarian Swiss person who'd object to sausage consumption; it's a national obsession. Zwingli also opposed clerical celibacy, with some self-interest given that he'd secretly married, and fell out with

Luther over the precise meaning of the Eucharist. 'Is it bread and wine or the body and blood of Christ? Discuss.'

Zwingli's revolutionary ideas spread across the country like runny cheese. Within ten years of that first sermon the country was split, roughly divided into Protestant cities and Catholic countryside. With both sides increasingly intransigent, war wasn't long in coming. At the Battle of Kappel (1531) Zurich lost to the Catholics, with Zwingli among the many dead – a simple stone memorial beside some linden trees now marks the spot of his death. And that was pretty much the end of him. In terms of reformers, Zwingli is far outweighed by Calvin, who transformed Geneva into a Protestant stronghold. But the fact that he was first, and Swiss (Calvin was French), makes Zwingli a fundamental figure in his country's history. Who knows what Switzerland, and its people, would be like today if he had never lived? Or, indeed, hadn't died prematurely.

His legacy is clear to see when sitting in the Grossmünster's compact nave, which is all hard wooden pews, bare stone walls and Romanesque arches, instead of the gilded chapels, overblown artwork and flights of fancy often found in Catholic cathedrals. It's possible to appreciate the simplicity and beauty of the church itself, and it's quite a calming experience. A covered stone font serves as the altar and the only real splashes of colour come from the vivid stained glass in the three tall apse windows; a modern addition, designed by Augusto Giacometti in 1932. Zurich's Protestants today are clearly less bothered than Zwingli about appearing frivolous. Across the river is the Grossmünster's slender sister church, the Fraumünster, which has even more colourful stained glass windows, though hers are delicate Chagall creations from 1970. Sublimely beautiful if just a little decadent.

The irony of Switzerland's city of excess being the birthplace of its Reformation is seemingly lost on Zurich's inhabitants. They like to think of themselves as well dressed, trendy, sophisticated people who live in a go-getting, hip city that's on a par with New York or London. I'm not sure Zwingli would approve. No wonder the rest of the country views them as too big for their Dolce & Gabbana boots. However, Zurich isn't all chi-chi boutiques and shopping excesses along Bahnhofstrasse. Niederdorf, Zurich's old town, has a distinctly medieval air to it, with no traffic, no big chain stores, no trams and no banks. This was where Lenin lived in exile until 1917 but it also used to be the city's red-light district; now the last survivors of those bad old days are a couple of exotic bars, islands of vice stranded in a sea of gentrification. Stepped alleyways branch off to the left and right, leading to a maze of narrow, hilly streets and pavement restaurants. It's a different city in here, a world away from the suited bankers and twenty-first-century hubbub across the river. Little squares with fountains, stout tower-like houses, front-room tailors, colourful window boxes, one-room bars. It feels like it's straight out of Zwingli's era, even though that was 500 years ago. So little has changed, and yet so much.

WARS OF RELIGION

In the three centuries after Zwingli's death, Switzerland was as fractured as everywhere else in Europe. The Swiss managed to stay out of the big conflicts, such as the Thirty Years' War, but fought each other more than once. It's hard to imagine the Swiss fighting anyone, let alone each other, but they were still doing it just over 160 years ago. In November 1847 the Catholics' last stand ended in defeat in the Sonderbund War, a very civil war that lasted less than four weeks and claimed fewer than 100 lives. Seven Catholic cantons, opposed to both the expulsion of the Jesuits and the liberalisation of Switzerland, had formed the *Sonderbund*, or 'separate league'. It was all top secret and highly illegal (how very un-Swiss), and when the Protestants found out, they weren't too pleased. So much so that, led by General Dufour and his new battle flag, they invaded and it was all over by Christmas.

Of course, the war was about more than religion. What started as squabbles over Mary's virginity and a priest's celibacy became nothing more than a power struggle. The mainly rural Catholic cantons had fallen behind the more urban Protestant ones, who believed that wealth was a reward from God. It helped that over the centuries waves of Protestant refugees from France, Italy and England had brought with them their expertise in such areas as textiles, watchmaking and banking. Cue lots of hard work to bring gains of both a worldly and a spiritual nature, also known as the Protestant work ethic.

To their credit, the Protestants didn't pursue a vindictive peace but a lasting one, one which would build a country for everyone, regardless of what they believed (except the Jesuits, who were banned until 1973). A new constitution, a new federation and a new-fangled idea called a referendum resulted in a unique political system, a crucial factor in the creation of modern Switzerland. Possibly the best outcome of any religious conflict in history.

A CLEAN AND PLEASANT LAND?

One thing that Swiss Catholics and Protestants can agree on is putting cleanliness next to godliness. There are few other countries as clean as Switzerland. It sometimes feels like an army of elves goes around every night making sure that everything from roadside verges to park benches is spotlessly clean. As my father once remarked, you could eat your lunch off the floor of a multistorey car park, which is so clean it makes the tyres squeak. Litter is rarely a problem. Even after day-long festivals, such as Carnival, the ankle-deep detritus and overflowing bins are dealt with promptly. However, take a moment to look beyond the pristine surface and you'll notice that Switzerland does have cleanliness issues: cigarette ends, chewing gum and graffiti. All three are everywhere.

Most Swiss smokers clearly don't regard fag ends as litter. They flick them to the ground so often that the area round a bus stop can look like a cigarette massacre, with little brown corpses littering the ground. It's perfectly possible to see a smoker carefully put his rubbish in a bin, take a last drag, then flick his still-lit end on to the pavement. Some communities, such as Bern, have tried to fight the flickers with on-the-spot fines of at least 100 francs, but with smoking banned indoors, the fag ends are piling up even higher outside.

Then there's the gum. The Swiss love chewing gum. Per head, they consume as much as those master masticators, the Americans: a jaw-dropping 700 grams per person per year.[2] Young, old, male, female, it makes little difference – but I think I know why. By repeating that slow, cud-chewing motion, they're revealing a subconscious desire to mimic the cows that fill their fields. It's just another sign that inside every Swiss person is a country soul trying to get out. No surprise, then, to learn that the German for chewing gum is *Kaugummi* (from the verb *kauen*, to chew, but it's very apt for an English ear: 'cow-gummi'). Living in a nation of copy-cows wouldn't be so bad if half of them didn't spit the gum out onto the ground. A lot of Swiss people, particularly young men, spit a lot, particularly with gum. Swiss pavements look like they have some particularly virulent form of measles, so numerous are the hundreds of dots that splatter the ground. It's a problem in most countries, but totally not what is expected in Switzerland.

The same goes for graffiti. Every morning I open the shutters of the bedroom window and am confronted with FUCK NAZIS scrawled in big black letters on the house opposite. While I might agree with the sentiment, though not literally, it's decidedly unattractive to have it plastered across the wall of a house in a normal street. But the Sprayers (as the graffitiists are known here) leave their mark everywhere, just like most dogs. As elsewhere, favourite targets are alongside railways, on road signs or billboards; some of the more colourful and artistic ones brighten up a dull bridge. Sadly, Swiss graffiti also appears on normal houses, historic buildings and windows. Most surprisingly, it's an act of rebellion that seems to be tolerated, or even accepted, by Swiss society as a whole. No one seems to notice it. Or, unusually, care, even in places where it matters a whole lot more than on an old warehouse or motorway flyover.

Neuchâtel is apparently the place with the best spoken French in Switzerland, and also has one of the prettiest old towns. Huddled beside a lake, it's a glorious concoction of steep alleys, cobbled squares and golden sandstone buildings, which Alexandre Dumas described as having been carved from butter. Crowning the whole ensemble are a turreted castle, hence the town's name, and a fairytale church. It's rather like a little slice of French heaven has been airlifted into Switzerland. But just to prove it really is Swiss, the graffiti along the road from the station into town is some of the most prolific in the country. It's so sad to see handsome medieval walls defaced by modern scrawl, but the locals seem to walk on by without noticing.

GREEN IS THE COLOUR

As if to make up for these three shortcomings, the Swiss are among the world's most ardent recyclers, with figures that put most other countries to shame. Most aspects of Swiss life are efficiently organised and strictly controlled, and recycling is no different. Supermarkets take back old light bulbs, plastic bottles and batteries, while paper and cardboard collection is free from the doorstep, and bottle and can banks are dotted everywhere. Sorting your rubbish is seen as a civic duty, rather than a personal choice. There are two possible reasons for this.

One: The Swiss may be neutral but they're eco-warriors at heart. Rather than doing anything too daring, like chaining themselves to trees or fighting whaleboats, they save the planet through recycling. And by voting Green. At the last general election the Greens were the fifth largest party, winning just over 7 per cent of the vote,[3] far more than the Green vote in the UK.

Two: It's cheaper. In a country where you generally pay for every bag of rubbish you put out, it's in your own interest to recycle. Rubbish is only collected if it's in the official pre-paid bin bags (which usually cost about £1 each) or in normal bin bags with the proper sticker; as with everything in this country, the system is different in each municipality. Suffice to say, the more you recycle, the less rubbish you have, so the less you pay. Saving your pennies is a good incentive for saving the earth.

Nevertheless, I have a sneaking suspicion that most Swiss recycle avidly because it means following the rules. How satisfying to look down a street on collection day (usually twice a week) and see a host of identical bin bags on the pavement. So uniform, so tidy. Even more rewarding is tying your bundle of newspapers neatly with string, knowing it will be collected. Leave it out in a paper carrier bag or badly tied and it will be left behind, most likely with a little sticker on it saying Unfit for Collection. And I'm not joking.

Whatever the reason, the Swiss are champion recyclers.

With batteries, for example, they manage a recycling rate of 67 per cent, well above the official EU target of 45 per cent (which fewer than half of EU members achieved in 2016).[4] If every EU consumer could drop off his old batteries (and light bulbs and Coke bottles) every time he went to the supermarket, rates would probably be higher too. Even better, in Switzerland the retailers are legally bound to take back empty soft-drink bottles;[5] so much better to have the collection costs paid by the likes of Tesco, with its £1 billion-a-week sales,[6] rather than a cash-strapped local council. These PET plastic bottles are then recycled into anything from egg boxes to fleeces. Who knew it takes 25 PET bottles to make a fleece jacket?[7] That's the kind of fact the recycling lobby uses to promote its cause, and it clearly works.

The most extreme form of recycling in Switzerland, though, has to be the graves. Visit a Swiss cemetery and the vast majority of the graves will be less than 25 years old, which partly explains why the graveyards are all so pristine. Apart from family graves, which are usually bought and paid for, most graves are rented for 20–25 years, with keeping the grave neat and tidy a part of the contract. After that the space is used again, very often by the next generation of the same family. Even the headstone is recycled if the family don't want to keep it; and let's face it, what would you do with Granny's gravestone? Put it in the corner of the sitting room? Or maybe make a feature of it in the back garden? Unwanted headstones are broken up to make ornamental chips and gravel. All so unsentimental, but an eminently practical solution to a lack of room; Switzerland is small and doesn't want to waste valuable land on the dead.

However, there is one place where the dead get plenty of space and that's in the newspaper death notices. It's definitely not a case of discreet three-line affairs, passed away peacefully, much missed, no flowers by request, that sort of thing.

In Switzerland it's more like a quarter-page black-bordered advert, complete with an appropriate quotation, the deceased's address, details of the service and the names of all the grieving relatives. Dying is a big deal in Switzerland, not least for the broadsheet newspapers, which have whole pages dedicated to the dead, both Protestant and Catholic. In death, as in life, both sides of the Swiss religious divide rest in peace.

THE PROTESTANT ROME

The Swiss Reformation began in Zurich but reached its peak in Geneva. Hear that name and you'll most likely think of peace talks, international conferences, private banks or a lake. Four centuries or so ago, the response would have been very different; apart from the lake, which was around back then too. In those days Geneva was the place to be if you were a Protestant, especially one fleeing the Spanish Inquisition or other Catholic heavies. It was a city republic, allied to but not part of Switzerland, and was the Protestant counterpart to Rome. And that's largely thanks to a Frenchman, Jean Calvin. He stopped over for a night in August 1536 and the city was never the same again. Under his rule, Geneva became the Iran of its day: a theocracy, with the God Squad firmly in charge.

From cradle to grave, the people of Geneva were expected to be all work and no play, with a ban on anything even vaguely fun: dancing, gambling, loud behaviour, theatre, drinking, luxury clothes. God was in charge and he was a Puritan with a capital P; his will was enforced by decree, curfew, prison and public execution. But not everything was banned. Hard work was fine, as was prayer and, more surprisingly, so was charging interest on a loan. The age-old religious objection to usury was put aside and, hey presto, the

Swiss banking industry was born. For this reason, Calvinism is seen by many as the origin of modern capitalism, though all that endless work might have played a role.

Arrive in Geneva by train and you don't get the best first impression of Switzerland's second largest city. In almost every city around the world the area near a train station is often the least attractive, and Geneva is no exception. True, it's not London's King's Cross, but in Swiss terms it's definitely down-at-heel, even if those heels are fake Jimmy Choos worn by ladies of the night. Actually they are ladies of the anytime-you-fancy, since prostitutes seem to be one of the few 24-hour services available in Switzerland. In Geneva, with so many diplomats and conferences coming and going, there's clearly plenty of demand and the supply to satisfy it.

Just a short walk downhill from the dubious bars is the tourist-board Geneva: a waterfront lined with palatial hotels, modern banks and neon signs, the lake dotted with sailboats against the backdrop of the French Alps, and the city's distinctive landmark shooting up 140 metres into the sky. The Jet d'Eau is one of the world's largest fountains but other than looking nice, especially when lit up at night, it does nothing more than give tourists something big to take a photo of.

For many Swiss Germans, Geneva is their least favourite city. This isn't because it feels decidedly un-Swiss (it's almost totally surrounded by France) or that it can seem as self-important as Zurich. It's about language. In common with most of the French-speaking part, almost every one of Geneva's inhabitants refuses to speak German. It's much like the British speaking French: they learn it at school but promptly forget every word once they're in the real world. You are more likely to hear English, numerically Geneva's second language, in the streets and shops. Or maybe it's not the lingo that's the problem but the sombre nature of everything and everyone. Too serious even for the Swiss, with no *joie de vivre* here in any language. The Protestant work ethic seems to have seeped into the buildings, the streets and the people. For sure there are lots of expensive baubles glittering in shop windows, but very few twinkles in people's eyes. Maybe they are all busy calculating how long they have to work to pay the rent, which in Geneva is about the highest in Switzerland. It's the main reason why, according to a 2017 survey, Geneva is the world's seventh most expensive city to live in.[8]

The heart of the city is not the lakefront or shops, but the hilly old town, which looks like a film set for *The Three Musketeers*, only without anyone hanging around in swirling capes and big hats. Much as in Zurich, it feels as if it hasn't changed in centuries, though the liveliness of Zurich is noticeable by its absence. Even on a sunny weekday, the narrow streets of tall stone houses are shady and almost empty, with the occasional café outnumbered by forbiddingly posh antique shops and shuttered windows. This is a city that forgot how to have fun even after Calvin died, and his influence is evidently still at work – as is the whole population. You only have to see his hard wooden chair sitting in the very bare cathedral to know what he thought about comfort and beauty. It's enough to give you a numb bum just looking at it.

The great man himself can be found in the Parc des Bastions. This lovely green space, where the city defences used to be, is home to the world's most imposing monument to the Reformation. A 100-metre wall of sandstone is dominated by four giant carved statues, all of them looking very severe and judgemental. With their long robes and grim beards they look like four Dumbledores, though they all have worryingly small heads. Of course Calvin is one of them, along with John Knox, founder of Scottish Presbyterianism, who sought sanctuary in Geneva. The Lord's Prayer in English is carved into the wall, and both the Pilgrim Fathers and England's Bill of Rights (which excluded Catholics from the throne) are also depicted. A world view of Protestant history, except for the absence of Zwingli, who is demoted to a mere name engraved in a nearby statue-less plinth. The fact that he was Swiss is clearly less important than the fact that he didn't speak French. Even as a Protestant, he was too Germanic for the good citizens of Geneva.

Today the city is no longer the Protestant stronghold it once was, with official figures showing that just 10 per cent of the population is Protestant.[9] It doesn't have Catholic holidays but is now Protestant in name only. Calvin must be turning in his grave, assuming it hasn't been recycled. Not that that would ever happen as celebrity graves tend to stay around forever.

OF MINARETS AND MINORITIES

The fact that only a tenth of Geneva's citizens still follow Calvin's faith shows how much the delicate Catholic–Protestant balance has changed. Until the sixties Protestants were the clear majority nationally, as they had been for ages. Then came the immigration decade, when thousands of Italians and Portuguese came to Switzerland to work. They were Catholic – and they stayed. Today, Catholics outnumber Protestants by a good margin, but only because over a third of them are foreigners.[10] Look at just the Swiss population – that is, excluding all the immigrants – and the gap narrows considerably.[11] The thing is, the Protestant–Catholic rift doesn't really matter any more. It no longer divides the Swiss the way it used to, and a new religious division has appeared instead.

Forty years ago over 98 per cent of the Swiss population was Christian; today it's just over two-thirds.[12] This national average hides the extremes, such as Canton Uri at 80 per cent Catholic and the city of Basel, where Protestants and

Catholics together are only about a third of population.[13] Part of that decline is due to the growth in the number of Muslims, mostly from ex-Yugoslavia and Turkey, who now constitute 5.1 per cent of the population; almost unbelievably, that's a higher percentage than in the UK.[14] For a country used to everyone being a Christian, it's a huge change and the growing pains are still being felt. As we'll see in the next chapter, Swiss politics has become a battlefield over immigration and integration, with religion a big factor. Switzerland is becoming a multi-faith nation, but its people need time to adjust and not everyone wants to, as the minaret vote of 2009 showed. Swiss change is not a fast process.

What is perhaps more telling is the meteoric rise in the number of non-believers. Almost 24 per cent of the population now lists no religion as its faith, a vast increase from 1 per cent in 1970.[15] This development is much more marked in big cities like Basel than in the staunchly Catholic areas of central Switzerland. It's most likely due to a loss of faith in the church or a decline in Protestant numbers, but I think it could just be a tax dodge. In most cantons you still have to pay a tithe, or church tax, which varies depending on your income, where you live and which church you belong to. It all sounds very medieval, especially as the tax is payable even if you don't actively go to church. The best way to avoid it is to leave the church officially and have no religion. Fine if you're a person, a bit harder if you are a company – in three-quarters of cantons businesses also have to pay the church tax, and in Canton Zurich it raises over 100 million francs a year.[16] The winner certainly doesn't take it all in Canton Bern, where lottery winnings are subject to an 8 per cent church tax.[17] Ouch!

Of the historic fault lines in Swiss society, the religious one is the least obvious today, mainly because it's the least clear-cut. There are French-speaking Protestants and German-speaking Catholics, and vice versa. Cantons are not split neatly into two camps, and there's no east–west or north–south partition. In fact, the jigsaw jumble that is the Catholic–Protestant divide is probably the least significant issue in today's Switzerland. For most Swiss people, where you live, how you vote and what you speak are all more important. Having helped create the Switzerland of today, Christianity has moved from conflict to consensus. A Catholic nun walking through Bern as the Protestant cathedral's bells ring would have once been unthinkable; today it's normal, at least for the locals. To me, it's still a moment to cherish. Not because of the wonderful bells, which ring at regular intervals all week, or because the only nuns I'd ever seen in England were in *The Sound of Music*. It's because it shows what a society can achieve if it tries. How sad, then, that these hard-won lessons of the past are being ignored by those determined to make Islam an issue. Religion could once again divide Switzerland, making the future seem much less certain than the past.

SWISS WATCHING TIP NO 3:
SOS – SWITZERLAND ON SUNDAYS

Sundays in Switzerland are still sacred, making a Swiss Sunday feel like being in England when it still had pound notes and Mrs Thatcher. From Saturday evening to Monday morning (or even 1 p.m. in some places) shops remain shut and shuttered, so that most town centres take on a *Mary Celeste* air. As for a day out at IKEA, think again; it may be out of town, but it's closed too. The only exceptions are train stations and airports, where shops can open every day of the year. Go on Sunday to a Coop or Migros in a big station like Basel or Geneva, and you'll probably have to fight your way round and queue to pay. It's like shopping just before Christmas, but every weekend. In fact, Christmas is the only time shops are allowed to open on Sunday. As with most things in Switzerland the rules are different in each municipality, but in most of German-speaking Switzerland, for example, some Sundays in Advent are designated as shopping ones. It seems that even respecting the day of rest takes second place to making money at the busiest time of the year. For the other Sundays, though, there's little chance of change. A recent referendum tried to restrict Sunday trading even further by preventing station shops from opening. It failed, thank God. Being used to 24-hour opening, it took me a while to adjust my shopping habits and I often still have to use the station shops for emergency milk. Swiss people, of course, are far too organised to run out of anything.

It's not only shopping that's affected. In many residential buildings you aren't allowed to do your laundry on a Sunday, or clean your windows, or do any DIY, while moving house is a big no-no. And it may be God's day, but you're not allowed to save the planet either. Before I knew any better I once did my recycling on a Sunday afternoon, and was soundly told off by a little old lady. I hadn't noticed the signs at the bottle bank, making it clear that using them on Sunday (and after 8 p.m. any other day) is not permitted, owing to the unacceptable noise. Heaven help anyone who breaks these rules by breaking some glass.

Public holidays also count as Sundays, at least in terms of what's allowed and what's not. So no Boxing Day sales, no mowing the lawn on May Day, no taking your empties to the bottle bank on New Year's Day, and no family outings to a DIY superstore. And it follows that the day before a public holiday is a Saturday (even if it isn't), when shops generally close earlier than normal. For example, in most cantons Maundy Thursday is a Saturday in shopping terms because the next day is Good Friday, which is a holiday, so a Sunday. But when the day before a holiday is actually a Sunday, then it clearly can't be a Saturday, since Sundays take precedence. This only happens on date-related holidays, such as Christmas, New Year and Swiss National Day (1 August), which wander through the week. Christmas Eve, New Year's Eve and 31 July are thus logically always Saturdays, except when they fall on Sundays, when they stay as Sundays. Got that?

This is all second nature to the Swiss, but it can be rather confusing to strangers, whether visiting for a week or staying for a year. It's easy to get caught out by shops and museums shutting early when you least expect them to, such as on the day before Ascension Day. Just to make it even more challenging, when the mobile holidays fall over a weekend there are no automatic replacement days to make up for that. A weekend Christmas in Britain means a four-day holiday, but in Switzerland it's merely another weekend and you go back to work on Monday 27. The only concession is the possibility of shorter hours on Christmas Eve, which, as we have seen, becomes a Saturday even though it's really a Friday. The double whammy is that when Christmas falls over a weekend, so too does New Year. Cue another normal weekend, another Monday return to work. There's no such thing as a free holiday in Switzerland.

With all these Saturdays and Sundays, real or otherwise, you'd think it would be chaos on the public transport system. Don't be silly, this is Switzerland. The main train network operates the same timetable every day of the year, including Sundays and all holidays, since they are exactly when many people want to travel. There's nothing more illogical to a Swiss person than the trains shutting down on Christmas Day, as they do in Britain. As for a 'Sunday service', in Switzerland that could only be in a church, not on a train. On Sundays the trains are packed, with skiers in winter, walkers in summer and tourists pretty much all year round. It's only at a local level, such as on city buses or suburban commuter services, that you get a reduced timetable on Sundays and holidays. The sole nationwide transport restrictions on Sundays are for heavy goods vehicles, which are not allowed out on the roads, including motorways. Now that is a good idea.

For the Swiss, Sundays are about rest and relaxation. They love seeing a film, going to church, being with family or going for a walk. Or maybe indulging in a bit of culture. Most museums open, though many close on Mondays to make up for the stress of having to stay open all weekend. So while some people, such as train drivers and cinema attendants, work like on any other day, for most Sunday is a day of rest, just as the good Lord intended. And for the bellringers it's the busiest day of the week, which is saying a lot as Swiss bells seem to ring all the time. The Swiss like nothing more than to wake up on Sunday morning to the sound of church bells, no matter what flavour of Christianity is involved.

FOUR

ASK THE AUDIENCE

Thick slabs of holey cheese and floury homemade ravioli, stylish bouquets of flowers and air-dried ham, rustic knobbly loaves and fresh-pressed apple juice. All that plus a bountiful array of seasonal fruit and vegetables, plump to the point of bursting. Nearly all the stallholders in Bern's Saturday market are farmers from the surrounding countryside, who come to sell their goods whatever the weather. It isn't so different from markets all across Switzerland, except for its memorable location – on the Bundesplatz, or Federal Square, the political epicentre of the country. It would be like setting up stalls in Westminster Square or on the steps of Congress – unthinkable for us, but normal for the Swiss.

That's not to say that politics isn't important in Switzerland – far from it – more that the Swiss are very practical about their land use. The Bundesplatz is no Tiananmen or Trafalgar Square; it's much more intimate. But its compactness hasn't stopped it being used for a multitude of purposes. It was once a car park, until a much-needed makeover gave it a smart (and very expensive) stone floor. As well as the market, the space hosts political rallies, open-air concerts and beach volleyball tournaments. A summertime pavement fountain with 26 vertical jets, one for each canton, is a source of endless delight for children wanting to cool off.

For all its multitasking the Bundesplatz is primarily a political space, lying as it does at the foot of the Federal Parliament, an imposing building with chunky green sandstone walls and a towering lantern dome topped by a golden Swiss cross. The grand building belies the fact that the Swiss parliament doesn't have much power; that lies elsewhere.

81

A PEOPLE'S REPUBLIC

Market day in almost any Swiss town is a good time to see politics in action. Not because there are speeches or party workers with stalls, but because that's the best day for collecting signatures. Walking through the centre of Bern means running the gauntlet of clipboard-thrusting pen holders wanting your name. These aren't charity muggers desperate for your cash, though such irritations also plague Swiss streets. And the papers are not futile petitions that will be delivered to the government without any prospect of anyone taking notice. This is not Britain. This is Switzerland, where the people have the power, and they use it. Collecting signatures is the first step towards a referendum, the basic tool of the direct democracy system. Don't like a government decision? Then collect names to change it. Want to create a new law? Then collect names to initiate it. Hate minarets? Then collect names to ban them. You get the picture. Signature seekers are quite high up in the annoyance stakes, but at least I can escape with four simple words: I am not Swiss. As a foreigner I can't vote, so there's no use in them collecting my signature.

For outsiders, it's hard to imagine how a country can function if every law and government action is subject to a popular vote. For the Swiss, it's hard to understand how any country can be run without just that. The Iraq war, rail privatisation and tax cuts – all would be so much less likely to happen in Switzerland, precisely because they would be subject to a referendum. The Swiss people can initiate legislation or destroy it; they can force the government into new policies or reject decisions it's already made. No one person or party ever has complete control – the people do. Forget China and North Korea; if any country deserves to be called a People's Republic, it is Switzerland.

For most of the country the ballot box is the main method

of expressing opinion, but in the canton of Appenzell Innerrhoden there's a different way. A way that has changed little since the fourteenth century.

DIRECT DEMOCRACY IN ACTION

The sloping main square is packed. Early birds have nabbed the front row, with the crowd ten deep behind them. Hardier souls are perched precariously on bicycle racks or the edge of stone fountains, while the lucky ones sit in comfort at windows overlooking the square. The shops and restaurants seem almost lost amid a sea of people, all in Appenzell for just one thing: the canton's parliament, or *Landsgemeinde,* which occurs every year on the last Sunday in April.[1]

Appenzell Innerrhoden is one of only two cantons (Glarus is the other) where an open-air parliament is still used to decide municipal affairs, vote on referenda and elect the cantonal government. Every citizen entitled to vote can attend and votes are taken by the raising of hands. Even though its sister half-canton, Ausserrhoden, abandoned its *Landsgemeinde* in the late 1990s, Innerrhoden shows no sign of following suit. Things change very slowly here. After all, this was the last canton in Switzerland to (reluctantly) give women the vote in cantonal matters. In 1991. No, that's not a typo. It was 1991, back when the first President Bush was fighting the first Gulf War, when both the Soviet Union and *Dallas* came to an end, and when Bryan Adams was number 1 for ever. At federal level, Swiss women had been able to vote since 1971 (itself shockingly late), but it took another 20 years before the men of Appenzell Innerrhoden gave up their stranglehold on cantonal affairs. And only then when forced to do so by a Federal Supreme Court decision in November the previous year.[2]

Today there are plenty of women in the small square wanting to exercise their hard-won democratic right. Exactly on time, at midday once the church service is over, drums roll, flags flutter, the brass band plays its tune and the dignitaries process from the church down the main street, around the square and on to the stage. The mass of spectators has to stand around the back and sides of the square, in ranks behind a rope barrier that separates off the inner circle, where the electorate is gathered. Between the two groups is a wide processional aisle, guarded by men in smart black uniforms and shiny helmets. Anyone wanting to cross the aisle has to show his (or her) voting card in order to duck under the rope and enter the central corral. Everyone has to stand, voters included, and endure the hot April sunshine.

The council members are solemnly dressed in black or grey robes, giving them a judicial air, but since they're standing on an elevated dais behind a wooden railing, they look as if they are on trial rather than giving judgement. In effect they are, as they have to face their electorate assembled in front of them. But before any debating can begin, the councillors and voters have to take the oath, exactly like the three men at Rütli. A forest of right hands shoots up, all with thumb and two fingers in position, and everyone swears together. To someone less cynical it might seem like a video for a Queen song, but to me all those arms raised in unison look spookily like a mini-Nuremberg rally. Just don't tell the Appenzellers I said that.

Once the session has begun, any voter can get up and speak on any issue being decided. No vote is taken until everyone who wants to has had their say, which can be a lengthy process. It's rather like being at Speaker's Corner in Hyde Park, though without the heckling. In fact it's remarkably quiet. Speeches are heard in silence, with no clapping or cheering or even murmurs of discontent; audience participation, it seems, is limited to listening and voting. It's all very civilised, if a little lacking in vitality. Each debate ends in a vote, with hands in the air for yea or nay and a winner declared without an exact count, and the session moves slowly on. The most excitement in the first hour comes when one voter faints in the heat and has to be helped out of the inner circle. Not that anyone really notices because the big issue of the day is up next. Naked hiking.

The *Landsgemeinde* always attracts a crowd and local TV, but today the audience is bigger and the reporters are international, all thanks to the naked hikers. A sharp rise in their numbers coming to Appenzell Innerrhoden led to a proposal banning the pastime, much to the glee of commentators from around the world. The debate is short and the vote overwhelmingly in favour, meaning that naked hikers now face a fine of 200Fr if caught.[3] What amazes me is not the result but that a few brave souls voted against it. In a flash, all their friends and neighbours know the truth: either they like walking in the altogether or they are softy liberals who would let it happen. And that for me is the problem with this whole process.

This is a demonstration of democracy in its purest form. Everyone has a chance to be involved and have their say, and those elected are forced to answer directly to their voters. But it can also exert such peer pressure that democracy itself is strangled. Imagine everyone in your town knowing exactly what you think and how you vote – and in Switzerland that doesn't just mean which party you vote for but, thanks to the referendum system, also your views on every other issue, from passive smoking and income tax to foreign policy and the age of consent. Literally standing up for your beliefs in the face of a huge majority could be a step too far for some people. It's a world away from secret ballots or hanging chads, but is it the best way for a modern democracy to function? I am less than sure.

The naked vote over, the crowd begins to thin even though the debates carry on. Gregor and I retire to the shade for some much-needed sustenance and end up sharing a table with an elderly couple. It turns out they're from over the border in Appenzell Ausserrhoden and they make a day out of it every year, now that Ausserrhoden no longer has its own *Landsgemeinde*. They clearly miss it. Unlike many other Swiss these two are happy to chat to strangers, and once they start there's no stopping them. They gladly tell us that the men in smart uniforms and helmets are the Ausserrhoden firemen, drafted in for guard duty. And that when it rains, you can have an umbrella up as long as you take it down to vote, so that all the raised hands can be seen. The most telling remark is that the *Landsgemeinde* is not only about debating and voting, important though they are, but about a sense of belonging. Thousands of voters from the whole canton, not just the main town, come in for the day to catch up with old friends, discuss the burning issues, go to church, eat a sausage and be part of the decision-making process. What is lost in anonymity is gained in community.

By the time we've all finished eating and chatting, the *Landsgemeinde* is over and the voters leave the square. Most are dressed in their Sunday best, which means lots of dark suits for the men, lending a funereal air to it all. Somewhat more bizarre is that many men are carrying a sword, more the Errol Flynn rapier type than a Crusader double-hander. Until 1991, the sword was the only symbol of being entitled to vote (and usually held aloft in each vote) and was handed down from father to son; these days it's a ceremonial accessory, though men can still carry it instead of an official card as proof of their right to vote.[4]

It might seem old-fashioned and parochial, but the *Landsgemeinde* is the most prominent physical incarnation of direct democracy, the bedrock of Swiss politics. At a municipal level such public meetings are fairly common, though usually held indoors, but otherwise direct democracy takes the form of a referendum.

BEGINNER'S GUIDE TO THE REFERENDUM

Politics in Switzerland is, in effect, a series of conversations rather than confrontations: the government is a permanent coalition, so has to talk to everyone to build consensus; parliament is never dominated by one party, so is a talking-shop on a grand scale; and the people get their say through the referendum, an integral part of the system.

Introduced as part of the revised Federal Constitution in 1874, the referendum is used for any and every issue in the country. At a local level, about shop opening hours or a new tram line; at a cantonal level, on anti-smoking laws or foreign language in schools; at a federal level, about joining the EU or changing sales tax. In short, the Swiss people are the final decision makers on almost every single policy, whether it affects their own neighbourhood or the whole country. This democratic freedom and the right to be heard are inalienable rights for the Swiss, who proudly view them as the source of their stability and prosperity.

Other countries use referenda, as do many US states, but no one does it quite to the same extent as the Swiss. They get to vote four times a year on whatever issue is up for debate. No wonder, then, that there are different types of referendum; it would be far too simple to have just one sort. Some are mandatory, some not; some start the legislative process, others end it; some require a simple majority, others are more complicated. It can seem rather like Eskimos and snow, with more than one word for the same thing, but here's a quick guide to the rules at national level:

✤ The obligatory referendum. This does what it says on the tin, and must follow any constitutional amendment or binding application to join international organisations like the EU.

✤ The optional referendum. Parliamentary decisions and legislation can be put to a popular vote, but only if 50,000 valid signatures are collected within 100 days. This threat of rejection by the voters is the main force behind making most legislation a compromise acceptable to the majority.

✤ The popular initiative. Anyone can propose a vote to change the constitution on any issue, as long as it doesn't violate either the constitution or international law. Proposers have 18 months to collect 100,000 valid signatures in order to force a vote, be that on abolishing the army (failed) or joining the UN (passed).[5] This can be thought of as the people's referendum.

✤ The counter-proposal. If parliament disagrees with a popular initiative, it can put forward its own alternative. Both are voted on at the same time and, bizarrely, both can be approved, known as a double yes. The one with the most yes votes is the winner.[6]

Much the same system operates at a cantonal level, with the big difference being the number of signatures needed to trigger a vote. For example, in Canton Bern a popular initiative needs 15,000 names, but an optional referendum only 10,000;[7] in Canton Fribourg it's 6000 for either type,[8] and Canton Aargau requires only 3000 for either.[9] It's all relative to the population.

The most important thing to remember about a referendum is that the people's say is final. If the vote is no, the legislation falls or the treaty goes unratified or the initiative fails. The government does not resign if it loses; it just goes back to the drawing board and tries to find a new compromise, which might of course need a new referendum. A yes vote approves legislation or forces the government to try to transform a popular initiative into law. But then there's the small print, which can mean that a yes becomes a no. It's all about a double majority, one from the people and one from the cantons.

For your average referendum, of which there are lots, a simple majority of the national vote is needed. Popular initiatives rarely manage even this; fewer than 10 per cent pass, making most of them unpopular initiatives. In addition to this electoral majority, all obligatory referenda and popular initiatives also need a cantonal majority. It's a mechanism to protect the small, and generally more conservative, cantons from being outvoted, but it gives them disproportionate influence. Each canton is equivalent to one vote, so Canton Geneva, with its 200,000 or so voters, is equal to Canton Uri with 25,000. The exceptions are the six half-cantons, which only count as half a vote each, so that even though there are officially 26 cantons, a majority of 12 is needed in a referendum.[10] In a close vote this can make all the difference. The irony is that changing this double-majority system requires a constitutional amendment, which needs double-majority approval. Since the small cantons are probably not going to vote for their own emasculation, it's unlikely to happen.

It may seem complicated but it's a system that works, albeit at a glacial pace. Transforming a popular initiative into an act of parliament, or getting a law passed by the people, can take years. Parliament approved giving women the right to vote in 1959, but it took another 12 years before the (male) voters agreed.[11] And since fewer than half of all referenda are passed, trying to win the voters' approval can be a long, fruitless task. Patience and a long-term view are needed, something the Swiss are rather good at: let's contemplate having a meeting about forming a working group to look at the possibility of setting up a committee to plan an initiative that will propose a law that might come into effect in five years. That's pretty much how the system works, and no one seems to mind that the rest of the world is moving at the speed of light. 'Change' would not be a winning theme in Switzerland.

STABILITY, PROSPERITY, COMMUNITY

The Swiss are right to see direct democracy, slow as it is, as the basis for their country's stability and prosperity. Simply being a federation isn't enough to sustain a nation; just look at what happened in the not so United States in the 1860s or to Yugoslavia in the 1990s. Involving voters four times a year, and not just once every four years, gives everyone the chance to have their say and feel included. True, the process can sometimes be hijacked by single-issue campaigns, but these are the exception. More often, the referendum process can save the day when things threaten to spiral out of control.

A good example is the Jura separatism of the late 1970s. Every municipality in question was asked to choose between staying in Canton Bern or joining a new canton, Jura. A series of local referenda resolved each problem, silenced the rioters and created the newest Swiss canton; a decision ratified by a national referendum, of course. Boundaries were not determined by decree but decided by the people affected, perhaps the only peaceful way to progress. Thus, some French-speaking Protestant communities along the new border could choose between being a religious minority in a Catholic canton or a linguistic one in a German-speaking canton. They chose the latter. Almost forty years later one Bernese municipality held another referendum and decided to swap sides: in 2017 the voters of Moutier changed their minds and decided to leave Canton Bern and belatedly became part of Canton Jura.

This attention to detail at a micro level gives the Swiss system the power and flexibility to deal with almost any issue, and not just because of referenda. Nationally Switzerland is divided into 26 cantons, but almost as important is the smallest subdivision of Swiss politics: the municipality, or *Gemeinde* in German, *commune* in French. Ranging in population from fewer than 15 to over 415,000, there are 2,222 Swiss municipalities,[12] though their number is declining steadily as small ones struggle to survive so voluntarily merge with neighbours. Each municipality is almost like a mini-republic, with decisions made by an elected council or, more usually, an annual general assembly of voters. It is responsible for basic services such as schools, the fire service, water supply, planning permission and health. More crucially, most of your income tax depends on which municipality you live in, and you can only become a Swiss citizen once you have been accepted into your municipality. It is the basic building block of Swiss democracy, but like every part of the system, the municipality is wholly answerable to its citizens.

At municipal, cantonal and national level, the referendum system works because it involves everyone. It forces the politicians to address the issues and engages the voters in the detail of the debate. Most Swiss people love nothing more than discussing whichever issue is coming up at the next referendum; they may end up not voting, but they'll have an opinion, usually a well-informed one. In the weeks preceding a referendum, it's hard to escape it. Every street corner seems to have a poster exhorting you to vote *JA!* or *NEIN!* (or *oui/si* or *non/no*), with smaller versions in the newspapers. Political discussion programmes on television, which are inordinately popular all year round, become obsessed with debating the ins and outs of immigration or health insurance. A member of the government pops up on television to explain the official line, which in itself is unusual because political advertising on TV is banned: no party political broadcasts, no ads paid for by the committee to re-elect the president. But there's no lack of information; all the voters have to do is decide.

Incidentally, for German speakers there's a clear distinction between voting in a referendum (*abstimmen*) and voting in an election (*wählen*). For once, English lacks the fine distinction in meaning. Then again, voting is much simpler in other countries – because if you thought the referendum was complicated, wait until you try to work out the Swiss voting system (see the Swiss Watching Tip at the end of this chapter).

GOVERNMENT BY COMMITTEE

With the people being asked to decide everything at every level every few months, it might feel like there's no actual government running the country. The Swiss system of municipalities and referenda does skew power towards the bottom (the electorate), but that doesn't mean there is no top. However, this being Switzerland, the top also has a unique structure, one which exemplifies the Swiss attitude to politics: no one person is in charge.

Switzerland is run by committee. Thanks to proportional representation and multiple parties, almost every ruling council at every level is a coalition of some sort. Each canton has its own rules about the size and make-up of its own parliament and council, so let's look at the federal structure to see how government by compromise actually works.

The government itself is known as the *Bundesrat*, or Federal Council. It consists of seven members and is a permanent coalition, with no one party or person ever in control. Each Federal Councillor is in charge of a department of state, such as the self-explanatory Finance or Foreign Affairs, or more nebulous Home Affairs, which covers everything from health and social security to statistics and culture. Or (my personal favourite) Defence, Civil Protection and Sports; Switzerland is possibly the only country to have a Defence Minister responsible for PE. The Councillors take it in turns to be president for a year, while still running their own department. Not that the President has any more power, but someone has to shake hands with visiting leaders and make a speech on 1 August.

The Federal Council is elected every four years by parliament, not by a popular vote[13] – the one time in Swiss politics when the people do not have a direct say. This is supposed to prevent party, linguistic or cantonal loyalties affecting the result, to deter presidential-style campaigns, and to define the Council as a consensual body above the political fray. It also made things boring and predictable, at least until 2003. Before that, a 'magic formula' was used so that the Council as a whole represented the four main political parties and reflected the different regions. And since Federal Councillors generally stay, and are re-elected, for years until they retire, resign or die, parliament was often little more than a rubber stamp. Then the general election of 2003 left the right-wing Swiss People's Party (known as SVP, or *Schweizerische Volkspartei*, in German) as the strongest party. It used its extra seats in parliament to oust a sitting Federal Councillor and elect its leader, Christoph Blocher, instead. Such a coup hadn't happened since 1872;[14] suddenly Swiss politics was interesting.

However, the best was yet to come. After the 2007 general election (Swiss elections are as regular as clockwork, every four years in October) the centre and left-wing parties combined to exact their revenge in the parliamentary Federal Council vote. Tall poppies don't live longer in Swiss politics, and Blocher lost his seat. The SVP stormed out of the government and, for the first time in decades, Switzerland had an Opposition, a powerful party not in the Federal Council. For a nation not used to party politics on this scale, the shock was palpable. Welcome to the real world!

Neither the parties nor the people seemed to know quite how to deal with this new-fangled confrontational politics; all that shouting and disagreement just wasn't Swiss. And the SVP discovered that being in opposition wasn't much fun, so when the Defence (and PE) Minister resigned from the Federal Council in 2008, his replacement was an SVP man. By 2016 the SVP had regained its second seat in the Federal Council so even it couldn't complain any more. Compromise politics and the 'magic formula' were back – cue collective sighs of relief from Swiss people everywhere. Sadly it also killed the best Swiss political joke: What's the difference between a Smart car and the SVP? A Smart car has two seats. And some people think the Swiss have no sense of humour.

Even though the government, in the form of the Federal Council, is made up of the largest parliamentary parties, that doesn't mean it has a free hand passing legislation. Parliament acts, in effect, as the opposition, counterbalancing the government. It can and does reject or reform legislation, as well as initiate its own, and of course it has the ultimate power in electing the Federal Council. But parliament is also a creature of compromise. It's divided between left, right and centre, but twelve parties have at least one seat, so loyalties and alliances are constantly shifting. Of course party politics is a major influence, but simply because no one party is in control, any legislation has to be the result of concession and debate. If it isn't, then it risks being rejected by the people at the next referendum. Despite the numerous parties and diffusion of power, Switzerland hasn't suffered the revolving door of governments seen in countries like Italy and Israel. The national desire for stability and *Konkordanz*, or consensus, is stronger than the parties or the system itself, and the Swiss would never let their politicians threaten the country's prosperity.

Having survived the complexities of people power and government by committee, you'll be pleased to learn that the simplest part of Swiss politics is parliament itself.

PART-TIME POLITICIANS

Like so many parliaments around the world, the Swiss Federal Assembly consists of two houses of equal status, both directly elected by popular vote every four years. In the *Ständerat*, or Council of States, every canton has two seats, with the six half-cantons logically getting only one each. This gives the smaller cantons a greater voice in the 46-seat chamber and prevents them from always being outvoted. The 200 seats in the *Nationalrat*, or National Council, are also allocated by canton, but based on their population: the largest, Zurich, gets 35 seats while six have the minimum one seat.[15] The Federal Assembly is the pivotal element in the Swiss political system as it elects the Federal Council (and one of its members as President) as well as the Federal Supreme Court. It was modelled on the US Congress, but with two big differences: it, and not the people, chooses the government; and secondly, there aren't just two parties and a couple of independents; Swiss parliament is an alphabet soup.

As well as the aforementioned SVP, there's the CVP, FDP, BDP, EVP, GLP etc., etc. And that's just in German – for example, in French the SVP is the UDC, short for *Union Démocratique du Centre*, a laughable name considering its right-wing policies. This multiplicity of parties is one result of proportional representation, introduced following the General Strike of 1918. That was the one moment in recent history when Switzerland verged on collapse, with the government paralysed and the army used against its own people. Nevertheless, this was no Russia or Germany, and it ended in a very Swiss way, with all-party talks and consensus. There were then decades with few strikes, lots of coalitions and countless parties. It's all too much for an outsider used to the two-and-half party politics in Britain. Perhaps the only way to get to grips with the system is to visit parliament itself, which offers free guided tours when not in session; that is, most of the year.

In official terms Bern is not called a capital city but merely the Federal City (or *Bundesstadt*) as it's home to both the federal parliament and government. But to you and me Bern is Switzerland's capital, and as capital cities go, it's one of the prettiest around. Set on a high cliff, it sits on a long, thin tongue of land, surrounded on three sides by the river Aare. At first glance the only hints of modernity in the pedestrianised old town are the shop signs and trams, since all the trappings of twenty-first-century consumerism are hidden within the arcades that line most of the main streets. These arcades – there are 6 kilometres in total – make Bern a pedestrian delight. Sheltered from rain and snow, and the summer sun, shoppers pack the arcades, reducing movement to a funeral pace. It was no surprise to the Bernese that in 2007 their city was rated one of the world's slowest for pedestrians.[16] Nothing happens quickly. Perhaps that's why Albert Einstein came up with the Theory of Relativity while he was living and working here; he had all the time in the world to contemplate the speed of light.

For the most part, politics also happens at a leisurely pace in the Swiss capital. It's quite common to see a Federal Councillor waiting for a bus, with no security in sight. That's of course assuming that you'd recognise him or her. Swiss politicians have a noticeably lower profile than their counterparts in other countries, with policies generally more important than people. Many of my Swiss friends struggle to name all seven Councillors and, as a new President is elected by parliament every year, it's hard to keep track of whose turn it is. Parliament itself is a part-time affair, sitting for only 12 weeks a year, in four three-week sessions. The Federal Council aside, there are few full-time politicians, with most having day jobs as lawyers, teachers, police officers or doctors. Swiss MPs don't get a proper salary but receive an allowance for staff, travel and accommodation plus a daily allowance for time spent on parliamentary duties; gravy trains are perhaps the only sort of locomotive you can't find in Switzerland. It's all very low key and low cost, in stark contrast to the building itself, which clearly cost a packet to build when Bern was designated as the Federal City (aka capital) in 1848.

Inside, it's all very Victorian (to my English eyes) with bombastic murals of Swiss history, neo-Gothic chandeliers and acres of carved wood. A vast stone statue of the three Rütli oath takers dominates the main entrance, though they look suspiciously like extras from *The Lord of the Rings*. Above their heads, the stained-glass dome shows the Swiss cross and coats of arms of all cantons at the time parliament was inaugurated (1902). That means Jura is an afterthought, stuck off to one side, much as it is in many Swiss people's minds. The overall effect is surprisingly un-Swiss: overblown, triumphant, nationalistic. Then again, it was built when newfound nationalism was all the rage, and even the Swiss succumbed to bigging things up. They may be Swiss but they are human too, not Vulcans.

Our guide tells us everything you could possibly want to know, such as that each member has his, or her, own seat and desk, not like the bum fight for a seat in the House of Commons. In the National Council they are grouped by faction, or political leaning, while in the smaller Council of States the seating plan is much more relaxed. And the speaker of the National Council is the highest-ranked person in the country. The President really is just a handshaking figurehead.

The weirdest part is when we are shown a ceiling mural depicting Swiss tourism in the nineteenth century. Three cherubs are dressed stereotypically to represent the three main markets: a blond boy in *lederhosen* for Germany, a black-haired boy in a stripy top for France, and a red-haired boy in shorts for Britain; for many Swiss, those stereotypes still hold. The guide then points out me and my sister (over from England for a while), both of us red-haired, and says: 'As we can see from our two English guests, the Swiss cliché of British people having red hair is as true today as it was then.'

Everyone else finds that funny, particularly the Swiss in the group. Red hair is something we Brits tend to associate with Celtic roots, but for the Swiss it simply means Britain in general. Where that stereotype came from nobody knows, but it's stuck. To the Swiss, the British are all well-spoken, red-headed tea drinkers who make funny films and good music but can't cook or deal with snow. Switzerland is largely an Anglophile nation that sees Britain as a kindred spirit, even if it persists in having a monarch as head of state – and she is usually referred to as 'Die Queen', as if there were only one in Europe.

In Switzerland, parliament inspires more confidence in the population than in many other countries. An annual Swiss survey rates people's confidence in public institutions, and in 2017 the houses of parliament did well, with both being ranked among the top five institutions in terms of public trust; the Supreme Court topped the list.[17] In contrast, political parties came in the bottom five (along with the army and the EU), showing that the Swiss can see a clear distinction between parliament and politics. As part-time politicians, Swiss MPs remain relatively normal and don't get carried away with their own importance. In Swiss eyes that's an essential trait in public life, where parliament is about serving the people not yourself. The good of the country is the only thing that matters, even if that means that a minority may suffer.

ONE IN FIVE

Politics, especially at election time, is usually concerned with tax and spend. British parties promise tax cuts and spending increases, while Bill Clinton won with 'It's the economy, stupid'. Swiss politics is different. Money is important, but as any tax changes or spending plans might face a referendum, they're not such a big deal. Promises usually become compromises, so the parties rarely come up with anything new, only to see it sacrificed for the sake of consensus. However, on one issue Switzerland is the same as most other democracies: immigration and integration.

Switzerland loves its statistics. Just about everything is counted, tabulated, assessed and published. Every town and canton has a website full of stats, imparting really useful stuff like how many people own their own homes or what percentage of the population is Albanian. But in a land full of statistics, one of the most surprising is that 25 per cent of Switzerland's population is not actually Swiss.[18] That's 2.1 million people, including me – I am a statistic, or at least part of one. It's almost unbelievable for a country to have one in four inhabitants not actually citizens; in Britain that would be over 16 million people, or roughly the population of London, the West Midlands and Greater Manchester combined. In the US it would be California, Illinois and Texas together. A lot of people.

Swiss nationality is seen as a privilege not a right, and as such is hard to get hold of. Being born in Switzerland doesn't count (unless at least one parent is Swiss): second-generation immigrants, known as *Secondos*, are still classed as foreigners, as are their children and grandchildren, and altogether they account for a fifth of the 2.1 million.[19] That's 404,000 people who were born and grew up in Switzerland but are not Swiss; sadly, they are nearly always lumped in with all the others as 'foreign-born' or 'born abroad' by lazy journalists. Many go on to become naturalised citizens, as shown by the 13 ex-*Secondos* in the Swiss team that won football's Under-17 World Cup in 2009. Or Ignazio Cassis, who was born in

Switzerland to Italian parents and in 2017 became the first ex-*Secondo* to be elected to the Federal Council. However, naturalisation (becoming a Swiss citizen) is a lengthy, expensive process, involving applying, and paying, for citizenship at municipal, cantonal and federal level. You can apply once you have lived in Switzerland for ten years[20] (compared to five in the UK)[21] and even then it can take up to two years, and cost thousands of francs, to become Swiss.

Nearly all the resident foreigners are European, and a look at the Eurovision Song Contest voting shows where many came from: in 2008 (the last year with a popular televote and no juries), the Swiss vote gave *douze points* to Serbia, ten to Portugal and eight to Albania.[22] In fact, the two largest immigrant groups are from Italy and Germany, but since Italy has only recently returned to Eurovision and no one Swiss would vote for something German, neither country got a look in. Ironically, Eurovision is about the only time foreigners can vote in Switzerland. Is that a real example of democracy in action? Or are the Swiss right to exclude so many residents from the political process? Who knows.

What is certain is that the Swiss economy depends on foreigners to an unsettling degree – a quarter of all wage earners in Switzerland are not Swiss and in some sectors such as the hospitality industry, almost half the workforce are foreigners.[23] But who else would do all the jobs the Swiss don't want to do? Just like in Britain and America, it's usually immigrants who clean houses, pick fruit, sweep streets and sell burgers. Without them, Switzerland would be dirty and its people hungry. This is a fact of life that many Swiss are unwilling to accept or face up to, until they are forced to.

THE BLACK SHEEP OF EUROPE?

To see how fundamental the immigration debate is to modern Switzerland, we need only look at some recent votes, starting with the 2007 general election and the explosive poster from the SVP: a cartoon showing three white sheep standing on a Swiss flag and kicking a black sheep over the border. For some, it wasn't just the image that offended but also the colours; red, white and black were the colours of the Nazi flag. Defaced by the left but defended by the right, the posters led to violent clashes on the streets of Bern, condemnation from the UN and British headlines like: 'Has Switzerland become Europe's Heart of Darkness?'[24] It was all quite a shock to most Swiss, who are used to their elections going unnoticed by the outside world. Sadly, the poster worked. The SVP won 29 per cent of the vote,[25] the highest ever for any party since the introduction of proportional representation.

That now infamous sheep poster may have been racist but it worked because it tapped into a wider feeling of xenophobia. It's not necessarily black foreigners who are the problem for many Swiss people, just foreigners in general, and especially ones from the former Yugoslavia. Often dismissed as 'Yugos', they face discrimination when applying for jobs, flats or even car insurance. And many of them are Muslim, a crucial factor in the minaret vote of 2009. It didn't matter that Switzerland had only four decorative minarets, the SVP launched a popular initiative with the goal of changing the constitution so that no more could be built.

And the party hit gold again with another aggressive poster in the same colours. This time the Swiss flag was covered in black minarets that looked just like WMDs, or Weapons of Muslim Destruction. Plus, for good measure, a woman clad in a black burka – nothing to do with minarets but great for giving voters the willies. Racist, xenophobic and inflammatory, but ultimately successful in winning a clear majority in favour of a ban.[26] It was a case of a far-right party winning a national vote by playing on people's fears of a religious minority. Sound familiar? Ironically, since only a third of Muslims living in Switzerland are actually Swiss,[27] most of them couldn't vote on an issue that affected them directly.

Perhaps the problem is that multiculturalism is a relatively new concept for the Swiss. No empire meant no colonial immigration. Whereas almost every British town has an Indian and/or Chinese restaurant, in many Swiss towns it's an Italian. Away from the more cosmopolitan big cities, that's about as exotic as it gets. Traditionally the Swiss themselves didn't move far from home, so that even someone from St Gallen can be dismissed as a 'foreigner' in Lucerne. Throw in a different language, religion or skin colour and integration becomes all the more difficult. Foreigners can feel like the proverbial square peg their whole lives, not helped by the fact that they are routinely blamed for the country's ills (few though they may be). Listen to the right wing and you might think there are no Swiss people in prison, no Swiss benefit cheats, no Swiss joyriders and no Swiss beggars. Only foreigners.

Of course, not all Swiss think like that. The country's conservative image hides a surprisingly liberal stance on social issues, such as drug use and assisted suicide – neither is actively encouraged but both are accepted to a much larger degree than in most countries. And let's not forget that Switzerland was the first country in the world where the people, rather than parliament or the Supreme Court, voted in favour of gay civil partnerships[28] (although gay marriage has yet to happen). Or that since the Second World War, Switzerland has a good record of sheltering refugees, be they from Sri Lanka or Kosovo, and helping them until they find their feet. Swiss politics may be in the hands of the people, but it's as paradoxical as any other aspect of modern Switzerland.

Those two votes were merely the latest incarnation of the SVP agenda of being not only anti-foreigner and anti-Muslim but also anti-EU and in fact anti almost everything. This is their recipe for success, which dates back to the momentous vote in December 1992 when a young Christoph Blocher led the SVP to defeat Switzerland's application to join the European Economic Area (EEA). Every other party, trade union and business organisation were united in supporting the government's European policy, with the EEA seen as the first step towards European Union membership. But joining the EEA was subject to an obligatory referendum and that's where Herr Blocher stepped into the picture. And won. But only just. With over 3.5 million votes cast, the No side won with a majority of 23,836, or 50.3 per cent.[29]

Unable to join the EEA, let alone the EU, the Swiss government instead manoeuvred itself into the unique position of being an almost member. It negotiated a series of bilateral treaties with the EU, each approved by referendum, giving Switzerland access to the single market in return for compliance on many issues – mainly covering trade and working relations – plus a contribution to the EU budget in the form of a voluntary donation to the Cohesion Fund that helps Eastern Europe. These bilateral treaties give the Swiss many of the benefits, and some of the costs, of membership without the integration. As a result, Switzerland is part of the Schengen Area, where there are no passport controls at the borders, and signed up to free movement of people, meaning that EU citizens can usually live and work in Switzerland and vice versa. That's why I (and 41,000 other Brits) can live here.

The EEA vote has dominated and determined Swiss European policy for the past 25 years, and will continue to do so for the foreseeable future. Switzerland's relationship with its mammoth neighbour affects practically everything, but especially the two key concerns of immigration and the economy. That political battle shows no sign of abating, as the most recent votes have shown.

WIN ONE, LOSE ONE

Swiss general elections are like the World Cup: they occur once every four years and the build-up is almost as important as the actual event. In this case, the qualifying round was fought almost a year before the final and the star of the show was that black sheep again. Having helped the right-wing SVP win the previous election, he was brought back in 2010 for his real purpose, one that made the minaret ban look tame. This time it wasn't just Muslims who were targeted by the latest SVP hate campaign, but all foreigners. The *Ausschaffungsinitiative*, or deportation initiative, was a popular initiative that proposed automatically expelling foreign criminals, from rapists down to benefit cheats, back to their country of origin. No appeals, no exceptions. For *Secondos* born and brought up in Switzerland that might mean being sent back to some tiny village in southern Italy that their grandparents left in the 1960s.

Funnily enough, the SVP's list of crimes worthy of expulsion didn't include corporate fraud, tax dodging or secreting away ill-gotten gains. Clearly those sorts of foreign criminals are welcome to stay, presumably because they aren't a threat to little old ladies, but most likely because they make the country richer and the SVP didn't want to alienate its friends in big business. Nor were traffic offences (which account for 55 per cent of all crime in Switzerland) mentioned, probably because 51 per cent of the offenders are Swiss.[30] It wouldn't do to highlight that. However, many other statistics to do with foreigners were liberally publicised; the trouble is that statistics sometimes don't tell the whole truth.

'One of the highest populations of foreigners in Europe' is a cry often heard, using the official 25 per cent as its basis. But is it right? In Swiss terms yes, but only because Switzerland's citizenship rules are very different from other countries'; if you level the playing field, the picture changes dramatically – then Switzerland has roughly 7 per cent foreigners, below the 8.7 per cent in Britain[31] and far less than the 12.2 per cent in Germany.[32] Two rules make all the difference. Immigrants in many EU countries can apply for citizenship after five years' residency, whereas in Switzerland it is ten.[33] Secondly, *Secondos* are treated better elsewhere. Children born in Germany, for example, are citizens if one parent has been a permanent resident for over eight years;[34] in Britain it is only a five-year minimum[35] (and in America all children are simply citizens at birth). Not so in Switzerland, where those circa 400,000 *Secondos* have no citizenship rights. Despite all that, or maybe because of it, the initiative passed with a small majority.[36]

One year later, however, the general election saw the SVP lose both seats and votes for the first time in 20 years. The SVP election poster had vainly proclaimed '*Schweizer wählen SVP*' (Swiss vote SVP), but in 2011 over three-quarters of them didn't. It seemed like the bubble had burst, and yet they bounced back again with another referendum victory on immigration. This time, in February 2014, it was an SVP popular initiative to limit mass immigration through quotas. It was very narrowly approved by the voters,[37] even though implementing it would bring Switzerland into direct conflict with the European Union. Immigration quotas aren't exactly compatible with the free movement of people, which Switzerland had signed up to, despite not being an EU member.

Quotas would break the bilateral treaties, so risking Swiss access to the EU single market, which is crucial for the Swiss economy. Not wanting to antagonise the EU or to damage the economy, parliament and government took three years to decide to do nothing, ditching quotas in favour of nebulous rules about hiring Swiss workers at times of high employment. Referendum results in Switzerland are not written in stone as they still have to be enacted by parliament, which is free to change the law as it sees fit. Of course, it didn't help that in the meantime Brexit had happened and the EU had bigger fish to fry, so the ever-pragmatic Swiss decided not to push too hard.

The SVP chose not to call another vote on the issue, which was probably a wise decision. When they did force a second vote on the implementation of the deportation initiative, they lost badly.[38] In the end the Swiss had had enough of xenophobic paranoia and divisive campaigning, especially at a time of economic and political uncertainty. Or maybe they merely came to their senses and realised that the SVP is a wolf in sheep's clothing, a party run by millionaires posing as men of the people. The SVP invented racially-tinged populism long before Brexit or Trump, and uses direct democracy to promote it, but it's actually direct democracy that also provides the necessary checks and balances.

As all these votes showed, the long-term issue is integration and Switzerland is not alone in not really knowing how to manage it; most other European countries face a similar challenge. The difference is that in Switzerland the hurdles are higher and the rules stricter than in most other countries. A legitimate defence of everything Swiss? Or the acceptable face of xenophobia and racism? The Swiss themselves seem unable to decide, caught between needing the extra workers but not really wanting them to be involved; trapped between the liberal urge to help those in need and the conservative push for greater controls; stuck in the stand-off between immigration and the economy. This is a nation torn by both an idealised view of the past and the insecurity of a multicultural future, seeing itself as open and tolerant but then not always acting that way. One thing is sure: it will be the Swiss voters who decide what happens, but it could be some time before they know what they really want, and what is best for the country.

To outsiders, Swiss politics seems unduly labyrinthine, with its multiple layers and complex distribution of power. It can also appear dull, especially to those used to the adversarial nature of British and American (or French or German) politics. But perhaps Switzerland should be the rule rather than the exception. If all democracies were as inclusive, then maybe the politics would be more about policy and less about personality. It could save billions of dollars if elections were less confrontational, and millions of lives if the people decided when to go to war. It could make such a difference. No system is perfect, least of all the Swiss one, but some are clearly better than others, and one that mixes direct democracy with a parliamentary system gets close to perfection.

Understanding its unique politics is the key to grasping much of what Switzerland and its people are about. The national model of consensus and compromise shapes the Swiss mind and permeates down to every level of society. Everything is looked at from every angle, open to debate and formulated to appeal to the majority. Spontaneity is not a Swiss trait, be that dropping by on friends unannounced or making a decision that hasn't been discussed to the nth degree. Almost everything is planned with the meticulousness of a train timetable; and I mean a Swiss one, not British, let alone Italian. For all its drawbacks, however, the Swiss political system is perhaps the best example of true democracy in action. Or, as Abraham Lincoln once said: 'Government of the people, by the people, for the people.'[39] He must have had Switzerland in mind.

SWISS WATCHING TIP NO 4: X DOESN'T MARK THE SPOT

Nothing is uncomplicated in Switzerland, least of all voting. As a visitor it's not something you will ever do, and even permanent residents may never get a chance. Only the Swiss can vote, which is probably just as well because they're about the only ones who understand the system (and I'm not sure all of them do). Other countries' elections involve simply putting an X in a box or punching a hole. The Swiss have the world's most complex proportional representation system; you almost need a degree in quantum physics to understand it.

The easy part is the Council of States. You get two votes if your canton has two seats, only one if you live in a half-canton. Candidates are elected if they get an absolute majority of votes cast; if the seats are not filled, there is a second round a few weeks later. You cannot vote twice for the same candidate, which seems blindingly obvious until you read on.

The National Council election is where things get serious. You have as many votes as seats available, which in Canton Zurich means 35 but in next-door Canton Zug only three. Each party produces a candidate list or, by presenting itself as various different factions, more than one. So the SVP might have lists for male candidates, female candidates, the youth section and an international section – four times as many chances to win seats. You could just use one of these pre-selected lists for your votes, giving them all to one party. But how dull is that? Far better to be creative by changing the list in three different ways:

♣ Strike. If you don't like a candidate, then cross his (or her) name off the list. Simple as that, he's lost your vote. You can strike as many as you want, as long as at least one name remains.

♣ Accumulate. Give your favourite candidates a better chance by voting for them twice. Write each name in again, having first struck off someone else. Parties can also do this by putting a candidate twice in a list. But two's company, three's a crowd — in both cases triple voting is *verboten*; that would be so unfair.

✚ Split. You want to vote CVP but your best friend is standing for the FDP. No problem. Just cross off someone on the CVP list and add his name instead. Even better, cross off two people and write his name in twice.

As if that weren't enough, it's possible to create your own list using a blank voting form. You can pick and mix from any candidates who are already on an official list — and still accumulate by writing in names twice, though don't get carried away and write in more names than there are seats. List making can be a daunting task in some cantons, such as in the 2015 general election when 873 candidates across 35 lists stood for the 35 seats in Canton Zurich.[40] That's some choice, but help is at hand. An independent website[41] asks your views on a host of issues, then matches your answers to the candidates' views. A few clicks and you have a personal list. All very twenty-first century.

With so many possibilities you could be in that voting booth for hours, crossing out names, writing legibly, asking for another form because you messed yours up. It'd be like taking an exam. To stop all elections turning into a votathon, the Swiss very sensibly do it by post for the most part. There are polling stations, often in the main train station, but not as many as you see in Britain. Like so many things in Switzerland, voting is a private affair (except in Appenzell Innerrhoden and Glarus, of course). Best of all, the polling stations close at 12 noon so results can be declared in time for the evening news. No waiting up until 3 a.m. to see if voters in Essex or Pennsylvania have swung the election.

Faced with all of that, it's no surprise that turnout in Switzerland is not very high, hovering below the 50 per cent mark for the last few general elections. This could be down to voter fatigue, not only from trying to work out the system but from being asked to elect local, cantonal and national councils, as well as voting in all those referenda.

It might also be because general elections rarely achieve much. The new Federal Council will be much the same coalition as the old one, with one seat changing hands if you're lucky. Parliamentary political swings are more obvious, as shown by the SVP recently, but the Swiss parliament is much less powerful than those in other countries, so the impact is lessened.

The average referendum turnout is even lower, normally around 40 per cent. This seems rather odd, given that in many ways a referendum has more direct influence than a general election; each vote really does count. Perhaps being asked to make judgements so often affects the level of participation. Or more likely, most voters are content with the status quo and prefer not to get involved or push for change. What is noticeable is that when something really important comes along, turnout shoots up: 69 per cent in the vote to abolish the army in 1989, and 78 per cent in the EEA vote of 1992.[42]

Even if turnout is low, the direct democracy system works to include people and galvanise them into action. An optional referendum has been held 182 times since 1874, while the popular initiative is even more popular. It was first introduced in 1891, since when 209 have been voted on at a federal level, the majority of them since 1971. That's an awful lot of committees formed, signatures collected, campaigns organised and speeches made. Never mind that only 22 initiatives succeeded in being passed,[43] such political participation is unheard of in many other democracies. More than anything, it reminds the elected politicians that the people are always there, waiting to pass judgement.

FIVE

WEALTHY, HEALTHY AND WISE?

Zurich may not be the capital city, but for many it is the face of urban Switzerland: compact and efficient yet cosmopolitan and exciting, especially if you live in rural Appenzell. It has everything a Swiss city needs: the lake-shore location, the Alps in the background, trams trundling past, spires piercing the skyline, no hint of pollution, and even a faint but definite whiff of chocolate in the air. No wonder it regularly tops the polls of most desirable cities in the world to live in.

But for many in the English-speaking world, Zurich brings one image to mind: grey-suited bankers. Back when the pound in your pocket was still worth twenty shillings, British Prime Minister Harold Wilson damned them to be known for ever more as the gnomes of Zurich. And he wasn't talking about the bearded men who look like mini Father Christmases and inhabit many a British garden. These gnomes were the secretive, greedy ones living underground with their piles of hoarded gold, the ones manipulating the world against the innocent pound sterling. Not exactly a flattering picture, but one which has stuck. Google that phrase today and up pop articles on Swiss banking that are still using it. It's even there subconsciously in Harry Potter, where Gringotts Bank is run by goblins, the gnomes' uglier cousins, also traditionally cast as the bad guys in fairytales. These days bankers are called much worse but Wilson lived in an age when they were, at least in Britain, still in the honest, dependable mould of Captain Mainwaring in *Dad's Army*. They were the ones you could trust with the family silver and turn to in a crisis, rather than them selling the silver and causing the crisis. How the world has changed.

The only gnomes to be seen in Zurich are the common-or-garden variety in the window of a seed shop: cheery fellows with pointy hats and colourful clothing. In Paradeplatz, the home of the big two Swiss banks, there are soberly suited men, all of normal stature and mostly beardless, though many stretch to a moustache, a facial feature that is worryingly popular with Swiss men. One or two also sport a *melon*, as a bowler hat is known locally, more as a fashion statement than a status symbol. Are Swiss bankers any different from other Swiss people? Not really, and certainly not in the way that merchant bankers in London are a breed apart.

Bankers in Switzerland are neither revered as masters of the universe nor reviled as the lowest form of pond life. Like many Swiss professions, they are just there, working their 42 hours a week, helping make the country a success. In fact, some people feel sorry for them – for the simple reason of clothing. In Switzerland, where smart casual is a way of life, the only men to wear suits are bankers, lawyers and politicians (and not even all of them). Invitations almost never state a dress code because that would break two cardinal rules: you are implying that you don't trust your guests to come dressed properly, and you are invading their privacy by telling them what to wear. Trust and privacy are paramount in all things Swiss, particularly when it comes to banking.

TRUST ME, I'M SWISS

A picture is said to be worth a thousand words, but sometimes only a word can give the real picture. In Switzerland's case, the countless photos of chalets, mountains and trains are fine for postcards but none sums up the essence of the country. For that you need one word: trust. Nothing reveals more about the Swiss, their country and their attitude to life better than that. Trust is what binds them together. When it comes to making the right decisions, they put their trust in each other, not their politicians. Shops leave display tables of goods outside unguarded, CCTV cameras are noticeable by their absence, and coats are hung at the restaurant entrance rather than over the backs of chairs. All because the Swiss trust one another not to break the rules or cheat the system. Of course theft, burglaries, benefit scams and tax dodges all still go on, but either there are far fewer of them or they're better disguised. However, living in a society based on trust presents bigger problems than a few fiddles and frauds; in such a society you don't ask questions and you expect everyone else to be as honest.

The lack of questions is not simply about trust but about privacy, something most Swiss cherish more than anything. You don't pry because you know your neighbours know that rules are there to be followed, not broken. You don't question someone's actions because they have given their word that they're all above board. The only time you interfere is when it's clear the other person has crossed the line. This is fine if everyone plays by the same rules, but in the real world that doesn't happen. When the Swiss are faced with dishonesty and deceit, they can appear both charmingly incredulous and alarmingly innocent. Or perhaps it's all an act and they're being totally disingenuous, and have just been turning a blind eye to what they don't want to see. When it comes to Swiss banks, it's hard to know what the truth is.

Of the many Swiss clichés, banking is perhaps biggest of them all, and it's true in one respect: Switzerland certainly has lots of banks. Alongside the big two (UBS and Credit Suisse) are 260 others, with over 3000 branches, altogether employing about 121,000 people.[1] That's a big chunk of the economy, but most of these are not the banks you read about in headlines or plotlines; most of these are the ones where the Swiss save their money, and they do a lot of that – on average, a Swiss person has three savings accounts.[2] But read *The Da Vinci Code* or watch James Bond, and you'd think that Swiss banks are there purely for numbered accounts stuffed with ill-gotten gains or deposit boxes hiding some long-lost treasure. Swiss banks pop up in books and films with predictable regularity, so that for the outside world they are all about secrecy, whereas for the Swiss the issue is privacy. That may sound like the same thing, but to the Swiss it's not. In many ways the banks are a reflection of the society as a whole; in both, there is an assumption of trust that everyone is doing what's right, and there is never any invasion of privacy or thoughts of dishonesty.

Swiss banks are regarded as part of the community, there to act as safe houses against uncertainty and guarantors of stability. It's this that always made them attractive to foreigners long before banking secrecy was legally protected. In contrast, the banking ethos in Britain and America shifted ages ago to making money and taking risks, bringing both the bankers and the economy more wealth. That's so very un-Swiss, but Swiss banks got sucked into this money-spinning whirlwind and have been paying the price. The head of UBS stepped down in 2011 after a rogue trader in London had lost the bank two billion francs. Having been bailed out by the government, fined for helping rich Americans evade their taxes and cut thousands of jobs, it hadn't been a good couple of years for Switzerland's biggest bank. Not forgetting the disastrous company dress code, which made headlines around the world: for women, it was skin-coloured underwear, discreet make-up and no black nail varnish; for men, how to tie the right knot, monthly haircuts and no scruffy beards. Both sexes should avoid garlic or onions at lunch and always have clean spectacles, as 'on the one hand this gives you optimal vision and on the other hand dirty glasses create an appearance of negligence'. That might just seem like Swiss attention to detail, but even that's outdone by the comment that wearing a wristwatch shows 'trustworthiness and a serious concern for punctuality'. What better advice does a Swiss banker need?

While the much derided guide was later quietly revised, it was perhaps symptomatic of Swiss banking in general: criticised from all sides, undermined by past overconfidence and weakened by its reluctance to adapt. The collapse of Wegelin, Switzerland's oldest private bank, and its federal indictment in the US are proof of how far Swiss banks have fallen. The Swiss banking system is no longer a stereotypically smooth machine, nor is its future as gold-plated as it once was. It might remain at the heart of Switzerland's economy, but it may well need a transplant some time soon.

For the Swiss, witnessing the downfall of UBS hasn't only been a lesson in national humiliation, it was as much about how the bank had broken its compact of trust with the people. Money can be earned back quickly, trust takes a lot longer.

TAXING TIMES

This assumption of trust that underpins Swiss society is ironically the source of so much conflict between Switzerland and the rest of the world, and all thanks to tax. In Switzerland the tax system is essentially the same as the unmanned farm stalls you see all across the countryside, where customers pay the right price for the produce they take. It's all about honesty. There is no pay-as-you-earn (PAYE) system for Swiss tax,[3] because that would let the government invade people's privacy. It's also quite difficult to administer, as very little of the (low) taxes in Switzerland are federal. The income tax you pay is based not only on what you earn but on where you live, with each municipality setting its own rates. Keep the same job but move house to another town, even within the same canton, and the tax will be different. Great if you live in a low-tax municipality, bad news for cities with a large commuter workforce. All those people using the trams and streets every day but all paying tax where they live, not where they work.

Instead of PAYE, everyone has to complete a tax return no matter how little they earn, as tax kicks in from the very first penny. And it's payable on capital as well as income, so if you're unemployed but own land, you could still have to pay tax. The upside of this is that there are all sorts of legal means to lower your tax bill. Having a mortgage, painting your house, taking the train to work, giving to charity or running up big medical bills can all count against tax. Perhaps the best is eating lunch. If you're employed, you can claim 15Fr a day because you have to eat lunch away from home. Essentially it's dinner money from the taxman.

The only tax that is automatically deducted from your pay packet is the one that isn't called a tax. It's the Swiss equivalent of National Insurance or social security to cover the state pension, unemployment and invalidity. These obligatory deductions add up to 12 per cent, though your employer pays half of that (if you're self-employed, you get stung for the whole amount). The bulk of that money goes into the state pension system, but alongside that most employees also pay into a company pension scheme and can then also choose to set up a private pension plan. Of course, money paid into the latter is usually tax-deductible. Of course it is.

The premise of the Swiss tax and banking system is that the government trusts the taxpayer to tell the truth. As long as you don't lie (that would be fraud), you might be economical with the truth by forgetting about a bank account (that's just evasion, which in Switzerland is punishable with a fine rather than a potential prison sentence), a slight distinction that most other countries don't acknowledge. For the Swiss, banking secrecy and tax declarations are all about not letting anyone invade their privacy. When one Swiss banker (and politician; the two are not mutually exclusive) was asked why anyone would hide their money from the state unless they wanted to avoid taxes, his answer was typically Swiss: there's no reason for the state not to trust its citizens, so no reason for it to be allowed to inspect an individual's finances.[4] It's a view of the world that continues to cause problems.

In the past few years, barely a month has gone by without Switzerland having a tax dispute with someone. With the Americans it's the UBS client list, with the Germans it's tax havens, with the French it's transparency, with the EU it's corporate tax incentives, and so the list goes on. In 2009 it all came to a head and Switzerland bowed to international pressure to cooperate over tax affairs. It agreed to help in cases of evasion, not merely fraud, and signed revised double-taxation treaties with other countries. Does that mean the end of Swiss banking secrecy? Probably not, though Swiss banks have had to change the way they do some business. The days of truly anonymous accounts and suitcases full of cash are long gone anyway, so now it's more a question of not marketing the banks as tax escapes, as UBS did in the States, and of being seen to be whiter than white. But cracking down on tax evasion isn't the same as declaring open house on privacy. There is a big difference.

Client confidentiality isn't, or at least shouldn't be, the issue. That's crucial for any bank in any country; you couldn't just walk into a British bank and get details of an account. And almost every country has its offshore places where the rich and powerful stash their cash out of the taxman's reach. Britain has the Channel Islands, France has Monaco and the US has the Caymans (or even Delaware, one of its own states). The issue is cooperation, and the Swiss should be good at that; they've been practising it at home for centuries. However, the problem lies in the fact that the Swiss hate others telling them what to do and how to run their country. It's *Kantönligeist* on a national scale, and is one of the main reasons Switzerland is not in the European Union. Letting Brussels run their affairs would be invasion of Swiss privacy on a grand scale. Being bullied by bigger countries usually has exactly the opposite effect to the one intended; the Swiss are nothing if not stubborn.

MONEY TALKS, BUT VERY QUIETLY

Whatever you do, don't mention the money. As we'll see, talking about the war isn't such a good idea in Switzerland either, but money is the love that dare not speak its name. The Swiss have it, and many have plenty of it, but they don't talk about it. Polite conversation never ventures down the road to riches, meaning that house prices are not discussed, sale bargains are not compared and salaries are not openly a talking point. Money is just there, in the background, seen but not heard. And often not seen either. In Switzerland, if you've got it, hide it. Flaunting is *so* not Swiss. Brash displays of wealth can be seen in Zurich more than most other places, but there it's as many Russian tourists as chavvy locals wearing fur coats and dripping bling. As for betting shops, nothing so vulgar can be seen on Swiss high streets, for one thing because the Swiss don't need to gamble to be rich, and for another if they did, they wouldn't want any of their neighbours to know about it. Betting is something best done in the privacy of your own home or in a casino – there are 21 legal ones dotted all over Switzerland.[5]

This aversion to mentioning money includes not putting any salary details in job adverts, because doing that would mean everyone else would know how much you earn. And that wouldn't do at all. So instead, as a prospective employee you must know how much the job should pay and how much you think you're worth. At the end of the interview comes the moment for discussing your monthly salary, and it's a surreal one for those not used to the Swiss system. You have to make an offer, which is met with a counter-offer, with both sides bearing in mind that most Swiss companies pay monthly salaries 13 times a year, not 12 – the 13th is for paying your tax bill (see below). Eventually you agree on a figure acceptable to both parties. It may sound more like bartering in a bazaar than a job interview, and very odd behaviour for people who don't like talking about money, but it's actually very Swiss. The subject may be money but the system is the same as always: communication and compromise are used to reach a consensus so everyone is happy.

Maybe the Swiss don't talk about money because Switzerland wasn't always rich. As a landlocked country with few natural resources and no empire, it couldn't compete with the great European powers. That all changed in the late nineteenth century with the advent of the railways and tourism, but well before that the Swiss had a reputation as good bankers. Even though, as a nation, they didn't have much money, they could be relied on to look after other people's. That had little to do with bank secrecy, which only became Swiss law in 1934, but was all about stability, honesty and security. In fact, it was all about trust.

THE WAR THAT NEVER WAS

Nevertheless, talking about money is infinitely preferable to talking about the war. The Swiss don't talk about that at all. Admittedly they weren't directly involved, but it's almost as if it never happened, as if it's the elephant in the room whenever Germany, or recent Swiss history, is discussed. Neither are there jokes or common cultural markers: traffic wardens aren't called 'Little Hitlers', TV sitcoms aren't made about the French Resistance and posters aren't often defaced with toothbrush moustaches. With Nazi insignia forbidden and *Mein Kampf* banned, the rules are the same as modern Germany, even though the Swiss weren't part of the Third Reich. The question is, why? It's as if they feel guilty about the past, ashamed of what they did, or didn't do. Better not to talk about it than have an uncomfortable conversation. How Swiss.

Part of the reason is Switzerland's love–hate relationship with its big neighbour to the north, which is often more hate than love. Germany is often referred to, half-jokingly, as the 'big canton' and the recent influx of thousands of Germans into Switzerland[6] has raised the tension rather than helped relations. The Germans seem to be the only ones who can make the Swiss feel inferior, and that's not an easy feat. It's partly about language. High German, as spoken by the new-comers, is much more direct and less fluffy than the Swiss German dialects so its speakers seem arrogant and rude, at least to Swiss sensibilities. German speakers sometimes face snide comments or worse, and that includes English people who have learned High German. But given that High German, rather than dialect, is the official national language, most Swiss are willing (albeit reluctantly in some cases) to switch.

The rise in German immigrants is largely thanks to the series of bilateral agreements negotiated between Switzerland and the EU over the past 25 years. As part of that Switzerland signed up to the free movement of people, so EU citizens[7] can usually live and work in Switzerland and vice versa. This didn't prompt a flood of Polish plumbers, as feared, but a wave of German doctors, nurses, teachers and thousands of others. The Swiss repelled one German invasion in the forties but have succumbed to another in the noughties.

As much as language and immigration the problem is history, specifically the Second World War. The Swiss did what they had to in order to survive. For sure, it wasn't perfect behaviour, but the Allies were hardly angels and many Swiss did try to help. However, it's their behaviour after the war that the Swiss perhaps feel most uncomfortable about. That boils down to two words: Nazi gold. They cover a multitude of things, but mainly refer to the gold shipped to Switzerland by the Nazis and the unclaimed Jewish assets sitting in Swiss banks long after the war ended. The issue with the former is that the Swiss didn't question where the gold originated – it's that whole trust–privacy thing again – so got their hands dirty with millions of francs in stolen loot. Acting in good faith can only be believed up to a point, after which it looks like being opportunistic. Which is exactly what it was. The Swiss still use that old Latin saying (but in German), *Geld stinkt nicht*, which translates literally as 'money doesn't smell' or, better yet, there's no such thing as dirty money. Never truer than in this case.

Luckily for the Swiss, the victorious Allies needed their money after the war, both to rebuild Europe and to help fight the Soviet threat. Trifles like $444 million[8] in gold were brushed under the communal carpet in the name of defending democracy. What happened to the gold? Who knows. Having dodged that bullet, the Swiss did the same with the second by ignoring it. Nevertheless, 50 years later it struck right where it hurt most, the Swiss banks. In 1995 the World Jewish Congress (WJC), backed by the US Senate, sued for the return of all unclaimed assets from dormant Swiss accounts. And that's when the Swiss made their biggest mistake. Instead of coming clean the banks fought back, denying responsibility, throwing up endless red tape, and generally making themselves look far worse than they already did. Then they asked for death certificates from concentration camp victims. Oh dear.

In the end they struck a deal with the WJC and handed over $1.25 billion. The Swiss government stayed out of it, but then had the decency to set up a commission to investigate every aspect of Switzerland's wartime behaviour. The critical Bergier report wasn't easy reading for anyone Swiss, but for once it made them talk about the war and their role in it. Soul-searching doesn't come naturally to them, but at least when they do it, they do it with the same thoroughness as everything else.

MATTERS OF LIFE AND DEATH

The strange thing is that the death certificate debacle won't have seemed so ridiculous to many Swiss people, not for moral reasons but because Switzerland is a bureaucracy as much as a democracy. Swiss red tape makes all others look pink. They love pieces of paper. To the Swiss mind, if it doesn't have a paper record, it doesn't exist. Job applications don't just need a CV and letter, they need copies of all relevant qualifications and work references. Every training course, every exam, every apprenticeship, every job, everything ends with a piece of paper to prove it. For any fairly normal application, registration or permit you have to copy countless bits of paper: school reports, degree, tax return, passport, visa, inside-leg measurement, dental records, etc., etc. And I'm only half-joking.

You sometimes even need to prove that you are unmarried, have no parking fines or live where you say you live. And for those, it has to be an official stamped piece of paper, not only your photocopy. Of course that's easy to get (for a fee) from your local municipal office because every person living in a municipality has to register with the authorities; you can't simply live somewhere without telling the powers-that-be. For a nation that relishes privacy, it's rather odd to live with such control. It feels almost like living in a police state, albeit a good-natured one that's officious but not vicious. Solzhenitsyn is said to have complained that the bureaucracy in Switzerland was worse than Russia.[9] It really is that omnipresent, but for the Swiss it's normal; they've been living with it ever since their birth certificate was issued.

Among all the many papers that every Swiss person needs, some of the most important are for insurance, another Swiss obsession. Taxes may be low, but insurance makes up for that by consuming 17 per cent of the average household budget.[10] There's insurance for almost everything, not just to give people yet more documents, but also to make sure they are prepared for any eventuality. Be prepared, and have the papers to prove it, is pretty much the Swiss ethos. Obligatory insurances cover old age, invalidity, accidents and unemployment, making them similar to the catch-all National Insurance in Britain. Then there's personal liability insurance which is almost mandatory, just in case, for example, you break someone's window and they sue you. But the killer is health insurance, with premiums so high, and still rising, that it's possibly the one reason Swiss people are moved to talk money. Only the US spends more per head on health than the Swiss.[11] That's how expensive it is.

There's no national health system in Switzerland. Instead, every permanent resident is obliged to take out basic health insurance, with those on low incomes getting some state help. Insurers cannot refuse anyone basic cover and must offer the same minimum cover, including maternity care but generally excluding such things as dental treatment. Prices can vary hugely, even for the required legal minimum. For example, in

Bern I have the choice of over 200 basic policies costing from 3300Fr to 8600Fr a year[12] (about £2500 to £6600).

The lowest figure comes with the highest annual excess or deductible, known as the *Franchise*; in other words the part I have to pay if I see a doctor or have any treatment. Under Swiss law, the minimum adult *Franchise* is 300Fr a year and the maximum 2500Fr, so there's no chance of people going bankrupt because they can't pay their medical bills. This being Switzerland, health services are a cantonal matter, so every canton has different rates, some nearly half the price of others. Live in Appenzell and you're laughing all the way to the (blood) bank; live in Basel and the insurance costs might bleed you dry long before you die.

Unfortunately, high insurance premiums don't make the system any cheaper. Every visit to the doctor is charged per minute and drugs cost more than abroad despite many of them being made in Switzerland. Supermarkets are not allowed to sell medicines, not even painkillers, so everything has to go through the doctor or the chemist. No surprise, then, that Switzerland is full of chemists: in my ten-minute walk into town, I pass seven and that's without going through the city centre. Entering a Swiss chemist is a daunting experience because everything is behind the counter, stored in drawers and cupboards. You have to ask a white-coated assistant for the simplest thing, and then try not to faint when you're charged seven francs for seven headache tablets. Enough to induce a migraine.

Healthcare in the US, or the lack thereof, may make headlines around the world, but few people are interested in the Swiss system. Apart from one issue: assisted suicide. Helping someone to end his or her own life is not illegal in Switzerland,[13] as long as it is done by an individual who isn't a doctor and has no vested interest in the outcome. So bumping off Great Aunt Hildegard to get her money isn't allowed, but volunteering to help a stranger who has chosen to end their suffering is okay. Two Swiss organisations, Exit and Dignitas, interpret the law, or lack of one, in such a way that since the 1980s organised assisted suicide has been an option in Switzerland. Exit only helps permanent residents in Switzerland whereas Dignitas is open to anyone, a policy that has been a tad controversial, initially abroad but then in Switzerland.

So far over 300 Britons, and many more Germans,[14] have travelled to Zurich and swallowed the lethal dose of barbiturates, having first paid Dignitas about 10,000Fr to cover costs (Dignitas is a non-profit organisation). It's this 'death tourism', especially for patients who are paralysed rather than terminally ill, that prompted calls for a change in the law. A recent referendum in Zurich proposed either banning assisted suicide altogether or outlawing it for foreigners; both proposals failed by a large margin. Almost at the same time, the pressure for change in Britain, where assisted suicide is banned, increased when the Director of Public Prosecutions issued new guidelines on the subject. Both moves are only the first step of many in an ongoing debate.

What is interesting is that in Switzerland the debate is far less emotionally charged than in Britain. There are few newspaper editorials from writers with more compassion for their pets than a dying relative. And certainly no hectoring from men chosen by God rather than the people; Switzerland may still be quite religious in many ways, but the church stays out of politics. The focus is much more on making sure the law is followed properly, which is very Swiss, and that assisted suicide shouldn't become a money maker, unusually not very Swiss. It remains to be seen which country will have the more constructive debate.

A SINGULAR CURRENCY

The one aspect of money that all Swiss have in common is pride in their franc. Before that came along in 1850, the Swiss money market was a mess. Every canton had its own currency, but there were also ones from the old Helvetic Republic, the monasteries, Italian city-states and a clutch of other countries. In total, around 8000 different coins were legal tender. Then someone had the bright idea of creating a single currency for the new federation, and the Swiss franc was born. Unfortunately, the cantonal mints couldn't cope with the demand, so the first Swiss coins were minted in Paris and Strasbourg. Not the best beginning for a national currency, although the Swiss franc has never looked back. It's one of the world's strongest currencies and the Swiss love it. So much so, they use it whenever possible.

Most Swiss pay the old-fashioned way, in cash. Perhaps that's why they have such big notes. Go to a cashpoint in Switzerland and it will give you your money in 100-franc notes, while a sure sign of being a tourist or newly arrived expat is that you apologise when paying for a drink with a 200-franc note. What to others is a small fortune in one note, for the Swiss is normal. Cashiers do not bat an eyelid when presented with three or four together. And even 1000-franc notes are accepted in most shops every day all across the country without a second glance – that's over $1000 in one purple piece of paper.

I'll never forget when I worked in Stauffacher Bookshop in Bern and had my first experience of a customer paying for a paperback with a 1000-franc note. I had never seen one before so wasn't really sure what to do. Should I hold it up to the light? Should I call my boss? Should I call the police? While I hesitated the customer simply stared at me staring at the note, clearly wondering why I didn't simply give her 976 francs in change.

Just as eye-opening was waiting in my bank in Bern one December, and trying not to stare open-mouthed at the elderly woman in front of me, who had asked for 17,000Fr in cash. It didn't take long as the cashier only had to count out 17 notes and pop them in an envelope. The woman picked up her money, put it in her bag and said she was off to do her Christmas shopping. Only in Switzerland.

Compare that to when I was in Britain some years ago to organise the deposit for my flat in Switzerland. Before I could withdraw my money from my account, I had to give 24 hours' notice and provide two forms of ID, not just for security but because the bank didn't have that much cash all at once. I needed to take my money to the building society but when it came, it was in bundles of tens and twenties, all badly sorted and rather worn. The cashier at the building society had a minor heart attack when I handed over the bag of notes. I felt like a bank robber.

Swiss notes are rarely tatty or crumpled. They are seldom stuffed into pockets but are treated with care, folded neatly into four or tucked carefully into a wallet. Their bright colours – yellow, red, green, blue, brown and purple – never seem to fade or get dirty; it's almost as if someone somewhere is washing the money. The fascinating thing about the banknotes is how much is squeezed on to them. For starters, an awful lot has to be in all four national languages: the name of the National Bank, the amount in words and the fact that the note is protected by law. Then come the 14 security features that make it one of the best-protected currencies. Standard things such as serial number, watermark and metal strip seem old hat against UV fibres or five different ways of showing the Swiss cross, including a see-through one which becomes the Swiss flag when you hold it up to the light. Or giving each note raised print, which also helps blind people feel the difference.

My favourite security trick is part of the current redesign of all the notes that has ditched the old portraits of Swiss notables in favour of broad themes. So instead of Le Corbusier on the 10-franc note, we now have the theme of 'Switzerland's organisational talent – expressed by time.'[15] One aspect of that is a tiny silver rail map of Switzerland along with the names and lengths of all the major rail tunnels written in teeny-tiny print. It's a nice factual counterpart to the rather garish abstract design of the new notes, which feature giant hands, globes and various random concepts.

CHANGING THE MONEY

With so many security features on their notes, the Swiss no longer need to print a whole separate set for use in times of crisis. There used to be a reserve supply of Swiss banknotes with a secret design, kept purely for if and when the currency was undermined by mass forgeries. The national bank could then recall all existing notes in circulation and replace them instantly with new ones of a different design. That's quite some undertaking, and one which exemplifies the Swiss commitment to their franc. Its continued stability and worth are of the greatest national importance, which is possibly why they are happy not to rock the political boat too much. The Swiss franc is strong precisely because it is Swiss: as solid, stable and reliable as the country behind it. The one big difference is that the franc changes far more often. Every twenty years a whole new set of notes is designed, printed and circulated. When that happened in 1995–8 the notes' sizes were also changed; it's a wonder the Swiss could cope with such radicalism.

Swiss francs used to be like pounds and euros, with the notes getting bigger as the value increased. This made it difficult to count them automatically in machines, something the Swiss love to do; with so much cash being used, who can blame them? The practical answer was to make all the notes the same width,[16] but still have them getting longer the more they are worth. Having the notes all the same width also means that they fit more neatly into a wallet, with no ugly edges hanging out and getting scruffy.

This practical aspect has not been lost with the new series of notes that are gradually replacing the old ones. The new 10-, 20- and 50-franc notes are already in circulation, with the series due for completion by the end of 2019. Each new note is smaller than the one it's replacing, but all the new notes are of equal width. And with typical attention to detail, each one is 7 millimetres shorter than the one above it (in value terms), so that by the time you reach the new 1000 francs, the note is a remarkable 158 millimetres long;[17] at least there's room for the extra zeros.

Design, production and upkeep of the notes are the responsibility of the Swiss National Bank. To show how much the Swiss value that, the bank has the most important address in the country: Bundesplatz 1, in Bern. Even parliament can't compete; it's merely Bundesplatz 3.

This ever-changing cycle of notes is possibly a reaction to having coins whose simple design has hardly altered since they were introduced. In all that time the most radical thing to happen was when Helvetia stood up in 1874; until then the Swiss equivalent of Britannia had been depicted sitting, but she's been standing ever since.[18] Then, over 100 years later, the creation of Canton Jura meant that the ring of stars (each one representing a canton) on the 2-franc, 1-franc and ½-franc coins had to shift to make room for one more. And that's about it. Coming from a country that changes its coins seemingly every few years, it's still decidedly strange for me to use coins that are older than I am. I occasionally get a 1940s coin in my change, causing me to pause and think how many thousands of hands have held it since it was minted. After that, I usually go and wash mine.

While their designs have stayed, the actual coins have had to change with the times. They used to be made of silver, but that was abandoned in 1967 when silver prices were so high that coins were hoarded or smuggled out of the country. And the Swiss don't really trifle with small change; the one and two *rappen*[19] coins were both abandoned, meaning no .99 prices. Very sensible.

The coins are such a constant that changes are fiercely debated, most notably in 1895 when a new design for the gold 20-franc coin caused uproar. It showed a Swiss woman with an edelweiss scarf against a mountain backdrop. Not too contentious, you might think, but certain gentlemen took exception to it. Or more precisely to her lock of hair flicked forwards across her forehead, making 'the woman look like a frivolous hussy'; not at all the image of Switzerland they wanted.[20] But 'Vreneli', as she is popularly known, was a hit with the public, who clearly didn't care about her wayward hair. Just as Vreneli is a generic Swiss woman, so the muscular, hooded man on the chunky 5-franc coin is a Swiss Everyman, a simple shepherd. Contrary to popular belief, he is not William Tell.[21]

THE IMPORTANCE OF BEING FRANC

Kreuzlingen is one of those nondescript Swiss towns that most people merely pass through, in this case on the way to its next-door neighbour Constance. The cathedral city just over the German border has always been a popular day trip for the Swiss, not only for its lakeside old town but for the shopping. In 2011 the steady trickle of Swiss shoppers became a flood, and the first casualty of the deluge was the local economy in Kreuzlingen. For years, its petrol stations had been full of cars with German number plates; Switzerland had the lowest petrol prices in Europe and profited from that. In real terms those prices were still much the same, but the mighty franc made them look very expensive. Suddenly the reverse applied: the Germans stopped coming and the Swiss were buying their petrol over the border. And for once, it was the franc that was at fault. From being a guarantor of Swiss security and stability and a source of national pride, it had caused an economic crisis in its homeland. It was the victim of its own success.

Low unemployment, minimal national debt, no housing bubble – while other economies crashed and burned, the Swiss was a beacon of responsibility and prudence, so the demand for francs exploded. With both the euro and US dollar collapsing, 2011 was the year when investors turned to the ever-reliable Swiss franc as a safe haven. It gained up to 30 per cent in value in just 15 months, rushing past parity with the dollar and then reaching it with the euro. Great news for Swiss going abroad, disastrous for Swiss industry dependent on exports and tourism. As quickly as the foreign visitors stopped arriving, the Swiss were leaving to shop in Germany, France and Italy. Same products, half the price. Not only that, but what had been the last resort for the Swiss tourist industry – loyal domestic guests – also started to disappear. Even the most patriotic Swiss realised that switching to a holiday abroad was a bargain not to be missed. The solid Swiss economy was battered from all sides – tourism down, exports down, shops closing down. Having survived the banking and housing crashes, Switzerland finally tasted economic distress, albeit of a very unusual nature. Only the Swiss could turn success into a crisis.

It was a summer of discontent. As complaints about high prices and low profits grew louder, the government offered two billion francs to help the export and tourist industries, but only got criticism in return. Supermarkets battled to show that they were cutting prices on imported goods, car dealers and electrical shops shouted about euro discounts, and hotels relied ever more on the Asian market. It is rather ironic that as hard as the Swiss try to stay aloof from the EU and its currency, they sometimes have no option but to succumb to economic and geographic realities. Refusing to join the party doesn't mean that you are immune to the noise. Eventually the Swiss National Bank stepped in and tied the franc to the euro at a minimum rate of 1.20, committing itself to spending whatever it took to achieve that. It proved to be an expensive decision, and ultimately a futile one. By 2015 the National Bank admitted defeat and was forced to let the franc float free again. Not even the Swiss are immune to the power of the money markets.

WHERE DEBT IS A FOUR-LETTER WORD

Cash is king in the Alpine Republic. Credit cards are a means of payment, not a way of life as they are elsewhere. One third of Swiss consumers don't have one at all and of those that do, only 17 per cent use it regularly.[22] Switzerland is a nation of savers who become spenders only when they can afford it; prudence is their middle name. To the Swiss mind, it's illogical to pay on credit when you can pay now in cash and keep control of your finances. And if you can't pay now, then don't buy it. You rarely see ads for buy-now-pay-later or interest-free credit because debt, either national or personal, is not a Swiss word. It's all about control, meaning that direct debit is not popular and certainly not a must for utility bills. Letting someone else take money automatically from your account does not sound like a good idea to most Swiss.

This reluctance to get into debt works for retailers too. They know that they can deliver goods without a deposit or credit-card number being taken, because their customers order things only when they can pay for them. And of course, they can be trusted to pay up when asked. For example, at Stauffacher Bookshop books are sent out with a bill rather than pre-paid by card, and customers have a month to settle. It's like being back in the 1970s. The same principle works for large purchases. When I bought a new fridge, it was delivered and installed without me paying so much as a penny in advance or giving a guarantee; the bill arrived a few days later. All very trusting; though if I didn't pay up, they knew where I lived.

The lack of debt also applies to the national economy. That's usually well in the black, thanks to a healthy trade surplus from precision engineering goods, but also pharmaceuticals and chemicals. Overall, Swiss GDP amounts to $669 billion annually,[23] of which financial services account for 13 per cent, a larger share than in most other countries.[24] It is the 19th biggest economy in the world, a crucial position because it means that Switzerland could be part of the G20 but wasn't invited. That snub still smarts.

Ironically, the recent economic crisis affected the Swiss far less than many G20 members, mainly because the housing market is as stable as the franc. No big booms or crashes because most people rent not buy. Only 38 per cent of Swiss own their own home, a figure that drops to 15 per cent in cities like Basel,[25] almost exactly the opposite of the British market. It's partly a cultural thing – owning property is not the be-all and end-all of life – but it's also practical, as you need a 20 per cent deposit. Some people rent the same flat all their lives, but that's seen as a risk-free, sensible option not a waste of money.

Everyone renting has its advantages. No property ladders mean no snakes, so while you might not make a fortune in houses, you're unlikely to lose one either. Negative equity, what's that? Estate agents are not ten a penny on the high streets, newspapers are not full of property ads and television isn't packed with endless variations of makeover, developing or relocation programmes. You have to watch German TV for those. To buy or not to buy is a question the Swiss ask about lots of things but rarely houses.

The best thing is that roads are not blighted by a forest of For Sale signs. Instead, you can see what look like four anorexic Martian spaceships sitting in vacant plots of land. These giant wooden or metal tripods show the dimensions of any new building, with their height and position corresponding exactly to that of the proposed building. This rule applies to every construction project in Switzerland, including high-rises, which need special Meccano-style pylons tethered with wires to show how tall they will be. It might look odd, but it gives everyone a good idea of what's planned and a chance to complain if they object. Planning permission not just by committee but by common consent.

Switzerland has a reputation for being expensive, and while that's true much of the time, not everything Swiss has a price tag. The Swiss like to say that nothing in life is free but some of the best things are. For example, almost every town has crystal-clear Alpine water gushing from public drinking fountains, many crowned by a colourful 'middle-aged' sculpture. That's not a statue of a man in cardigan and slippers (middle-aged is a common mistranslation of *mittelalterlich*, or medieval) but more likely blind justice or a baby-eating ogre. Then there's the gift wrapping. The nice thing about Swiss shopping is not the choice of watches or, sadly, the level of service, but the wrapping. This is free, even at Christmas when the wait for the wrapping table is longer than that at the tills; the Swiss are not ones to look a gift-wrapped horse in the mouth. Perhaps that's why they have ended up as wealthy as they are, by looking after their own – and other people's – pennies.

Wealth and health. Historically, these have been the two main reasons for coming to Switzerland for longer than a ski trip. It was all about protecting your wellbeing, be that physical or financial, and dodging the grasp of the Grim Reaper or the taxman. In the nineteenth century there was no place to get bed rest like a Swiss sanatorium. Long before Davos became an economic talking shop, it was one big convalescent home. Robert Louis Stevenson wrote the last part of *Treasure Island* while recuperating in Davos, and the town went on to have a starring role in Thomas Mann's sanatorial epic *The Magic Mountain*. These days a sanatorium is more likely to be called a wellness hotel or spa resort, but the idea is the same: come to Switzerland and get healthy. It worked for me. And now that Swiss banks are going to be playing by something approximating the rules, the taxman will probably catch up with you before the tall man with the scythe.

The Swiss live long and prosper. They are one of the healthiest and wealthiest nations on earth, where an average life expectancy of 83.4 years, second only to the Japanese,[26] is matched by a per capita GDP of $80,000, second highest in the world after Luxembourg.[27] Nevertheless, as we have seen in this chapter, they don't always make the wisest decisions, sometimes out of necessity or greed, but usually because they trust others to be honest. And in that, are they unrealistic or altruistic? Naive or calculating? Probably all of the above, which makes them no different from most other countries; they just wrap it up more attractively.

SWISS WATCHING TIP NO 5:
NOT AS EASY AS 1-2-3

Counting in a foreign language should be easy. Even if you are linguistically challenged, you can probably stretch to *un, deux, trois* from memories of school French. Or *uno, dos, tres* if you've ordered beers in Ibiza, and you might even manage *eins, zwei, drei* from countless war films. But in Switzerland, mastering 1-2-3 is up there with learning your ABC (for that, see the next chapter).

The issue is not the multiple languages, which are rarely used together unless you happen to be playing multilingual bingo. Imagine how time consuming that would be: two fat ladies eighty-eight, *zwei dicke Frauen achtundachtzig, deux grosses dames quatre-vingt-huit, due grasse donne ottantotto*. No, the real issue for number novices is how the Swiss use their numerals. In English, numbers, such as a phone number, are generally given one digit after another: 021 364 7958 (all Swiss phone numbers, including mobiles, are ten digits) is said as ten distinct numbers with a slight pause between the three groups; a Swiss person would typically say that same number as zero twenty one, three sixty four, seventy nine, fifty eight. Not too difficult to follow in English, but in German, numbers are all backwards: zero one-and-twenty, three four-and-sixty, nine-and-seventy, eight-and-fifty. Try writing that down as someone is saying it and you're bound to get a wrong number. Literally. You have write the 0, then leave a gap and write 1, go back to the 2, jump over to the 3, over again to the 4, back to the 6 and so on. Perhaps this numerical leapfrog is a way of breaking up otherwise scarily long German numbers. That 364 would be written as *dreihundertvierundsechzig*, which is quite a mouthful.

The Swiss way of saying phone numbers may sound odd, but at least as far as the languages go, it's logical. The same can't be said for the emergency numbers. In a country where everything is organised to the last millimetre, how is it possible that each emergency service has its own number? That's federalism taken to ridiculous lengths. You have to ring 117 for the police, 118 for the fire brigade and 144 for an ambulance. What happens if you dial the wrong one by mistake? And if you need a policeman and a fireman, do you have to ring twice? It would be laughable if it weren't so serious. Plus the fact that directory enquiries is 1818; no surprise that the fire service sometimes get callers asking for the number of the local pizzeria.

It's not only phone numbers that are all over the place but addresses too. In Swiss terms, the British Prime Minister lives at Downing Street 10, as the number comes after the street (except for holiday chalets, Swiss houses rarely have names since that would be too individual for the house as much as the owner). But the postcode then comes before the town name: the Stauffacher Bookshop where I used to work can be found at Neuengasse 25-37, 3001 Bern. So much for Swiss logic.

Dispensing with written digits and using your fingers instead may not help either, as Swiss people use a thumb rather than index finger for number one. So four is shown with the thumb and first three fingers, instead of folding the thumb into the palm and holding up all four fingers. And that's not the only use the Swiss have for their thumbs. The first time a friend proffered me his fist clenched around his thumb, I didn't quite know how to respond. He was too old to be fist bumping and too polite to be itching for a fight. All he wanted to do was wish me good luck. For that, the Swiss don't cross fingers, they hold a thumb.

Making things more complicated are the local variations on normal numbers. Until I came to Switzerland I thought I could count in French and German. To show that they are really Swiss and not some French province, the people of Romandie have their own versions of 70 to 99. In the bingo example above, the frankly ridiculous *quatre-vingt-huit* would be *huitante-huit* in Switzerland. Easy once you know. As for Swiss German numbers, they were the cause of one of my more embarrassing expat moments. A newish friend was giving me his mobile number, patiently saying each number in turn, but in his Bernese dialect. The last three digits were 896, which sounded something like *achty-noony-sechsy*. All I heard was 'afternoon sex'. Unaccustomed as I am to being propositioned in the vegetable aisle of the Coop, my face went as red as the tomatoes behind me. Apart from my blushes, the other outcome was me learning Swiss numbers asap. The one that still makes me smile is five: in Bern the ugly German *fünf* becomes *füüfi*, which brings a little white poodle to mind.

However, there are even bigger number problems than that. The Swiss, like most other Europeans, use a comma for a decimal point, so inflation might be 3,4%. To complicate things further, an apostrophe is used to replace the comma in numbers over four digits, so this book might sell 1'000'000 copies. Then, if it were to sell a thousand times that number (that is, 1 plus 9 zeros), in Switzerland that would be a milliard; a Swiss billion is a million million (1 plus 12 zeros). That means it's scarily easy to mistranslate numbers, and that much harder to become a Swiss billionaire.

Time can also get lost in translation. For example, friends would arrange to meet me at *halb sieben*, which was easy enough to understand as half seven, and I'd be an hour late. The next time, I'd clarify the time in both English and German, as my mastery of German numbers was clearly not quite beyond kindergarten level, and the same would happen. To be an hour late once is a misfortune; to manage it twice looks like carelessness, as Lady Bracknell might have said if she'd been Swiss. It all comes down to the mistranslation of time idioms. There I was simply translating *halb sieben* to half seven and presuming that it meant 7.30. Silly me. *Halb sieben* actually translates as half six. Obvious, isn't it? Translate the number and deduct one.

The problem is that in English half seven is a shortened form of half-past seven, whereas in German *halb sieben* translates as halfway to seven o'clock, 6.30. A whole hour earlier. And even with other English speakers there's a chance they mistake an English half seven for a translated Swiss one; once you've been here long enough, that's how your mind starts to work. My solution? Switch to saying six thirty, or better yet arrange everything for on the hour. Seven o'clock is crystal clear to everyone – or is it? Many Swiss tend to use the 24-hour clock, even in speech (it must be from reading all those train timetables), so I have taken to saying *neunzehn Uhr*, or 19.00, so there's no outside chance of anyone being 12 hours late. It makes me sound very military, or maybe just very Swiss.

SIX

WAR AND PEACE

very year a national survey asks the Swiss people what three things they associate with their own country. And almost every year two themes come top of the vox pops: peace and security, and neutrality.[1] In the Swiss mind those two go hand in hand; they value their status as an oasis of security in a troubled world, but maintaining it is only possible through upholding their neutrality. These are the two wheels of the Swiss bike; lose one and you lose both. Incidentally, the third factor to be mentioned changes almost every year: democracy, freedom, landscape and education have all featured in the list. None has the consistency of neutrality, which is seen as a fundamental part of the Swiss identity, both at home and abroad, the most sacred cow in a land of many. That's partly due to the strict rules the Swiss impose on their own neutrality, but also to the ongoing links to one organisation, the Red Cross. It may be nominally independent, but for many the Red Cross is as much a Swiss creation as army knives and holey cheese. That it exists at all is down to one man, who should be the most famous Swiss person of all time, but few people have heard of him. After all, this is the man who gave the world a conscience. And gave Switzerland a world role.

It's hard to imagine what the world would be like if Henry Dunant had never been born: no Red Cross so no humanitarian aid, no Geneva Conventions so no rules of war, no YMCA so no Village People. Without him such a terrible world might exist. Even if assessing his global effect is too much, what about his part in the making of modern Switzerland? If Dunant, and thus the Red Cross, had never existed, how

139

different a place would Switzerland be? Or, almost as important, how different would it be *seen* to be?

Time to find out more about this most Swiss of international institutions, and also about its creator. Time, in fact, to go back to the most international of Swiss cities, Geneva.

A WORLD VILLAGE

Small as it is, Geneva is the physical embodiment of Switzerland's much-cherished internationalism and neutrality. It is home not only to the Red Cross but also to the European end of the United Nations and many of its subsidiaries, such as UNICEF and the World Health Organisation. Over the years, a whole menagerie of other international organisations has mushroomed, making Geneva truly a world city. Some, like the World Trade Organisation, are well known; others you might not have heard of. The International Road Federation, anyone? Or the International Textiles and Clothing Bureau? How about the International Organisation for Standardisation, which sounds almost Orwellian? And then there's the International Union for the Protection of New Varieties of Plants, though I can't imagine it is too busy. These are just a few of the 24 international bodies with headquarters in Geneva, which, along with about 250 non-governmental organisations stationed there, employ over 31,000 people.[2] That's the equivalent of everyone in Windsor working for one of these organisations: a city within a city. With so many diplomats, international civil servants and other hangers-on, it's no big surprise to discover that 48 per cent of Geneva's population is not Swiss, one of the highest percentages in the country.[3] Perhaps that's why Switzerland itself has a diplomatic mission in Geneva, though its official role is to liaise with the UN and all the others.

Many of these organisations are in the city's International

Quarter, clustered around the monumental Palais des Nations. Built to house the ill-fated League of Nations between the world wars, it was then converted to become the UN European HQ. And that was despite Switzerland not joining the United Nations until 2002, when it became the 190th member, and only then after a close referendum. A little more than 54 per cent said yes,[4] but that narrow victory represents quite an earthquake in Swiss terms; a previous attempt in 1986 failed after managing to score just 24 per cent approval.[5] The intervening 16 years had seen the end of the Cold War and 9/11, which were enough to persuade a majority to overcome fears of compromising Swiss neutrality and being bound by UN resolutions. Letting the people decide foreign policy may seem rather strange to anyone brought up in any other country, but to the Swiss it's perfectly normal.

The International Quarter is one of Geneva's posher, leafier suburbs, where gracious villas stand in manicured gardens, making the UN building, with its severe, almost Stalinist architecture and forest of flagpoles, appear rather ungainly. But it's nothing compared to the ghastly concrete entrance to the Red Cross Museum, which sticks out like a sore thumb. Maybe its 1980s ugliness is intentional, there to remind us that the world has as many thorns as it does roses. For proof of that you need only look at the property next door, the Russian Embassy compound, which has razor wire all along the top of its outer walls. Welcome to the neighbourhood.

INSIDE THE RED CROSS

On Swiss television news the Red Cross, which pops up with alarming regularity, is known in German as the IKRK. The full name is rarely given, as for Swiss viewers it would be condescending to explain what the letters stand for; imagine if the British news always gave the full version of the NHS or American the FBI. But for non-Swiss viewers, the letters IKRK signify nothing. At first I thought it was referring to some separatist movement in the Middle East (it was a story on the war in Iraq) or a weird offshoot of the Ku Klux Klan (in a story about Hurricane Katrina). Or, most worryingly, how IKEA was helping reconstruction in both places. Even when they interviewed some chap from the Red Cross, the caption just read so-and-so from IKRK. They love captions on Swiss news, especially when interviewing people, which usually means thrusting a big grey microphone into the interviewee's face, something the BBC stopped doing about 20 years ago. Every time they come back to the interviewee for another soundbite, up comes the caption again, to remind you who the talking head is. This is not because the Swiss have memories like goldfish but because a viewer might have tuned in halfway through and need to know who is speaking. It certainly makes the news livelier, with captions flashing on and off screen every few seconds.

But back to my white supremacist furniture dealers in the Middle East. The letters actually stand for the *Internationales Komitee vom Roten Kreuz,* aka the IKRK. That's the organisation's official name and on its website it refers to itself almost exclusively in those terms, even in English, when it becomes the ICRC (short for International Committee of the Red Cross). For sure those four letters have never been seen or heard together in the British news, where the more informal Red Cross is used, not least because it's easier to say with a straight face. Having to say 'icy arsey' more than once might make even the most serious newsreader smirk. Of course, the ICRC being Swiss in origin, there is a logical explanation for the long-winded name. Each country has its own Red Cross (or Red Crescent) society, which is why those giant food-aid bags always have 'Gift of the American Red Cross' stamped on them; although I thought it was the Americans showing off again. Overseeing all the societies is the ICRC, which really is a committee, currently composed of 17 members,[6] who take decisions by consensus. It's all very Swiss, as is every member of the committee. This is to ensure its neutrality, as having other nationalities on the committee might compromise it. For example, how would a Russian member react to a need for aid in Crimea, or Syria about Aleppo? Remaining unbiased would be hard, and the ICRC would end up as impartial as ice-skating judges and Eurovision juries. So to refer to it as merely the Red Cross, as we lazy English speakers do, is technically inaccurate, and the Swiss are nothing if not accurate; they make the world's best watches, after all.

So, in true Swiss spirit, let's give the museum its full title – the International Red Cross and Red Crescent Museum – and then go back to being English and reduce it to something more manageable. This is one of Switzerland's best museums, managing to be informative, unpatronising and thought-provoking, while all the time exploring the effects of inhumanity. Most of all, it is moving. It would take a hard heart not to be touched by the sight of six million index cards in stacks a third of a mile long, each card representing one prisoner of war in the First World War; just the surname Meyer (one of the most common in German) stretches to 14 boxes of cards. My soft heart is left wondering what happened to each of those men, or to the 45 million POWs in the Second World War, whose index cards thankfully are not on display; they would be too much to see.

A truly engrossing display is made up of four cards from those millions so that we can experience four individual cases. For example, Malcolm Watson of the Royal Navy Air Service, who was captured at Menin on 5 October 1917. His family requested more information from the Red Cross on 24 October and on 8 November were told of his incarceration at the officers' POW camp in Karlsruhe. All quite quick and efficient, given the circumstances of war. Or the story of Karl Schuster, a Prussian chef who was one of 4,625 German military and civilian internees in Switzerland in November 1916. He was captured in Zeebrugge on 6 August 1914 as a civilian enemy national not eligible for army service. Such people were routinely imprisoned but often transferred to neutral countries, in his case to St Gallen where he was interned with 113 other Germans. Two lives that were a tiny part of a vast conflict, but their stories make it seem all too real.

Making that personal connection is what the Red Cross Museum does very well, with video testimonies from witnesses and survivors of all manner of tragedies, from civil war and famine to earthquakes and the effects of climate change. Watching these people tell their stories made me thankful that I live in peaceful neutral Switzerland.

BORN IN BATTLE

The opening section of the museum introduces Monsieur Dunant and his personal campaign to change the way countries behave in wartime. In 1859, he was a 31-year-old banker who cut a rather dashing figure with mutton-chop sideburns and a penchant for white suits. He was also desperately seeking an audience with Napoleon III, about whom he had something of an obsession; the fact that the third Napoleon was rather busy fighting the Austrians in northern Italy doesn't seem to have deterred him. Off he went to Lombardy, arriving just as one of the bloodiest battles of the war had finished.

Nearly 40,000 dead and dying soldiers littered the battlefield at Solferino, with next to nothing being done for them. Dunant sprang into action and for three days organised the locals, bought provisions and tended to the wounded from both armies. It was a bloody, traumatic experience that changed his life, and our world, for ever. Determined to make a lasting difference, he wrote a slim book, *Un Souvenir de Solferino*, about the battle, its aftermath and his idea of creating a society of qualified volunteers to provide care in wartime. Dunant paid for the 1600-copy print run, which these days might be called vanity publishing, and sent it to the great and good (and royalty and politicians) across Europe. It was an instant success.

Apart from being lionised by Charles Dickens, Victor Hugo, the Queen of Prussia and the Empress of Russia, Dunant initially saw few concrete results. Then in 1863 he met with four other Geneva men, including the seemingly ubiquitous General Dufour,[7] and formed the International Committee for Relief to the Wounded, a body that would later become the ICRC. That led to an international conference and the original Geneva Convention, which is on display in the museum. Signed in Geneva's Hôtel de Ville on 22 August 1864 by 12 states and comprising only 10 articles, it sets out the rules governing the treatment of wounded soldiers on the battlefield. Most importantly, it recognises the neutrality of medical staff, vehicles and buildings, as well as stating that all combatants shall be cared for. And Article 7 says that 'a distinctive and uniform flag shall be adopted... a red cross on a white ground'.[8] An iconic symbol of hope and trust was thus created. What's more of a surprise is that there are actually four Geneva Conventions. Three more followed for the treatment of wounded sailors, prisoners of war and civilians in wartime, plus additional Protocols to protect victims of armed conflicts, including non-international ones.

Despite its heroic work over the years, the Red Cross hasn't always got things right. Not every country was willing to get on board with the whole neutral-and-fair thing. It might have been a Swiss man's idea, but Switzerland waited two years before creating a Red Cross society, which is actually quite speedy in Swiss terms; remember, it waited 57 years to join the UN. The US was much worse, dithering around until 1881 before joining. And if you thought political correctness and religious oversensitivity are modern afflictions, think again. Muslim countries objected to the cross, so as early as 1876 the Red Crescent was recognised as the alternative, though it took another half century for it to be adopted officially. That of course has led to a Red Star, for Jews, and now the Red Crystal, presumably for Hindus, Buddhists, Sikhs and non-believers. It's taking things a bit far and threatens to dilute perhaps the biggest factor in the organisation's success: instant recognition.

PEACE IN WARTIME

The Red Cross's greatest challenge – and failure – came during the Second World War. None of the then three Geneva Conventions (the fourth was added in 1949) was designed to deal with mass incarceration and murder of civilians, and the Red Cross failed to adapt its policies and procedures to the reality of concentration camps. Another problem was the relationship between the Red Cross and Switzerland, both officially neutral. The former feared that any intervention in Germany would be seen as taking sides, so embarrassing its host nation, and undermine the organisation's work, limited as it was. Having a member of the Swiss government on the Committee might also have had something to do with it. The Red Cross, both collectively and individually, helped where it could, but there was no public condemnation of the death camps, even though it was later proved that the ICRC knew exactly what was going on.

Switzerland itself behaved little better. Neutrality can be

difficult at the best of times, and this was definitely the worst of times, with Switzerland an island surrounded by the Axis powers and threatened with invasion. But the invasion never came, and the myth of Fortress Switzerland, with its mountain bunkers and ever-ready army of sharpshooters, was born. The Swiss saw (and many still see) the war as their finest hour, when they stood up to the might of Germany. Hitler might well have been deterred by the prospect of snipers in mountain hideouts, but it's more likely that he got distracted by bigger things such as invading Russia or rescuing a collapsing Italy. And it didn't do him any harm to keep the Swiss neutral. That way he could still use their Alpine routes for non-military transport, benefit from their engineering expertise, and hide his gold in their banks. Switzerland had little choice but to play along – it's hard to deal equally with both sides in a conflict when one is 1000 kilometres away and the other controls your access to the outside world and its supplies – though it possibly did more than strictly necessary to accommodate Germany.

A neutral country is often caught between the devil and the deep blue sea; landlocked Switzerland chose to deal with the devil. During the war that wasn't so much of a problem; that came later when the Allies viewed the Swiss as, at best, moral cowards and, at worst, collaborators with evil. But if Switzerland turned away Jewish refugees, then it acted no differently from Britain or America; it was just closer to the problem. If it pressured the ICRC into silence, it was trying not to give Germany any flimsy excuse for invading. If it traded with 'the enemy' (which meant either side, of course), it did so to survive. Every action, and inaction, can be interpreted two ways; it just depends on what you want to see. With the benefit of hindsight and of winning the war, the West's condemnation of Switzerland's wartime record has never gone away, but it's probably only justified in one area.

As we have seen, the words 'Nazi gold' came back to haunt Switzerland and its banks long after the war was over.

The Red Cross and its host nation eventually parted company, with the latter becoming an 'international legal personality'. That's not a cross between Michael Palin and Perry Mason, but puts the organisation on the same legal footing as the UN. The ICRC is still based in Switzerland but, like an embassy, its premises are no longer Swiss; they are international territory. And in contrast to Switzerland being forced to face up to its wartime record, or maybe because of that, the Red Cross voluntarily admitted it made mistakes in dealing with the wartime genocide: 'The ICRC today regrets its past errors and omissions. This failure will remain engraved in the organisation's memory.'[9] Well said.

Today the Red Cross is a global player, but its founder never quite achieved the same success as his creation. Henry Dunant went from hero to zero so quickly and completely that even in his own country few people would be able to tell you much about him. The Swiss are generally a modest lot; they dislike egoism and view self-promotion as something not to be encouraged. But even by their standards, Dunant deserved much more recognition than he got. So what happened to him after his good deed was done?

THE END OF THE ROAD

Henry Dunant's life, which began by the shores of Lake Geneva, ended above the lake at the other end of Switzerland. These two lakes sit like giant bookends on opposite sides of the country and share a few similarities. Both are essentially a giant bulge in a big river – Lake Geneva is a swelling of the Rhone, Lake Constance of the Rhine. Neither is entirely within Switzerland, and each has a completely different name in its native language. In French Lake Geneva is *Lac Léman*, derived from the Latin *Lacus Lemannus* and used by locals (and English speakers trying too hard to be locals) on both sides of the border. The English name for Lake Constance is a logical extension of the main settlement, a German city which tried but failed to join the Swiss Confederation in the sixteenth century. But in German the lake is called *Bodensee*, literally 'floor lake', a name that makes sense when you look at a map of Germany: the lake is very clearly at the bottom of the country. Never mind that for the Swiss and Austrians, who both use that name, it's totally nonsensical (see the map of eastern Switzerland on page 275).

Lake Constance never features much in British travel articles, television programmes or holiday brochures, which all seem to concentrate on the Italian and Swiss lakes. Maybe it's a German thing; for all its historic towns, grand castles and many sausages, Germany isn't top of most British holiday lists. But for Germans the lake is a prime tourist destination, and even with the summertime crowds there's something rather magical about sitting on one of its promenades eating ice cream. It feels so very un-German. In contrast, the Swiss shore is too dull for words, with depressing towns and nothing much for visitors; no wonder the German side is full of Swiss day-trippers, though that's probably also because Germany is cheaper. Pop into Müller (a German equivalent of Boots or Walgreens) in Constance and pretty much everyone in there will be Swiss, buying up a six-month supply of perfume, toiletries and medicines. I know, because I'm usually one of them.

Instead of lining the lake with handsome towns, the Swiss hid them inland, as if trying to keep them secret. It didn't work. You can't build such gems as the extravagantly baroque cathedral in St Gallen or the impossibly quaint village of Appenzell and not expect people to find them. But the place that became Dunant's home for the last 23 years of his life was neither of those; it was Heiden, a small town in the half-canton of Appenzell Ausserrhoden, the Protestant one of the pair that's marginally larger than its Inner twin. In those days Heiden was firmly on the convalescent map as one of the places to come and recuperate, thanks to its clean air and its railway. The former made it ideal for a spot of R&R, the latter made it possible to come directly from the big German cities without changing trains. The line up to Heiden from the lakeside is one of two rack-railways in Switzerland that uses a normal gauge. If that means as little to you as it did to me, the simple explanation is that most mountain railways need rails close together (narrow gauge) to cope with the corners, whereas normal lines have a wider space between the tracks. Maybe it's enough to know that the arrival of this railway in 1875 started Heiden's boom time, which lasted until the First World War. And it was during this period that Dunant lived, and died, here.

Today Heiden is a shadow of its former self, though its past glories can still be seen around the town square. One of the grandest buildings is the *Rathaus*, a pale three-storey affair with that simple, symmetrical elegance that looks Georgian to my English eyes. One look around the empty square and it's immediately apparent how uniform the architecture is. All the buildings appear to be siblings of the *Rathaus*; they all seem to have been built at the same time, in the same style and in the same colour, mostly varying shades of off-white. It's almost as if it were a new town built from scratch. An info board in the square reveals why: Heiden burned to the ground in a *Föhn*-assisted firestorm in 1838 and was rebuilt in classic Biedermeier style, roughly equating to Georgian in Britain.

Heiden sits on the edge of the undulating Swiss Plateau 400 metres above Lake Constance, one of Europe's largest lakes. Even on sunny days, the horizon can be shrouded in blue mist so that water and sky merge in the distant haze, making it feel like Heiden is at the edge of the world. In fact it's just the edge of Switzerland: Lake Constance is shared with Germany and Austria, with the borders somewhere mid-water. It's a tranquil scene, and one which apparently Dunant enjoyed on his regular constitutionals. At one spot, the one with the best view of the lake below, there is even a little park named in his honour, complete with a large sculpture, though the angular 1950s affair is rather out of synch with the man and the town. But to get the whole story of Heiden's most famous resident we need a trip to the hospital, an imposing grey-stone building that's a larger version of the ones in the main square. It's no longer a hospital but now houses the Dunant Museum, as this, or at least one room of it, was Dunant's home from 1887 until he died on 30 October 1910.

ONE MAN AND HIS MUSEUM

It's a Sunday, but even by Swiss standards there's not a lot happening in Heiden. Maybe that's why it's such a good place for R&R; there's actually nothing else to do but rest. Having walked through deserted streets and empty squares, I was beginning to think the town had been abandoned. Then at the museum I finally meet a living, breathing person. Luckily, my one human contact is very welcoming (maybe she's glad to see someone as well) and offers to play the short introductory film in English, purely for my benefit. As we walk across the hall to the TV room I notice she is wearing red shoes, which makes my day. Only one person to be seen in Heiden, but she really is Swiss.

For a comprehensive but easily digestible overview of one man's life, there can be few better small museums than this. In four rooms, it manages to explain and illustrate the man and his work so well that you come away with a very clear picture of him. Unfortunately, it's not a happy one. For all his good deeds and overwhelming humanity, by the end he was a deeply sad, bitter, sick and lonely old man, largely forgotten by the world. It's a far cry from being feted by royalty and hailed as the author of one of the nineteenth-century's most influential books.

Henry Dunant was born on 8 May 1828, the eldest of five children in a very Calvinist family. As a young man he set up the Geneva branch of the YMCA, and then went on to be the driving force behind that organisation's conversion into a worldwide phenomenon; without him it might have remained a parochial English charity. But it was the Red Cross that was the high point of Dunant's life. When his idea became a reality, international law was created and the seeds of international cooperation were sown. How sad, then, that the rest of his life was largely a disaster. In 1867 he went bankrupt, as did the bank where he was a director. For Geneva society there were (and probably still are) few worse crimes than being involved in a bank's collapse. Dunant was forced to resign from the Red Cross, expelled from the YMCA and driven into exile in Paris. He never saw his home town again. He flitted around Europe, often homeless and hungry, before ending up in Heiden, an ill hermit with a white beard and long coat.

In among all the man's artefacts, the museum has one document in pride of place on a wall. It looks like a school certificate, with Dunant's name and the year 01 written by hand in ink. This piece of paper is proof that the world, at last, remembered Dunant and honoured him for what he had achieved. On 10 December 1901, he was the recipient of the first Nobel Peace Prize. True, he had to share it with Frédéric Passy, founder of the French peace society, but I know which man, and which organisation, has had a greater impact on the world. As for the prize money, Dunant never touched it and it remained in a Norwegian bank account until his death nine years later. In his will, he provided for a free bed in Heiden hospital for anyone too poor to afford treatment – a humanitarian right to the end.

His was truly a riches-to-rags story, not only financially but in terms of fame and family as well. There can be few other people in history who dined with kings but foraged for food in Paris dustbins, who created an international organisation with a multimillion-dollar budget but was a bankrupt businessman, who helped save thousands of lives but died in a lonely hospital room. His lasting legacy is the Red Cross, which employs over 14,000 staff worldwide and has a tax-free annual income of 1.6 billion Swiss francs,[10] or roughly the same as the GDP of Belize.[11] More importantly, it saves lives every day all over the world. I hope he's smiling in his grave.

As perhaps the clearest physical example of neutrality and humanitarianism, on the whole the Red Cross has only strengthened Switzerland's image abroad. The big difference between the two is that while the Red Cross deals with the aftermath of the latest war, Switzerland prepares for the next one; two sides of the same coin, just as their flags are the reverse of each other's. Neutrality, Swiss style, is not only about being impartial, it's about being prepared. Very prepared.

MILITARY TRAINING

The train ride from Geneva to Bern is quite unlike any other in the country. On a map, Lake Geneva resembles a croissant in a down-turned mouth position, with Geneva sitting at the bottom left, which might explain the city's outlook on life. By the time the train passes Lausanne, at the top of the bend, it's possible to look down on both arcs of the lake. Azure water sprinkled with golden sunlight stretches as far as the eye can see, while rocky peaks tower over the opposite (French) shoreline and villages cling to the steep slopes either side of the railway line. Okay, if it's raining and you're sitting on the wrong side of the train, all you'll see is grey, wet stone. However, sit on the right side and it feels like being beside a small sea, making Switzerland seem a little less landlocked. As enchanting as lakes are, they're not the same as the sea, but beside this lake there's a feeling of openness and flatness that is hard to find elsewhere in Switzerland. Ignore the mountains, and the very French architecture of high sloping roofs and iron balconies, and you could almost be beside the Channel.

Tear your eyes away from the grandstand splendour and focus on the detail, and you won't believe you're still in Switzerland. Vines are everywhere: three lines beside the train tracks, long stretches that reach practically into people's houses, marshalled rows marching down to the water's edge. Every possible square inch seems to support a vine so that villages appear to be afterthoughts, hemmed in on all sides by cascading terraces of plants. These 30 kilometres of south-facing slopes are in effect one giant vineyard, known as the Lavaux, dating back to the eleventh century. Switzerland may not be as famous as its neighbours for its wines (and I'm excluding Austria from that sentence), but the Swiss love to drink them almost as much as the imported ones. A bottle of Switzerland's finest is always a good option as a thank-you present.

This stretch of landscape may look rather un-Swiss – the plethora of vines, the lack of cows, the dearth of green fields – and yet it still all looks so very Swiss – organised, tidy, regimented yet somehow beautiful. It's as if the landscape has evolved in complete harmony, with man and nature working together for the benefit of both.

But even with the vines and wines, this train trip can seem like almost any other in Switzerland. Not because of the multilingual announcements, or the efficiently friendly conductor, but because chances are you're sharing the carriage with a group of soldiers. For many visitors it can be rather unsettling to see a bevy of beer-drinking soldiers carrying assault rifles on public transport. That's often the biggest surprise of a trip to the world's most peaceful nation. It may be neutral, but Switzerland is certainly not pacifist. Far from it. It is a highly militarised country, with uniformed soldiers a common sight in trains and towns; it can often feel like the whole country is mobilising for the First World War every weekend. Nevertheless, the Swiss think nothing of it. For them, it's just a fact of every Swiss man's life.

From the age of 20 a Swiss man must complete 260 days of compulsory military service,[12] either all at once or in annual stages, before he reaches 34. After his active service time is up, he remains in the reserves for a further ten years and must regularly practise shooting his rifle. Objectors used to go to jail, but in the 1990s the law was finally changed to allow community service instead, though it's a longer stint of 390 days.[13] The Swiss government is looking into extending this obligatory service to women too, but currently they can join in voluntarily; unsurprisingly few do, so that women make up less than 1 per cent of Swiss soldiers.[14] It all adds up to an army of over 200,000 that can be called up at any time to defend the country. But the big question is, against whom?

Having a permanent army in waiting doesn't come cheap. Defence annually eats up over 4.5 billion Swiss francs, 7 per cent of the national budget, or more than agriculture.[15] Admittedly agriculture now only accounts for 4 per cent of the Swiss economy (despite all those cows) but it's still quite an achievement for a neutral country that hasn't been attacked in over 200 years. When a Swiss man is away on his military service, the government pays 80 per cent of his salary.[16] Given that, in total, 6.5 million days are needed every year,[17] that's quite a bill for the taxpayer. Not only that, each soldier gets his own rifle and two uniforms to keep at home, so that he is ready at a moment's notice to shoot the enemy and be properly dressed for it. The weapon has to be kept locked out of sight, but this doesn't stop guns from being used in around 200 suicides a year, giving Switzerland the second highest rate of gun suicide in Europe.[18] With about 3.4 million guns in Swiss homes,[19] the country has the world's fourth highest rate of gun ownership per head, beaten only by the USA, Serbia and Yemen.[20]

But just having lots of guns isn't enough to defend a country against those as yet unknown enemies, so the Swiss have tanks and planes too. Lots of them, so that when ranked per capita, Switzerland is third in the world for numbers of battle tanks, after Saudi Arabia and Russia but way ahead of the USA; for fighter jets, it has the same number per capita as Russia and twice as many as Germany.[21] The only thing missing is battleships, not too surprising given the country's geography, but in fact the Swiss military does have 11 patrol boats in service on Lakes Geneva and Constance.

As if being armed to the teeth wasn't enough, Switzerland is also prepared for anything else that might be thrown at it. Everyone has access to a nuclear shelter, because you never know when the bomb will drop. Mine is in the primary school down the road, but for most people it's in their cellar, as almost every Swiss building has a cellar. Most house a laundry because most Swiss don't own a washing machine. Instead there are communal ones in the cellar for all the flats in the building to use. Some laundries have few rules about usage; others have a rota so that everyone gets a turn at washing their dirty laundry in public. Just imagine, having only two days a month (not including Sundays, when it is forbidden) when you can do your washing. It's so uncivilised. But at least you'd survive a nuclear blast if it was on one of your laundry days.

Then there are the sirens. No one warns you about those so the first time they start, it sounds like war has broken out. As you contemplate running to the nuclear shelter, a glance out the window shows that everyone else is acting normally. Either the Swiss are frighteningly calm in a crisis, or they know something you don't. And that something is that at precisely 13.30 on the first Wednesday in February the siren system is tested. At least it has a use beyond warning of an imminent attack from God knows who – it's also used for flood, avalanche and other natural disasters.

Perhaps the worst side of Swiss militarism is the export of weapons. A lot of them. It defies my logic to see how a country that preaches peace and neutrality can sell weapons to 70 different countries, with the Top Ten importers including Germany at number one but also those peaceful nations of Saudi Arabia and Pakistan.[22] Per capita, the Swiss are one of the largest arms' exporters in the world, selling more than either the British or the Americans.[23] Armed neutrality is one thing when it's a matter of self-defence; it becomes a whole different issue when you are exporting death. To declare yourself neutral in a conflict, and even offer mediation, is laughably hypocritical if you're selling arms to one side; the Swiss get over that by selling arms to both sides. What are morals when there's money to be made? War is an extension of business by other means, as Clausewitz might have said if he'd been Swiss. Just as when it exported its men as mercenaries or accepted gold from anyone who had it, Switzerland is still profiting from wars fought by others. A referendum on banning weapons' exports was defeated in 2009; clearly most Swiss aren't willing to put their mouth where their money is.

FORTRESS SWITZERLAND

Having been to the lakes at the far east and west of Switzerland in search of peace, I am now standing beside one in the middle of the country, looking at war. Or more precisely, at how Switzerland survived a war. On the tranquil shores of Lake Lucerne (see map on page 30) is an old army bunker, buried deep inside the mountains so that from the outside it's barely visible. Festung Fürigen opened in 1942 as part of the vast network of Swiss underground defences against a German invasion. The army stayed until 1987 (clearly no one told them the war was over), since when the bunker has been preserved as a museum. And quite a spooky one at that. Wearing an army greatcoat (it's only about 10°C inside), I walk down long, dank corridors with roughly hewn sides and flickering lights. Marshalled rows of rifles, huge guns that can fire shells 12 kilometres, an emergency operating room and atomic air filters (added in the 1950s) prove that this was not built for peace. The cramped bunk rooms and one shower for 100 men show that it wasn't designed for comfort either. This was part of Fortress Switzerland. In the event of a German invasion, the cities would have been abandoned and the army would have retreated to these mountain hideouts and fought to the last man. This is armed neutrality in its most extreme, and arguably most successful, incarnation. It's an engrossing sight and one which exemplifies the Swiss be-prepared mentality.

Nowhere in the world does neutrality like the Swiss. They've been at it for almost 500 years, so they know exactly what's involved in not getting involved, not taking sides and sitting on the fence. Or do they? Switzerland exports more arms per head than Britain, has the world's fourth highest gun ownership rate and spends more on swords than ploughshares. Armed neutrality is a very Swiss concept, one that defines both the country itself and its relations with the outside world. And it's still popular with the Swiss, with polls continually showing that both the army and neutrality are seen as necessary; that's possibly no surprise, given that the former is one of the few sources of cohesion in a fractured country and the latter an essential part of Swiss national identity.

Shortly after he became Defence Minister in 2008, Ueli Maurer said he wanted the Swiss army to be 'the best in the world'[24] (though no sign of him, as Sports/PE Minister, promising the same for the Swiss football team). A lot of Swiss would agree with his goal for the army, even if they couldn't say why it's necessary, but not all of them: in a 1989 referendum, over a third of voters said yes to abolishing the army.[25] And things are changing, albeit at Swiss speed. Since 2008 soldiers have had to keep their ammunition in the arsenal, not at home.[26] This is rather odd given that their guns are in the cupboard, but with the rifle seen as a symbol of both Swiss manhood and the state's trust in the individual, that is unlikely to change soon.

If your only knowledge of history and international law came from war films, you would at least know that the Geneva Conventions are good things, there to protect POWs and define the rules of war. And after watching Steve McQueen trying to jump the border fence on a motorcycle or the Von Trapps walking over the hills, you'd also know that Switzerland is the safest place to be in wartime. But the world is not as simple as Hollywood. War and peace are not black and white, or in German *schwarz* and *weiss*; combine the two and you get *Schweiz*, the German for Switzerland. How apt for a country that lives in that grey area of armed neutrality, striving for peace but continually preparing for war. This seemingly untenable position may be why Switzerland has survived unscathed for centuries.

However, you only have to look at Belgium's fate in two world wars to see that being neutral with an army doesn't guarantee anything. So perhaps it's Switzerland's mountainous location at the centre of Europe, and not only its army, that has been its saviour. Whatever the reason, Swiss neutrality has been a success. Despite its dark side, such as an obsession with invasions that might never happen, it has succeeded in producing not only the Red Cross but also peace for its citizens. And there's a reminder of that success in every town.

Once you've visited a few Swiss towns and villages, one thing stands out. Not the time-warp medieval centres with their sculptured fountains; not the stencilled decorations and overhanging roofs; and not the sturdy churches and pristine graveyards. It's the lack of a stone cross in every village centre, no engraved lists of dead sons on a town cenotaph. That took me a while to notice. Such things are part of the fabric of nearly everywhere in Britain and France, but in Switzerland they are almost non-existent. How strange for a place to be so close, both geographically and culturally, but for it to have a completely different collective memory of the last hundred years. The two world wars affected the Swiss but just not in the same immediate, every-family-lost-someone way. And in November you can really see the difference: no poppies, no two-minute silence, no Last Post. There's no Remembrance Day in Switzerland because the Swiss have nothing to remember. For all its imperfections and contradictions, armed neutrality has at least given the Swiss the luxury of no lost generations. How lucky they are.

SWISS WATCHING TIP NO 6: LEARNING YOUR ABC

My IKRK moment highlighted one important fact about life in German: it's like living in alphabet soup. On a daily basis you are faced with gaggles of capital letters, as every noun begins with one and then almost everything is reduced to its initials. Part of the comprehension challenge is that the full version is often not spelt out because it's blindingly obvious to everyone else. So to you and me a BH could mean anything, but to a German speaker it's clearly a bra (*Büstenhalter*).

The Swiss equivalent of the Foreign Office is known as the EDA or, to give it its brain-achingly full name, *das Eidgenössische Departement für auswärtige Angelegenheiten* (the Federal Department for Foreign Affairs). Or there's AHV, the Swiss German word for a pension, which actually stands for *die Alters- und Hinterlassenenversicherung* (old-age and survivors' insurance). Quite a mouthful, even if you have still got all your own teeth. Even something as commonplace as traffic has to get in on the letter craze. A lorry is known as an LKW, short for *Lastkraftwagen*, whereas a car is a PKW, or *Personenkraftwagen*. Thankfully, the more obvious *Auto* is also used.

As for the train system, it goes the whole hog. Swiss Federal Railways becomes SBB (short for *Schweizerische Bundesbahnen*) in German but, since this is multilingual Switzerland, it's in French and Italian too. So we also have *Chemins de fer fédéraux suisses* and *Ferrovie federale svizzere*, both of which are reduced to their initials. All this means that trains (and timetables, merchandise and tickets) are emblazoned with nine letters: SBB CFF FFS. Not exactly a catchy acronym.

Reducing words to letters is the best solution to two problems. First, everything has to be precise, hence using IKRK and not *Rotes Kreuz* (or Red Cross). If something has a proper name, then that's what should be used. But problem number two is that German is full of tongue-twister phrases and ridiculously long words. As Mark Twain so memorably noted in *A Tramp Abroad*, German words such as *Unabhängigkeitserklärungen* are 'not words, they are alphabetical processions'. By the way, that mouthful in the last sentence meant declarations of independence. Reducing words to their initials is the best practical answer, and certainly saves on column inches, air time and brain aches. Of course we do it in English – BBC, OBE, MRSA – but not nearly to the same degree.

Dealing with the abbreviation mania raises a big – and unexpected – problem in learning German: the alphabet. You may laugh, but it's true. It's not like Russian, where a C is an S and a P is an R, but while German letters look the same, they all sound different. And with so many initials to deal with, not to mention spelling your own name, the alphabet is one minefield that can't be avoided.

First, the good news. About half the letters are similar to English, but with a German accent: the likes of ess, ix, eff, and zett (S, X, F and Z) present little problem, while kuu, kaa, ooh and haa (Q, K, U and H) are fairly obvious. Then come six letters with a simple vowel change, where an English -ee sound becomes an -ay: B, C, D, G, P and T in German all roughly rhyme with bay. The only one to cause any consternation is G, which becomes hard in German, so changes from gee to gay. Every time I used to hear someone mention the old G tram in Bern I had to smile; it was probably the world's only 'gay' tram. As for the G-spot, well, we just won't go there.

Easy letters done. Now, If I say ay I mean A but the Swiss mean E, which I pronounce as ee but for a German speaker that's an I. Confused? I usually am. Throw in a German A (aah) sounding like an English R, and spelling can be a nightmare. I now clarify if German or English letters are being used when spelling out loud, especially with people who speak both languages. The tendency to revert to your mother tongue when spelling is surprisingly common, even for people who are otherwise fluent in a second language. It must be something so instinctive, going back to our very first words, that it's hard to un-learn.

Last come the special cases. In German Y and J are oop-see-lohn and yot, but then a J becomes a Y in speech. For example, jaguar and jungle are horribly complex: jaguar is spelt the same but said 'yaguar' while jungle sounds the same but is spelt *Dschungel*. And then the two letters that cause the most trouble for many German speakers. I've lost count of how many willages, wegetables and wisits I have heard about. As for when a friend was telling me about an aunt living in Vancouver, well quite. It seems to be a quirk particular to German speakers, which is most peculiar as a *V* in German is pronounced as a hard *F* (as in *Vater*, meaning father) while a *W* is a *V* (as in *Wasser*, or water, and Ve have vayz and meanz, if you watch too many war films). Interchanging the two letters is the least logical – and therefore least Swiss – thing to do. It would make more sense to say fillage and fegetable but that never happens. Having asked Swiss friends about it, many say that they can't hear the difference between veal and wheel, though I'm sure they'd notice once they started eating. The odd thing is that many Swiss people speak French and have no problem with *V*s in that language; you never hear *woulez-vous*.

Following on from the *BCDGPT* rule above, a *V* should logically go from the English vee to a German vay. But vay is German for *W*, as in vay vay vay is the www with which websites start. So it's easy to see how *W* and *V* could get transposed – or is it? *V* is pronounced fow (to rhyme with cow not low), which makes that archetypal German car a Fow-Vay, a name that means little until you realise it's an abbreviation of the German for 'people's car'. As with so many German words, Volkswagen was reduced to its initials and conquered the world.

Just when you think you've mastered the whole letter thing, you sit down to use a computer and end up with something like 'lovelz piyya'. That's because on a Swiss keyboard the *Y* and *Z* are swapped over, *Z* being used much more in German and French than English. The other 24 letters are the same but most punctuation keys are different to make room for the six accented vowels: *ä, ö* and *ü* in German and the French *à, é* and *è*. If I type without looking my sentences are often dotted with rogue apostrophes, umlauts, hyphens and exclamation marks. It's enough to make you go crayz+, or maybe even crazy!

SEVEN

MADE IN SWITZERLAND

Resourcefulness is, ironically, exactly what is needed by a country that has few natural resources of its own. With no coal or iron, not enough arable land to feed itself, and no colonies to provide endless raw materials, Switzerland has always been reliant on trading with its neighbours to survive. It helped that the Swiss had a trump card: control of the mountain passes everyone else wanted to use. And they have proved very adept at making the most of what they have, and filling the gaps by being the ultimate import–exporters: they import what they need, create something out it, then export it for profit, helping to make the Swiss economy one of the most successful in the world.

Part of that success has been a knack for innovation. Penknives and watches may be what the Swiss are most famous for but, as we'll see in this chapter, everyday things such as toilet ducks and cellophane were invented in Switzerland. It's typically Swiss to create a world-beating product then not shout about it; modesty in all things. The irony is that this is essentially a conservative country where change is often viewed with suspicion. 'Stick with what you know best' could be a life motto for most of its people; luckily for cleaners and chefs everywhere, the Swiss talent for invention can be stronger than their desire to retain the status quo. In social terms progress may be glacial at times, but technologically speaking it can be remarkably speedy. There's no greater impetus than material gain.

This sense of inventiveness, combined with the Swiss reputation for quality, has produced more than one world-famous product. Perhaps the most ubiquitous, and most copied, is the humble penknife, Made in Switzerland's best ambassador.

WHERE THE KNIVES COME FROM

It feels like a rite of passage, something every Swiss man has to go through before being accepted into society. And I'm not talking about blowing his first alphorn or shooting his first gun; I'm talking about making his very own Swiss Army Knife, from scratch. Actually, it's something very few Swiss people have the opportunity to do. Assembling this icon isn't something we mere mortals can do whenever we want but an organised few get the opportunity to make their own. Organised because places at the workbench are limited and much in demand. Just as well one friend of mine is Swiss enough to book ahead for both of us. So one grey Saturday in September, Markus and I set off into deepest Switzerland on a quest to make the ultimate symbol of Swiss manhood.

Our goal is the town of Schwyz; the same Schwyz that christened the country and is home to the Rütli charter (for more on this see Chapter Two). It was here in 1884 that Karl Elsener opened his cutlery business, going on to develop the penknife that made his name. On the map the trip looks easy, but when we get off at Schwyz train station it soon becomes clear that we are not where we thought we'd be; SBB has obviously gone to the Ryanair School of Geography. Schwyz station is not in the town of the same name but in Seewen (or more likely Seewen-Schwyz), a bus ride away. By the time we realise that, the bus has gone, as it only waits a few moments for connecting passengers. For once the Swiss transport network isn't the epitome of perfection, which is comforting in a way; it makes it feel almost human. There's no choice but to walk; 20 minutes later we're in Schwyz, ready for our penknife moment.

Victorinox may not be a household name everywhere, but in the English-speaking world most people have heard of a Swiss Army Knife, particularly anyone who watched *MacGyver* in the late 1980s; there was hardly a problem he couldn't solve without using his trusty red tool. The knife's initial popularity was largely down to American GIs taking them home after the Second World War; if it weren't for them, the Swiss Army Knife might have remained exactly that. As it is, its compactness and hardiness helped propel it into the epitome of Swiss design and craftsmanship. Funny, then, that the knife we all know and love isn't the one Swiss soldiers normally used. The original soldier's knife, first introduced in 1891, was black and had only four tools, with no corkscrew, which was not deemed to be essential for survival. The newest soldier's knife, issued to all army recruits, is green and bigger than a Swiss Army Knife. And it still has no corkscrew. The penknife that found world fame was actually the Swiss Officer's Knife, patented on 12 June 1897, which was never army issue but had to be bought privately. Clearly a corkscrew was (and still is) essential to being an officer, as that knife had one from the beginning.

Penknives aren't a new invention, but Elsener changed the internal workings so more blades could be added without increasing the overall size. That first Officer's Knife has been the template for all the company's penknives ever since, with more additions over the decades. Every tool imaginable has been incorporated into a Swiss Army Knife: nail file, wire stripper, magnifying glass, altimeter and now USB stick. Not all made it, though. The best part of the exhibition is seeing the prototypes that never got produced. Ones with a mini-fork or a comb look faintly silly and the potato peeler is just laughable, but those are almost normal compared to the one with a pencil sharpener. Apart from ruining the design (the prominent bulge makes it look pregnant), the sharpener is clearly superfluous in a tool that already has two blades.

The knife-making process takes place under the careful supervision of Daniela and Joe, two friendly Victorinox employees. At the workbench, Daniela patiently guides me piece by piece in the art of building a penknife. Start with three tiny brass pins, and three tinier rings, on a base plate. Then attach a spring and the first three tools (bottle opener, can opener and reamer) and pull a one-armed-bandit handle to push it all together. Position the middle plate and compress everything by pressing the foot pedal. Next come a second spring and the last three tools (small blade, large blade and corkscrew). Pull the handle, add the top plate, press the pedal and out comes something resembling a naked penknife.

While that basic assembly took me about five minutes, an experienced worker can do it in 45 seconds. At least the next bit is less technical. Hammer down the protruding brass spikes, add red plastic covers, squeeze in a vice, oil the blades, pop the tweezers and toothpick into their slots, clip on a key ring and my knife is ready. A Victorinox Spartan penknife, measuring 91 millimetres, weighing 59 grams and with 12 standard features. Holding it in my hand, I feel almost Swiss.

An hour later in the factory shop, it becomes clear just how big the Victorinox family of knives is. My Spartan has so many siblings. There's the Sportsman, which rather strangely has a nail file in it, something not so useful to most sportsmen; the Manager, one of the few penknives actually to have a pen; the Angler, with a fish scaler that doubles up as a ruler, though it's only 7 centimetres long so is clearly for measuring minnows; and the Camper, Explorer, Ranger and a host of other suitably rugged names, although I'm not too sure the Escort fits in with the rest. Top of the range is the SwissChamp, containing 22 tools with 33 functions, including five different types of screwdriver. Who could ask for anything more? In fact, Victorinox has 100 different models of Swiss Army Knife and produces 28,000 per day (that's 6 million a year),[1] which seems a lot until you discover that it makes twice as many household and chefs' knives.

For me, the strangest member of the Victorinox family is the one aimed at children. Whereas in other countries kids have my first bike, my first Sony or my first Little Pony, Switzerland gives its children My First Victorinox. It comes in red or blue with two tools: a large blade and an all-purpose affair that opens bottles or cans, strips wire and drives screws. Admittedly the blade has a rounded tip rather than a point, but it's still rather disconcerting to see two wholesome children on the box proudly displaying their first potentially lethal weapons. Then again, Swiss children are far too sensible to do anything silly with their penknives.

Markus doesn't see the problem, but then he probably grew up with a *Sackmesser* (the Swiss German word for a penknife, which I'm convinced is misspelt; surely it should be *Sak-messer*, short for Swiss Army Knife?) instead of a rattle. He's an officer in the Swiss Army and has the uniform to prove it, but he couldn't resist buying the new soldier's knife. It was love at first slice. There's nothing guaranteed to get a Swiss man more excited than a new penknife. Most of them already own one and carry it at all times, but show them a new knife and let them play with all the different blades and their faces light up. They're all still Boy Scouts at heart.

TEN THINGS YOU NEVER KNEW WERE SWISS

Other than milk chocolate, the Swiss Army Knife is possibly the best known invention to come out of Switzerland. I exclude watches, at least until the end of this chapter, as the Swiss are famous for making rather than inventing them. But that red Army Knife isn't the only Swiss invention that has left its mark on the world; there are plenty of others. Since the Swiss aren't that good at blowing their own trumpets (too busy with alphorns), many of their best creations aren't known for being Swiss. So here are ten things that you probably didn't know were invented in Switzerland.

Velcro

More properly called 'hook-and-loop fastener', Velcro (which should probably be VELCRO® as it is a registered trademark) is possibly the most useful Swiss invention ever. It was the brainchild of Georges de Mestral, a native of Canton Vaud, who went out for a walk with his dog and ended up changing the world of children's trainers and strippers' trousers. Far from getting irritated at all the burrs sticking to his clothes, he inspected them under a microscope and decided to invent a man-made version. That's the sign of true genius – producing an extraordinary idea from an ordinary moment. And as befits all great inventors, although he wasn't taken seriously at first he never gave up. In 1955 he patented his invention as 'Velcro', a contraction of *velours* and *crochet*[2] (French for velvet and hook respectively). It's so useful for so many things, but such a shame he didn't also invent an easy way of getting all the dust and hairs out of the hooks.

Absinthe

There can be few other drinks with a reputation like absinthe, also known as the Green Fairy. This highly potent spirit (up to 72 per cent alcohol) is made from wormwood and green anise and played a starring role in late nineteenth-century culture, particularly at the Moulin Rouge. It was first made in 1792 in Couvet, Canton Neuchâtel, by a Dr Pierre Ordinaire, who touted it round as an extraordinary all-purpose remedy.[3] At least that's how the story goes. What's certain is that once Pernod Fils started mass production in France, there was no going back. Until absinthe was banned, at least. A Swiss referendum in 1908 changed the constitution to ban the drink,[4] with France and the US following suit, though it was never prohibited in Britain. The Swiss ban was overturned in 2005 and absinthe was once again available in its homeland.[5]

The division sign

Two dots bisected by a line. It's such an everyday symbol, pressed by millions of fingers using calculators, that it's hard to imagine anyone inventing it. The ÷, or *obelus* to give it its technical name, was first used by Johann Heinrich Rahn in his text *Teutsche Algebra,* published in Zurich in 1659.[6] Funnily enough, it doesn't appear anywhere on a normal computer keyboard; you have to use / instead. Rahn is also credited with inventing ∴ to mean 'therefore' in algebra.

LSD

In November 1938, Albert Hofmann was a mild-mannered Basel chemist working at Sandoz Laboratories, now part of pharmaceutical giant Novartis. He was researching rye fungi to find a cure for migraine, but accidentally discovered LSD, though it took him five years to realise its mind-bending qualities. LSD, or acid to its friends, then became the drug of the hippie era before it was made illegal. Its full English name is lysergic acid diethylamide, but LSD is actually (in typical Swiss fashion) an abbreviation of the original German, *Lysergsäurediäthylamid.* The formula is an equally uncomfortable mouthful, $C_{20}H_{25}N_3O$, but with all those Cs and Hs it looks very Swiss. Herr Hofmann died in 2008, aged 102,[7] so dropping a bit of acid clearly never did him any harm.

Stock cubes

Real chefs may hate them, though even they must use them, but most of us couldn't cook without a stock cube. And for that we have to thank one Julius Maggi, a half-Swiss, half-Italian man from Frauenfeld, who created the first *Bouillon-würfel*. These days you can get any variety you fancy, be that fish or porcini mushroom, but the original bouillon cube was made from beef. The Swiss Maggi cube (1908)[8] pre-dates the ones from both Oxo (Britain, 1910)[9] and Knorr (Germany, 1912).[10] Maggi, now part of Nestlé, is one of Europe's biggest brands and probably best known for its dried soups, also something Julius invented.

Cellophane

If you think plastic food wrapping is a modern creation, think again. It also dates back to 1908, when Dr Jacques Brandenberger from Zurich came up with a cellulose-based transparent film, which he called cellophane.[11] By 1912 he'd perfected both the product and the process, but initially cellophane was used mainly for the eye-goggle part of gas masks during the First World War.[12] It then found its true calling as the perfect food packaging, still its main use today, as any trip to the supermarket will prove. Best of all, because it's made from cellulose (the fibrous part of most plants) it's totally biodegradable.[13] As if inventing one food covering wasn't enough, the Swiss went and did it again two years later...

Aluminium foil

Tin foil, as we normally still call it in English, used to be made of tin. Then a Swiss company, Dr Lauber, Neher & Cie., Emmishofen,[14] worked out how to make it from aluminium and in 1910 opened the first aluminium foil rolling facility, in Kreuzlingen just near Constance. Chocolate bars and leftovers were never the same again. Personally, I still miss the foil that used to cover a KitKat. Running a nail between the chocolate fingers was almost as satisfying as eating them afterwards. How ironic, then, that it was a Swiss company, Nestlé, which ditched the foil and switched to plastic after buying Rowntree, the original British creator of KitKats.

Electric toothbrush

The Swiss love looking after their teeth; most seem to spend a small fortune on their mouths. So it's no wonder that a Geneva man came up with the world's first electric toothbrush. Back in 1954, Dr Philippe-Guy Woog helped the cause of dental care by creating an oscillating, motorised toothbrush.[15] Called the Broxodent, it was an immediate success despite not being battery operated – you had to clean your teeth while plugged in. Trust the Swiss to come up with not one but two inventions to help in the battle for hygiene, though only the most fastidious cleaner would use them together . . .

Toilet duck

Cleaning the loo isn't the nicest job, but at least it's easier since the advent of the toilet duck. On 18 June 1980, Walter Düring created his first *WC-Ente* (as it's called in German) in his factory in Dällikon, near Zurich.[16] At that time, the family business was famous in Switzerland for Durgol, a decalcifying liquid invented by Walter's mother. Her son's gadget would give the company a worldwide brand. Anyone who has to clean the loo has been thankful ever since, especially if someone has just thrown up after being forced to listen to another type of duck . . .

The Birdie Song

Originally called *Der Ententanz* (or duck dance), this ridiculous dance-along song was composed in 1963 by a Swiss waiter called Werner Thomas.[17] It began life as a sort of polka played on an accordion in an après-ski club at Davos and just kept on going. Its high point came in the early 1980s when the absurdly popular 'La Danse des Canards' in France and 'The Birdie Song' in Britain stormed the charts. In total, there have been 370 versions in 42 countries selling over 40 million copies.[18] Some duck, some dance, as Churchill might have said, though I'm sure he would never have flapped his arms on the dance floor. In 2000 it was voted the most annoying song of all time, beating other classics such as 'Teletubbies' and 'Barbie Girl'.[19] My vote would have gone to fourth-placed 'Agadoo'.

Forget 'The Birdie Song', what about the cuckoo clock? Where's that in this list of great Swiss inventions, I hear you ask. Visit almost any souvenir shop in Switzerland and a whole array of these carved wooden wall clocks will be on display, so you could be forgiven for thinking they are a national treasure. In fact, they're just a money-spinner and the Swiss never turn away a tourist franc. The customer is always right, even if they're buying something which originated in southern Germany. Take a trip to the delightfully named Furtwangen in the Black Forest and you'll learn all about the real origins of the cuckoo clock. Perhaps Orson Welles should have gone there before he added the famous line in the film *The Third Man* where his character Harry Lime disparages Switzerland for having 500 years of democracy and peace only to come up with the cuckoo clock.

With the notable exception of that clock, Switzerland is justifiably renowned for its timepieces. And for its time-keeping. Is it just a coincidence that the most punctual nation on earth also makes some of the best watches? Maybe not.

A CLOCKWORK COUNTRY

Time is important in Switzerland. The clichés about personal punctuality and the country running like clockwork are true to a degree. I do have Swiss friends who are habitually late, the trains don't always run exactly to the second, and not everyone wears a watch. But they are the exceptions in a country where tardiness is generally regarded as a deadly sin and opening times are followed to the number. Almost every Swiss person has a mobile phone, but rarely has to text to say they're running late as they still manage to be on time for meetings, dates and outings. But how do the Swiss define being 'on time'? For many it actually means a fraction early, as timing it to the second is hard even for the Swiss; for most it means within five minutes of an arranged time.[20] Few wait longer than 15 minutes before giving up and leaving. Better never than late, it seems.

When it comes to timekeeping, almost everything in Switzerland seems to be run with military precision, including the cinemas. Films nearly always start on the hour or half-hour, sometimes on the quarter but never at annoying times like twenty past or five to. And most still have an interval, which comes exactly halfway through the film, no matter if that's in the middle of a scene or even a line of dialogue. It may be timed to perfection, but the interval is nearly always badly timed as far as the viewer is concerned. Nevertheless, the Swiss seem to like the intrusion, using the wee break not just for that but to buy the overpriced popcorn, sweets and drinks which make the pause worthwhile for the cinemas. Just like everywhere else, time is money in Switzerland.

With everybody tacitly agreeing to the same rules, the easiest way to confuse Swiss people is to bring a measure of doubt into any question of time. English-style dinner invitations of the formal '6.30 for 7' or informal 'come about 7ish' will not be understood because they are not clear. In the first case most of your guests will turn up at 6.34, in the second at 7.02. When it comes to time, flexibility is rarely an option.

Take this scenario: it's a national holiday, so everyone is off work. It's 34°C in the shade and the riverside open-air baths in Bern city centre are like Brighton beach, with barely a blade of grass to be seen between the towels and bodies. Good business for the café with a long summer evening ahead and hundreds of people spending money on food and drink. But what happens? Exactly at 6 p.m. everyone is kicked out. It's a holiday, so closing time is earlier than normal. Never mind that countless people are there, or that it's the hottest day of the year, or that it's just plain mean. Closing times are there to be followed. The only people grumbling were foreigners; the Swiss all left without complaint because to them it was clear that if closing time is 6 p.m., then that's when it is. It dawned on me then that there's something more important to the Swiss than money: time. Combine the two, and you have the Swiss idea of heaven, or the watchmaking industry as it's known to the outside world.

WATCHING THE CLOCKS

Think of the ultimate in Swiss quality and precision, and you'll more than likely be thinking of a watch. Watchmaking is the Swissest of Swiss industries, and one of the country's success stories. While many of the companies involved are small, watches are big business overall. In 2017 the Swiss exported 24.3 million timepieces, which is tiny when compared to China, the world's largest exporter (688 million watches).[21] The Swiss concentrate on quality over quantity, and nowhere is that more apparent than in the prices: the average export price of a Chinese watch is $4, a Swiss one $827; no wonder the Swiss watch industry is worth $19.9 billion in exports alone.[22]

And it's all Calvin's fault. In his quest to make Geneva the perfect puritan city, he banned jewellery in 1541, so forcing craftsmen to turn to a new trade: watches.[23] It turned out so well for them that 60 years later they formed the world's first Watchmakers' Guild.[24] A century on, they had become so successful that Geneva just wasn't large enough for all of them and many took to the hills to set up shop in the lower reaches of the Jura mountains. Some of the most famous names in Swiss watchmaking are to be found in the region along the French border: Omega and Swatch in Biel/Bienne, Tag Heuer in La Chaux-de-Fonds, Zenith and Tissot in Le Locle. No wonder the towns involved like to make the most of their connection to the industry; together they are now known as Watch Valley. It's the perfect place to go for a crash course in all things horological, starting in La Chaux-de-Fonds, the spiritual home of Swiss watchmaking (see the map of Romandie on page 184).

Just a few kilometres from the French border, this is the city that in its nineteenth-century heyday was famous for its craftsmen and their watches, cementing the Swiss reputation for masterpieces. La Chaux-de-Fonds is also a prime example of 'modern' town planning. Burned to the ground in 1794, it was rebuilt on a grid pattern, with rows of identical four-storey houses designed for the watchmakers' needs. With 39,000 inhabitants, it still counts as the third largest French-speaking city in Switzerland; it's also one of the highest in the whole country, sitting at 1000 metres up.

I anticipate great things from my visit – but I'm disappointed. La Chaux-de-Fonds isn't exactly beautiful. It's easy to become spoilt in Switzerland with all its chocolate-box towns and medieval buildings, but by any standards this is not an attractive place. It feels like a cross between some neglected French provincial town and a leftover of Tsarist central planning. Bleak is probably the best word. Maybe it looks better in high summer, though I can't imagine there's much in the way of street life even then, but on a cold January day it feels like I've been transported to Siberia. This is a town that will never win any beauty contests, though, along with nearby Le Locle, it became a Unesco World Heritage Site in 2009 for its industrial past and urban planning (rather than its aesthetic qualities). Apparently the two are 'outstanding examples of mono-industrial manufacturing-towns which are well preserved and still active'.[25] No wonder Karl Marx described it as a 'huge factory-town' in *Das Kapital*,[26] though he probably meant that in a good way. I suspect he never actually visited what could possibly be Switzerland's drabbest city.

There are, however, a couple of pearls to be found, thanks to Le Corbusier, the architect formerly known as Charles-Edouard Jeanneret and the most famous local boy made good. Another contender for that title is Louis Chevrolet, the car man, but I'll stick with Le C as at least there's something of his to see in La Chaux-de-Fonds. And buildings are so much more interesting than cars. And warmer when it's cold and snowy outside. And when you get to look around a house as simple yet splendid as La Maison Blanche, you realise that there's more to Swiss homes than wooden chalets. Its open-plan rooms and clean lines are way ahead of their time, looking more 1930s than 1912, the year the house was built. Across town is Le Corbusier's second early triumph, the Villa Turque, a dream house. And for the likes of us, that's what it will remain. Designed for a local watch bigwig, it's now owned by Ebel, a watch company I'd never heard of, who are probably the only ones able to afford such a home, with its double-height reception room, vast bay windows and sensuous curves.

Houses apart, Le Corbusier (and indeed Chevrolet) is noticeable by his absence. In true Swiss style there's little to commemorate the town's famous sons; doing that might be verging on pandering to celebrity. Or perhaps it's sour grapes, given that both men only really found fame once they'd left home. Instead the town concentrates on its watches, which can never be accused of having egos bigger than their makers.

The watches are honoured with their own museum, probably the ugliest building in town, and it's potentially quite a long list of contenders. Thank goodness most of the concrete monstrosity that is the Musée International d'Horlogerie is hidden underground. Back in the days when people knew no better (that is, 1977) it was awarded the Prix Béton prize for a museum. That's a prize for buildings made of concrete (*béton* is French, and also Swiss German, for concrete), preferably as grey and rough-looking as possible, if this winner is anything to go by. The only advantage is that its drab walls make the museum's collection appear even more luminous: ornate pocket watches, an elegant sun-pendulum clock, early wristwatches for First World War soldiers, and mystery clocks seemingly with no mechanism. But the most noticeable thing is the near silence. Ticks, tocks and the occasional beep and chime are the only sounds to break the hush. It gives the museum a rather reverential air, part temple, part library.

Despite not being a watch-spotter, I can't help but be transfixed by the detail and craftsmanship on display. And become engrossed in the developments that have led to the slim wristwatches we now take for granted: first spring, first self-winder, first battery, first quartz and so on. Among the cases of watches from Swiss companies, my favourite is perhaps Girard-Perregaux, a local manufacturer. Not for its watches, which look much like any other, but for the company motto: 'Watches for the few since 1791.' No hiding the fact that they are ridiculously expensive and elitist. I'll stick with my trusty Swatch, which I learn has ten stages of assembly, rather like an Airfix kit. The secret of its success was halving the number of components to 51, so cutting production costs and retail prices alike. Its launch in 1983 helped rescue a Swiss watch industry that was floundering in the face of an Asian-led quartz revolution. If Swatch hadn't come along, maybe today Swiss watches would all be Girard-Perregaux, luxury trinkets for the very rich.

WHAT'S IN A NAME?

As Swatch, Rolex and Omega – and indeed Girard-Perregaux – have proved, the Swiss watch industry is all about its names. Its success is based on having brands that mean quality and reliability. It's about who you are as much as what you make, even if the mass market has never heard of you. The Federation of the Swiss Watch Industry lists official websites for 230 brands,[27] many of which I suspect most Swiss people aren't aware of. For example, Juvenia, Glycine and Vulcain have been around for decades but I'm betting none of you recognise them as watches; they sound more like face creams or sci-fi characters. Maybe their popularity is limited by the odd names (or more likely their prices), but then there's the very English-sounding West End Watch Co., another new brand to me that was in fact launched in 1886. And it's Swiss, despite the name.

The Swiss themselves love watches, or at least watch shops. Almost every town has one, though perhaps they're only there for the tourists. A typical city centre has a striking abundance of three types of shop: shoe, bread and watch. It's hard to walk more than a few metres without passing one or all of the above, which is handy if you need a baguette for supper or a pair of red shoes. Or indeed want to splash out a small fortune on a new watch. That's where the watch shops differ from the other two: they cover the whole price range, from 40 to 40,000Fr, as if it were quite normal for a high-street shop to sell something that costs half a year's salary. What makes it more bizarre is that, except for Zurich, Swiss cities aren't big enough to have a posh shopping district, so you can get some unlikely neighbours.

For example in Bern, you can walk past a pharmacy, Burger King and cheap-and-cheerful Tchibo, only to find a very fancy shop indeed, Gübelin. Behind its plate-glass windows are baubles that would look more at home on Bond Street or Fifth Avenue, not just around the corner from lap dancers. The most expensive watch on display is from Patek Philippe with a jaw-dropping price tag of 42,000Fr. A sign beside it says 'Complicated Watches', which could be a justification for the astronomical price but is actually a Patek Phillippe series of watches, all with prices that make a 5000Fr Rolex seem quite reasonable. Gübelin has branches in six other Swiss cities,[28] which is truly mind-boggling. Seven places in Switzerland, none larger than Bristol, can support a shop selling 38,000Fr watches. The bigger issue is: who buys them?

My favourite watch shop is Christ, which is far more affordable than Gübelin and far less intimidating to go into. Its prices are almost sane, with many under 1000Fr, so that you don't feel like you have to flash a platinum card to get through the door. Prices aside, I like Christ purely for its name, which in German has a short *i*, as in mist. There are nine Christs in the Bern phonebook, not including the four branches of the watch shop or Christ International Furniture Transporters (how apt), but what makes me smile is that the shop fascia has three words on it: *Schmuck Christ Uhren*. This merely means that the shop sells jewellery, *Schmuck* in German, and watches, or *Uhren*. Heaven knows what an American visitor from the Bible Belt thinks about having the Son of God next to a slang word for an idiot. To make things worse, according to my dictionary schmuck is derived from *shmok*, a Yiddish insult meaning penis. Of course, for a German speaker the two versions of schmuck are worlds apart thanks to a subtle vowel change. The American schmuck rhymes with 'luck', whereas the German *Schmuck* is closer to 'look'. Tomayto, tomahto, you might think, but vowels are very important in German.

BORN TO BE SWISS

The one saving grace in having Christ as a surname is that the Swiss don't go in for naming their boys Jesus. Almost half of them may be Catholic, but this isn't Spain. Even if it were, Herr and Frau Christ would most likely not be allowed to call their son Jesus (see below for more on that). They would probably choose Leon instead, a popular name for new baby boys in German-speaking Switzerland; if he was born in Ticino he'd be Leonardo, or in Romandie then it'd be Nathan.[29] The regional name variations are much more marked than in most other countries because of the languages. Those three boys' names, each popular in their own linguistic area, barely get a mention in the other two. Leon is very definitely a German name in Switzerland, along with Jonas, Elias and Tim. French speakers are more likely to be called Louis or Maxime than any of those, and Ticinese boys Alessandro or Mattia.

What makes Switzerland interesting is that a man can have a very Italianate name but have been born in Zurich and speak only Swiss German. The newspapers and television are littered with Matteos, Fabios and Nicos, most of them *Secondos* who have probably never set foot in Italy. But some boys' names cross the linguistic divide: Liam and Luca are popular in all three regions, and for the country as a whole, Noah is number one.

Girls' names show a bit more continuity across Switzerland. For sure there are the regional quirks, such as Chloé or Zoé in Romandie, Giulia or Martina in Ticino, and Leonie or Lena in the rest of the country. But oddly similar names – such as Lara, Lea and Mia – are popular in all three regions.[30] Nevertheless, looking through the Swiss official list for 2016, you have to wonder why 25 girls were called Océane. Perhaps being so far from the sea made their parents wistful. Or vindictive, except that wouldn't be allowed.

Names, like everything else made in Switzerland, are taken seriously. When you decide on your child's name, it has to be approved by the civil registrar. If it's deemed to harm the child's well-being or be offensive to a third party, you can't have it. For once there are few set rules, but shocking, insulting or laughable names are forbidden;[31] if this were transplanted to Britain, Richard Head would be a no-no and Mary Christmas might not make it either. You also can't give a boy a girl's name or vice versa, and surnames can't be used as first names. Biblical bad boys Cain and Judas are both *persona non grata*, as are any names that are places (such as Brooklyn or Paris) or brands (Pepsi or Armani).[32] As for making up a name just because it sounds nice, that would be far too free-spirited and creative. Not forgetting that sticking out from a crowd is not something most Swiss strive for. Better to be a Doris Müller among the many with that name than to be the only Gaynor in the village.

ONE BRAND THROUGH TIME

Name recognition means everything in the watch world. A few brands achieve such a status that they stand out. Omega is one of them. Thanks to its being the official watch for the Olympics, Nasa and James Bond, it's often seen as the archetypal Swiss watch. And rather handily for me, it has a company museum that you can visit for free, although by appointment only. It wouldn't do for just anyone to turn up whenever they want; that would be so very un-Swiss. Despite my best efforts, no watch company was willing to show me round its premises; industrial espionage and all that. So I settle for a tour of the Omega museum in Biel, having duly booked first by phone.

If I thought La Chaux-de-Fonds was ugly, I changed my

mind once I got to Switzerland's Slough, as Markus memorably described Biel. Or more correctly Biel/Bienne, the largest officially bilingual town in Switzerland.[33] Everything comes in French and German, making all the street signs, timetables and adverts that much bigger. To be fair to Canton Bern's second city, it's only the postwar bits that are depressingly unattractive. Biel/Bienne has two assets that Slough could only dream of: its own lake (Bielersee/Lac de Bienne) and, hidden in the middle of all that architectural mediocrity, a true pearl of an old town. This is the city's secret heart, straight from the pages of a novel and filled with ochre-painted buildings, carved fountains and creeper-clad bistros.

Omega and the other watch companies didn't relocate here for the lakeside ambience. It was all about transport, particularly rail, which made Biel (it's easier to stick with one name) far more accessible than La Chaux-de-Fonds up in the hills. Omega set up shop in an old spinning factory in 1880 and is still there, a five-minute trolley-bus ride from the centre. Its museum may focus on one company, but essentially it's a timeline of the whole industry, from the intricate early pendant watches right through to high-tech ones that can cope with being 1000 metres under water. Quite why that's necessary isn't clear; I'm happy if mine survives an inadvertent swim or shower. You can see how a company founded by Louis Brandt in 1848 eventually chose a brand name with a more international feel (1894), which led to the first fake (Onega in 1908). Or how little adjustments came along, such as the winder on a wristwatch switching from the left to the right, or the second hand being added in the 1940s.

But it's the modern era in which Omega shines. Where else can you see the watch President Kennedy wore at his inauguration or the one that was chosen to go to the moon? Incidentally, the astronauts wore their watches over their space suits, fixed with a giant strip of Velcro; one Swiss product helping another. Perhaps the most useful thing I learn from my guide is why all the watches in the museum, and in most shops, are set at 10 past 10. It's simply to avoid anything being obscured, such as the date window or tricksy little dials or, most importantly, the company name. It really is all about the name.

Watches and penknives, along with cheese and chocolate, are perhaps the best-known products to be made in Switzerland. Part of their success has been that they come with that 'Swiss made' label, guaranteeing quality and reliability. For the Swiss themselves, it's no different. If anything, such a label encourages domestic sales, despite the higher prices that usually come with it. The Swiss love to buy Swiss, which is possibly why such a small country with few natural resources can sustain a manufacturing industry. Some Swiss companies, such as Logitech for computer mice and Sigg for water bottles, flourish on the world market, but many brands are household names only nationally. While you've probably never heard of Freitag, Kuhn Rikon or Riposa, almost any Swiss person would recognise them as makers of shoulder bags, kitchen appliances and mattresses respectively.

A consumer study of brands in Switzerland showed that of the Top 20 most popular, 13 were Swiss,[34] and I'm guessing that Ragusa, Thomy and Zweifel mean little to non-Swiss readers (they are all food brands). What's noticeable is that apart from Swatch and Toblerone, the Swiss brands you might expect to be there aren't. No Nestlé, no Omega, no Victorinox. And no Rolex, which does however appear in the Top 20 in Britain – a list that's almost the opposite of the Swiss one, with 11 foreign brands against 9 British.[35] Perhaps Brits just aren't as patriotic as the Swiss when it comes to shopping.

That so many Swiss brands have conquered the world is thanks not to industrial might but to technological know-how. Although Switzerland might be small, it thinks big in terms of research and development. It has 26 Nobel prizewinners, mainly in the fields of science and medicine; per capita that's far more than most other countries. The Swiss may debate everything to death and take years to accept real change, but if they can see a material benefit, then often they are first in line. Maybe knowing that their society and economy are so stable gives them the impetus to try new ideas in other fields. Certainly something has helped make this quiet nation of conformists come up with more than its fair share of inventions.

Made in Switzerland is such a hallmark of good craftsmanship that everyone wants to mimic it. A fake Rolex, a copycat Toblerone and an ersatz Army Knife can be found all around the world, and even in Switzerland itself. But the real things still maintain their standards, and their appeal, without compromising on quality or perfectionism. Rather like the Swiss themselves.

SWISS WATCHING TIP NO 7: A YEAR IN THE COUNTRY

Life in any country is all about the rhythm of the year. Not just its seasons, but its festivals and customs, holidays and traditions, all of which combine to make the year as individual to a country as its flag. In Switzerland, where so much happens at municipal level, festivals aren't mere footnotes on a calendar, they're part of everyday life. Well attended and well organised, they are hard to miss (not that you'd want to) and every town seems to have its own.

For example, in April's *Sechseläuten* Zurich celebrates the end of winter by burning a giant paper snowman. Bern's big hurrah is *Zibelemärit*, or onion market, in late November, with every possible way of selling an onion and running confetti battles in the streets. In December Geneva commemorates the *Escalade*, a failed Savoyard invasion of 1602, with torchlit processions and vegetable soup (it's a long story). Then there are the cheese-sharing, cow-fighting, bell- ringing and flame-throwing festivals, to name just a few, that show how widespread such celebrations are, as if they are an affirmation of community spirit. Local knees-ups aside, the country follows a similar annual pattern.

Silvester, as New Year is called (referring to 31 December being St Sylvester's day), starts the year with not so much a bang as a damp squib. Few fireworks, no midnight chimes, no Times Square countdown, in fact not a lot. Swiss television largely ignores it, either showing celebrations from abroad or something as mundane as a quiz show. To those of us used to more, it's a big anti-climax, though I have got quite attached to the Swiss German tradition of watching an old comedy on TV. *Dinner for One* was recorded in English in 1963 and is cult viewing for many Swiss. And Germans, Danes, Swedes, Finns and various other nations except the UK. Few native English speakers have ever heard of it, let alone seen it, but it's actually a very funny sketch about a 90th birthday dinner for Miss Sophie, waited on by her increasingly drunk butler. 'The same procedure as every year' is a quote most German-speaking Swiss will instantly recognise.

Many Swiss festivals have their own particular food, and the first is *Dreikönigstag* or Epiphany on 6 January, when a special sweet bread is sold in almost every bakery. The seven-part cake looks like a child's drawing of a daisy, with six petals and a central round. One part has a little plastic king baked into it – whoever finds that gets to be king (or queen) for the day. I'm still waiting.

Perhaps the biggest annual event is Carnival, or *Fasnacht*. It's the one time when the Swiss really let their hair down, wear outrageous clothes, get ridiculously drunk and generally behave like the rest of Europe. Many towns and cities, Catholic or Protestant, get in on the act with fancy-dress parades, marching bands, confetti cannons, paper lanterns and food stalls. This is February (or March, depending on Easter) and it's Switzerland, not Rio, so costumes are more substantial than a dental-floss bikini and gold body paint. Basel takes *Fasnacht* very seriously, beginning in the darkness of Morgestraich at 4 a.m. on the Monday after Ash Wednesday, with drummers drumming and pipers piping to kick off three days of celebration that take over the whole city.

After all that excess, things are quiet with everyone too busy eating fondue, skiing at the weekends and waiting for spring. One sure way of judging when winter is over is to visit a newsagent. Since October, the postcard racks will have been filled with winter wonderland scenes and snowy extravaganzas; as soon as they've been replaced with snow-free cards you know that spring has sprung. I'd never seen seasonal postcards before, but the Swiss view them as a logical extension of the distinct seasons. Another sign is supermarket shelves full of massed ranks of chocolate bunnies in cellophane packets. Swiss Easter eggs tend to be half shells filled with pralines; hollow bunnies of all shapes and sizes are more common. As delicious as they are, there's something vaguely sinister about hundreds of bunnies looking at you with chocolate eyes. No wonder I bite their heads off first.

By May, the cows are up in the high pastures, the shops are packed with asparagus and everyone has put their winter coats and boots down in the cellar. It's a May Day tradition to have a workers' demonstration in cities like Zurich and Bern, but recently the demos always ended in attacks on McDonald's and battles with the police. Not something you associate with the Swiss, but the anti-capitalism, anti-globalism, anti-Americanism, in fact anti-anything feeling has grown quite strong in a country that traditionally sees itself as pro-individual.

Summer in Switzerland can feel like one long walk-and-grill season. Everyone seems to spend every spare moment up a mountain or down by a lake, inevitably ending up in some sort of open-air meal. The Swiss like nothing more than sticking a sausage on a stick, grilling it over an open fire and eating it with a hunk of bread, a squirt of mustard and a can of beer. If they're not doing it out in the woods, they're barbecuing in the back garden or on the balcony. Peak sausage season is July when the schools, and much of the country, are on holiday. Even in busy city centres some shops and restaurants close for their annual break despite it being high season for many tourists. But the best part of a Swiss summer is the swimming — not in the sea but in rivers and lakes. When it's hitting 30°C, there's nothing better than jumping in cool water and it isn't just a countryside activity: in Zurich, Lucerne and Geneva, people dive into the lakes to cool off. In Basel, it's the Rhine and, best of all, in Bern the crystal-clear Aare. You don't even have to swim as the river's fast enough to carry you downstream; it's rather like being on a liquid travelator.

On 1 August or Swiss National Day the whole country seems to partake in a giant walk–grill–swim fest that culminates in huge firework displays. After that it's back to school, with posters going up everywhere to remind drivers that children are back on the streets — most Swiss children walk to school, often unaccompanied. Once the cows have come back down from the high pastures and the last of the near-daily thunderstorms has rumbled off, then summer really is over.

The tastiest season is autumn when the Swiss go wild for anything with pumpkin, venison and chestnuts. Especially chestnuts, which by November are being roasted and sold from little wooden huts in every town. The bags they come in even have a little section for the empty shells. So very Swiss. As winter returns, so do the snow and the fog, which can envelop whole valleys for days on end. The only way to escape is to take a cable car up above the fog line and sit on a sunny mountain top. At 11.11 on 11 November, when much of Europe is commemorating its century of loss, the Swiss get out their brass bands and garish costumes. This marks the traditional start of the Carnival season, which culminates in the festival itself the following spring.

Advent is, in many ways, bigger than Christmas itself. Advent crowns, with four candles, can be found everywhere, Christmas markets pop up all across the country, shopping is often allowed on Sundays, and every child gets an Advent calendar. These can be glittery cardboard affairs, but are more normally a series of 24 little boxes or pouches, each containing a gift. All through Advent, Swiss kitchens are full of people baking mini-cookies, ready to offer to guests or take as presents. By Christmas, everyone seems rather glad to have a quiet time around a tree with real candles. That's right, no fairy lights but proper candles in clip-on holders. Health & Safety would have a fit. There's no traditional meal, no TV marathon, no getting legless and no crackers – one thing many Swiss people have never pulled. And of course, there's no ten-day holiday. It may be Christmas, but everyone still has to go back to work.

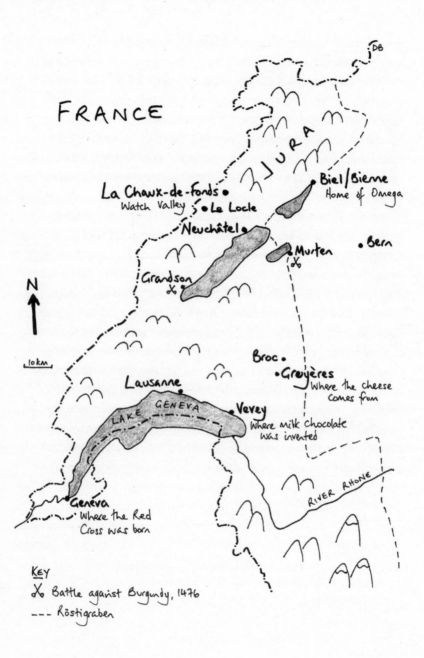

FRANCE

JURA

La Chaux-de-Fonds •
Watch Valley • Le Locle

Neuchâtel •

• Biel/Bienne
Home of Omega

• Murten
✕

• Bern

Grandson
✕

N

10 km

Broc •
• Gruyères
Where the cheese
comes from

Lausanne •

LAKE GENEVA

• Vevey
Where milk chocolate
was invented

RIVER RHONE

• Geneva
Where the Red
Cross was born

KEY
✕ Battle against Burgundy, 1476
- - - Röstigraben

EIGHT

THE HOLE TRUTH

Life in Switzerland may seem like the epitome of modernity, with all those precision products and hyperpunctual trains, but actually it's not. Tradition is as important as technology, and the Swiss love nothing more than combining the two. You can download some yodelling onto your smartphone, text your friends in Swiss German (normally a purely spoken language) and may even have your say in the referendum online. And when it comes to that most traditional of Swiss products, modern machines have been seamlessly grafted on to centuries-old methods. Cheese is where tradition and technology really do come together.

Put Swiss in front of the word cheese and you're probably now picturing exactly this: a big slab of yellow rubbery stuff with holes in it, the kind that Jerry runs into when hiding from Tom. This is Emmental, to give it its proper name (Swiss cheese is the insipid generic term used across North America) – the cheese with the holes, the cheese that is one of the iconic symbols of Switzerland, the cheese that tastes as synthetic as the plastic it's wrapped in. Surely there must be more to Switzerland's most famous export than that? The hole cannot be the best bit. Time to discover the truth about Swiss cheese, the hole truth, and where better to start than Emmental, the biggest cheese in Switzerland.

WHEN NO MEANS NO

With some notable exceptions, such as Baby Bel and Stinking Bishop, most cheese takes its name from where it's made:

Roquefort, Cheddar, Edam, Gorgonzola. Unlike those, Emmental is not a town but a region of central Switzerland near Bern, with the river Emme at its heart. The name becomes clear once you know that the German for valley is *Tal*, not far removed from the English word 'dale' (German *ts* often change to English *ds*: *trinken* means to drink and *unter* is under). That makes Emmental scarily close to Emmerdale[1] in meaning, though perhaps Wensleydale is a better analogy. There aren't too many crashing planes, exploding buildings, lesbian love affairs or murders in peaceful, rural Emmental. This is Switzerland, after all.

Since there's no town called Emmental to aim for, it's not obvious where to go and how to get there. It doesn't look very far on the map, about 30 kilometres east of Bern, but there's no one place that looks to be an obvious starting point. A visit to the Bern tourist office is in order, which proves to be less straightforward than anticipated. My request for some information on Emmental, possibly the most famous part of the local area, gets a shake of the head and a sorry smile.

'It is too far away,' the man explains.

I am so taken aback that I'm left spluttering. 'But it's part of Canton Bern, a really famous part. You must get lots of people asking about it.'

He nods. 'Sometimes.'

By which he probably means every day. Most Swiss people understate everything from their own wealth to the winter temperatures. If they say they only speak a little English, they're probably nearly fluent; just a few people in the market, and you know it was packed. The Swiss never oversell themselves or anything else. Even with this proviso, however, I had presumed that the Bern tourist office would actually have information about other places in the same canton. This was somewhere on the doorstep, a place which attracts thousands of visitors a year. It would be like me going into the York tourist office and being told that the Dales are too far away to be of interest. He seems to notice my incredulity and tries to explain.

'We have not the room,' he says, his voice echoing round the huge space where we are standing, 'because we need it for the informations [sic] on other parts of Switzerland. This is the capital city so we must have things about Ticino or Geneva.'

As polite as he's being, I can see I'm getting nowhere. A no in Switzerland is always a no; it's never a no disguised as a yes or even a maybe, even though Italy is just across the border. And it never changes. Before I leave, I ask where to find information (no -s) on Emmental.

'You should go there and ask in the local tourist office,' he suggests.

I sigh. Of course. I have to go there before I can find out anything, even though I don't really know where *there* is.

Finally, he says something helpful. 'Start in Langnau. They will help you.'

With something concrete to go on, I smile and leave.

According to the timetable, the local train takes 40 minutes to cover the 33 kilometres to Langnau,[2] probably because it stops at every cowshed along the way. After that, with train lines few and far between in Emmental, it's either getting around by bus or calling in the cavalry. My parents are over from England for a visit. With a car. I dial their number.

IN SEARCH OF CHEESE

The first stop is a mere two minutes out of Bern main station, and my fears of the train stopping this frequently begin to grow. Nevertheless, when I see the station name I have to smile. It's my favourite place name in the whole of Bern: Wankdorf. What a great name for English speakers to laugh about, even more so because most Swiss just don't get it. But there's more. Wankdorf is the Swiss Wembley, home to the national stadium, grandly called the Stade de Suisse, as if they know that having international matches at somewhere called Wankdorf is just asking for trouble. It hosted the 1954 World Cup final, won by West Germany, but that old stadium was demolished in 2001 (it really is like Wembley) to make way for a new 32,000-seat affair that is all solar roof panels and clear sight lines.[3] Its biggest events so far have been the Euro 2008 championships and a Robbie Williams concert. You can guess how much he enjoyed saying that name. The rest of the time it is home to Bern's football team, which has the unlikely name of Young Boys. You couldn't make it up. Young Boys playing with balls at Wankdorf. It almost makes Sheffield Wednesday look like a normal name.

It never takes long for the countryside to appear on a Swiss train ride – the cities just aren't that big – and on this route the countryside is majestic. The backdrop of snow-dusted mountains looks too stunning to be real, almost as if a giant artist decided that the green foothills and wheat-filled fields weren't picturesque enough, so he painted in a monumental horizon. Nowhere in Switzerland is very far from the Alps, but sometimes it's easy to forget they are there: out of sight, out of mind. The Swiss have perfected that art; it still takes me by surprise.

On most maps Langnau appears followed by i.E., and once there you realise what the letters stand for, making it very clear that this is the place to start any cheese trip: Langnau im Emmental. It's a modest country town, with a sprinkling of old wooden buildings, flower-laden balconies, sturdy churches, small shops and a supermarket. Rather like a British market town of similar size, only with fewer brick buildings and free parking. Tucked away in a hideous modern building that's out of step with its grand old neighbours is the tourist office, with its informative Emmental Cheese Road map/guide. Out of sheer curiosity I ask for information on Bern. 'Too far away' is the now familiar answer, as if I'm asking about Outer Mongolia.

A horn beeps behind me; the cavalry has arrived, and we head off in search of the cheese with holes.

INTO THE HEART OF EMMENTAL

We take to the back roads and it quickly becomes clear how hilly Emmental is. I was expecting something much flatter, with plenty of open fields for all those milk cows. True, there are lots and lots of cows (and not many sheep, making it doubly different from Emmerdale), but most have to graze while sloping uphill. Or down, or maybe even at an angle, but rarely on the level. It shouldn't be a surprise, given that the Alps are just an hour to the south, but these really are big hills. In any other country they'd probably be called mountains, given their height. The one behind Langnau climbs up to 1036 metres, which is not much smaller than Mt Snowdon, but compared to that craggy bleak rock this looks like a cuddly hillock covered in green velvet. Then again Langnau is 643 metres above sea level, making the 'mountain' appear to be a hill of only 393 metres. Everything is relative.

Even with the lumpy landscape, much of the countryside is farmland, though on a small scale. No vast tracts for combine harvesters to churn through, no long-distant vistas of rippling cornfields, no miles of polytunnels shining in the sun. Instead, semi-wooded hillsides crowd in on the rushing streams, cows munch away in lush sloping meadows, and the farmhouses appear at astonishingly regular intervals. A decent-sized back garden looks bigger than some of these farms, but they more than make up for it by having the largest farmhouses I have ever seen. Each is like a vast wooden barn with a tiled roof the size of a football pitch sloping almost down to the ground on both sides. The hugeness of it is offset by rows of dinky little windows beneath the overhanging eaves and geranium-filled boxes across the whole of the A-shaped front. So photogenic, so Swiss.

The scenery is too inviting, and the weather too agreeable, so we downgrade lunch from a slap-up restaurant to an outdoor picnic, complete with the best thing Swiss supermarkets sell: hard-boiled eggs, cooked, cooled and ready for just such occasions. They're even called picnic eggs on the packet. What a great idea! And they have prettily painted shells, like at Easter, so that you don't get them confused with raw ones. Such is the Swiss attention to detail. We tootle north, following the Emme downstream through a trail of villages, each looking as if they've only just realised the twenty-first century is here. Take away the few trappings of modern life, such as the asphalted road, cars and overhead wires, and much of Emmental wouldn't appear to have changed in the last few decades. And in that, it isn't so different from anywhere in rural Switzerland.

A SLICE OF COUNTRY LIFE

While the world around it has been travelling at a hare's pace, Swiss country life has been taking the tortoise route, preserving its traditions while adding a few modern comforts here and there. Flag-throwing festivals, yodelling clubs, traditional costumes and folk music: the customs of the past are very much part of present-day life, and almost every community has its own variations that are treasured and celebrated as a matter of course, not as something wheeled out for the tourists.

For example, all across Switzerland the herding of the cows up to the high Alpine pastures in spring is cause for great celebration. Cows are decked out in flowers, bells and flags, and often compete in beauty contests, with the winner being queen for the summer. There's another chance for a procession and a party in the autumn, when the cows are brought back down again. For sure, it's a popular sight, with many townies coming for the day, but it's more about doing things the way they've always been done. Even if that means having to listen to, and claim to enjoy, *Hudigääggeler*, the Swiss version of oom-pah-pah music, usually played by a trio of men on an accordion, a double bass and a clarinet or tuba. After about two songs it all sounds the same, but the Swiss love it, so much so that it's often on television, at prime time on a normal channel, not at 3 a.m. on some cable network watched by 17 insomniacs.

Then there are the three traditional Swiss sports, *Hornussen*, *Schwingen* and *Steinstossen*, all summertime affairs. A mad mix of golf and baseball, *Hornussen* is a team game, where one side catapults a plastic puck into the air while the other team tries to bat it down with giant paddles. It's particularly popular in Emmental. *Schwingen* is rustic wrestling that takes place outdoors in a sawdust ring. The *Schwingers* are usually big men, cheesemakers or carpenters in the real world, wearing what look like giant hessian nappies over their clothes. The winner gets a wreath or a cowbell – no cash prizes here. Just as burly are the *Steinstossers*, who hurl stones as far as possible. It's like shot putting, except that the stones range from 4 up to 50 kilograms. Every three years all three sports, along with yodelling, alphorn blowing and flag throwing, take part in a *Schwing- und Älplerfest*, a sort of Swiss cultural Olympics. The *Schwingen* winner is crowned the king of the *Schwingers* and wins a prize bull. After becoming *Schwinger* king for the third time, carpenter Jörg Abderhalden was voted Swiss Personality of the Year[4] – that's how big the sport is.

Nothing seems to change quickly in Switzerland, which is exactly how most Swiss like it. Come back in 20 years and it's highly probable that lunch will still be at midday, *Hudigääggeler* trios will still be playing at cheese festivals, and the shops will still be closed on Sundays. All that is what makes it a fascinating place, full of a living sense of history and such a feeling of community that I wonder if it will ever change. Of course, progress has a will of its own, so that even the most traditional parts of Swiss society have to move on.

CHEESE IN THE MAKING

Old and new seem to be able to coexist quite comfortably in Switzerland, and one place to see them together is the show-piece of Emmental cheese-making: the dairy at Affoltern (also an i.E. village). Here you can, along with coachloads of over-excited Swiss grannies, watch the famous cheese being made and learn all about the process from multilingual handsets. Separated from the cheesery by huge plexiglass screens, you can look down on the vast vats of swirling milk and still catch a whiff, especially downstairs where the huge cheese rounds sit in storage racks. It's like sticking your nose into someone else's shoe.

I now have the recipe for perfect Emmental cheese. Take one cow. Feed it 100 kilograms of fresh grass per day, mixed with 85 litres of water, and let it ruminate. Milk twice daily, giving you up to 22 litres of the white stuff. Add rennet and stew at 32°C until it coagulates. Slice with a wire whisk and gently heat to 55°C. Pour the curds into a mould and press for one day, turning it occasionally. Immerse in a brine bath for up to 24 hours. Leave to ripen in a cool, damp cellar for a minimum of four months, regularly turning, washing and rubbing the cheese. Slice and eat.

It takes 12 litres of milk to produce one kilo of Emmental,[5] which means that an awful lot of milk goes into a whole Emmental. It is truly a big cheese: each round is one metre in diameter, about 25 centimetres deep in the middle and weighs up to 120 kilograms.[6] That's why you almost never see a triangular wedge of Emmental; it's always in oblong blocks because pie-slice-shaped pieces would be 50 centimetres long. Not too handy for the average cheeseboard. As for the holes, they are actually trapped CO_2, released by the bacteria added at the final stages of production. The technical term for the holes is eyes, which must make Emmental the peacock of cheeses, and their size can be controlled by changing the cooking temperature or curing time.

Hole technology is not the only thing I learn in the show dairy. I also discover what a difference an ER makes, and it's nothing to do with hospitals. Emmental is, apparently, the generic name for holey Swiss cheese made by that method, wherever it's produced. But Emmentaler (with an extra ER) is a protected brand, made only in a specific area of Switzerland, using raw milk less than 12 hours old and coming from cows fed with fresh grass or hay.[7] Each round is numbered so its origin can be traced, and each has the AOC (*Appellation d'Origine Contrôlée*) stamp of approval, just like certain wines.

The wonderful thing about most Swiss cheese is that it's made on a small scale. Cheese is not a cottage industry – Switzerland produces 185,000 tonnes of cheese every year, over a third of which is exported[8] – but much of it is made in the hundreds of village dairies using milk from local farms. True, most dairies have embraced modern technology; they're not all still cooking milk in copper pans over wood fires, though there's a chance to see that at this dairy. In an old wooden house, a suitably rustic gentleman is making cheese the traditional way, in an enormous cooking pot hanging over a fire. Even away from the cheese-making room, the building reeks, almost as if it's actually built of cheese. Maybe it is, like a Swiss version of a gingerbread house, and it's only age and the smoke that make the walls look like brown wood.

THE CHEESIEST TOWN AROUND

While Emmental is the archetypal German-speaking Swiss cheese, Gruyère is its French-speaking counterpart. Together they can make a perfect fondue (though the more traditional *moitié-moitié* fondue uses Vacherin fribourgeoise instead of Emmental). Two languages, two cheeses, both Swiss and both used in the ultimate Swiss dish, French and German combined in culinary harmony.

In a country full of picturesque towns, few make a better first impression than Gruyères (the town name, unlike the cheese, has an -s for some reason). High above the valley floor is a castle perched on top of a craggy rock, with a cradle of higher hills all around. Think Rapunzel meets a mini-Edinburgh. Swiss castles tend to be more fairytale than militaristic. Instead of battlements, keeps and curtain walls, you get towers topped by dunce's cap roofs, covered ramparts, and a core that is more château than fortress. Gruyères castle fits the part but also manages to look quite forbidding, more Dracula than Rapunzel.

Since Gruyères is out in the sticks between Bern and Lausanne, it's a long train ride from anywhere – but worth the effort. Walking up the hill from the station, I soon realise that coming by train was the easiest option. Much less stress. Overflow car parks, one mainly for coaches, line the road up the hill and are already dotted with vehicles. Car park number one, beside the town walls, is full even though it's only mid-morning and this isn't peak season; imagine the crowds in high summer, when Gruyères receives most of its one million annual visitors. Not bad going for a place with only 170 permanent inhabitants.

Gruyères is actually quite small, more village than town, with just one street – but it's quite a street. Wide enough to hold a football match, its cobbled expanse first slopes downhill to a central fountain and then up again, narrowing dramatically to squeeze through the castle gates. Handsome medieval buildings run down both sides, their stone walls nearly all whitewashed, their eaves overhanging, their window boxes bursting with colour. As an ensemble it is almost too photogenic to be real. It looks like the set for *Chitty Chitty Bang Bang* and I half expect the Child Catcher to come rattling through in his black carriage, cracking his whip and sniffing for children.

Look a little closer and it's clear that almost every building is either a restaurant or a tourist shop, which spoils the aesthetics a little. Dairy products of every description spill out on to trestle tables outside each shop: cheese, cream, fudge and, my personal favourite, *confiture de lait*. This Swiss version of *dulce de leche* (a smooth caramel spread) is perfect on fresh, squishy bread; it's nothing short of heaven in a jar.

All the restaurants have terraces opening out onto the square and seem to have the same menu, involving 101 ways to eat cheese. It feels like walking down Gerrard Street in London's Chinatown and trying to find a restaurant that offers something different. I always thought Chinatown was actually one giant restaurant, with a central underground kitchen and little trains transporting all the food around to the different dining rooms. Perhaps Gruyères is the same.

Reservations are essential in such a busy town, especially for a larger table (I've brought my visiting English family along for the ride), so I pick a place at random. The stressed waitress makes it abundantly clear that our table will only be held for ten minutes, after which it's a free-for-all. Having to feed so many people all year round obviously leaves some people unable to remember the basic concepts of friendly service. Then again, Swiss service is often as direct as the people themselves: few sugary niceties, few frilly edges, including on the aprons, and certainly no 'Hi, my name is Heidi and I'll be your waitress today'. Far too familiar for the Swiss.

By the time we return from a castle visit, being very careful not to be late, the sunny square is buzzing. All the restaurants are packed with people eating their fill of cheese, most of it melted in a pot.

A CHEESE AND WINE PARTY

Fondue is Switzerland's gift to the culinary world. Swiss Germans might disagree on it being the national dish, but as much as they like potato *Rösti*, and they really do like it, it's just not that popular elsewhere in the country. Fondue, on the other hand, can be found in places well beyond its origins in the French-speaking cantons: in the streets of Zurich's Niederdorf, the chalets of St Moritz and the resorts of the Bernese Oberland. It might have a French name (from the French verb *fondre*, or 'to melt') but fondue is truly a Swiss dish.

In case you were too busy strutting your stuff on a flashing dance floor or just didn't live through the 1970s, here's a fond reminder of a typical dinner. Fondue is, essentially, a cheese and wine party all in one pot. Everything's melted together in a ceramic pot, known as a *caquelon*, and then kept warm over a squashed Bunsen burner placed in the centre of the table. You spear cubes of bread on to a ridiculously long-handled fork, then dip it into the gloopy-cheesy-winey concoction, twirl rapidly and attempt to get the dripping cube into your mouth without dribbling. Drop the bread in the pot and you pay a forfeit, maybe having to kiss your neighbour, though that depends on how much wine you've both had. And who your neighbour is.

Of course, for the Swiss fondue isn't a fad food that disappeared about the same time as kipper ties. It's a traditional dish that's been around for ever, but it's usually a winter comfort food, their version of stew and dumplings or shepherd's pie. It's generally only tourists who eat fondue when the thermometer hits double digits, and in that the Swiss have got it right. Who wants to be eating hot cheese when it's 30ºC in the shade? But much to the constant amusement of the locals, that's exactly what hordes of tourists do.

Equally shocking, no doubt, is having to watch visitors break the three cardinal rules of eating fondue:

❖ Firstly, and most importantly, your fork should never touch your tongue, teeth or lips as you eat, purely because it has to go back into the pot every time.
❖ Secondly, don't drink anything fizzy, especially sparkling water, as you eat, otherwise what is anyway a fairly indigestible meal will turn to lead. It's more normal to drink white wine or black tea, by which the Swiss mean tea that isn't green or herbal; in English, we just call it tea.
❖ Lastly, once all the fondue has gone, the bottom of the pot is encrusted with a layer of cheese hardened to a crisp by being closer to the heat. Never leave *la religieuse* uneaten, but don't take it all for yourself. For most Swiss it's the best part of the meal and is there to be shared.

Contrary to popular belief fondue is not the only Swiss cheese dish; there's also raclette, which originated in the Valais region of southern Switzerland. Like fondue it's perfect for a sociable dinner, and most supermarkets sell the special table-top grills and ready-sliced raclette cheese. Traditionalists – that is, most Swiss people – eat raclette only with pickled onions and little gherkins as accompaniments, though some wacky types throw in pineapple, baby corn cobs, cherry tomatoes and apple. I'm one of the eccentrics, but a misshapen gherkin will probably be the most exciting thing to go with a raclette in Gruyères. It's that kind of town.

As anticipated, my raclette appears with accompaniments of the traditional (severely limited) variety, although the grill itself is rather special. A large oblong of cheese sits under what looks like a mini version of those outdoor heaters you see in pubs and bars. The top surface melts and I scrape it off with a wooden spatula – hence the name, from the French *racler,* to scrape – straight onto the small boiled potatoes, still in their jackets. It's a typically heavy Swiss dish; those long winters and vigorous walks mean that the Swiss don't eat dainty food in minute portions. If it's big and hearty, then it's Swiss. Definitely no room after that for the time-honoured Gruyères dessert: meringues with raspberries and thick double cream.

Gruyères is the cheesiest (in every sense) town in Switzerland. It's undeniably sweet, even more so in winter when snowflakes outnumber visitors, but its blatant exploitation of the cheese theme grates a little. True, it has the authentic history to back up its marketing, even if the quaintness feels a little contrived, but somehow it feels so different from Emmental. Compared to the traditional rural life along the Emme valley Gruyères is so commercialised, there for the tourists who descend in their thousands from all over the world. There's further proof of that in Gruyères' show dairy, down at the bottom of the hill. Unlike its Emmental counterpart, it isn't free. Not only that, but you can pay in euros as well as Swiss francs.

DOWN AT THE CHEESERY

The audio tour is narrated by Cherry, who's a likeable enough guide, talking us through her life, which basically involves chewing lots of grass, having her udders squeezed twice a day, and walking up to higher pastures in spring and down again in autumn. Not exactly a thrill a minute but as lives go, it seems comfortable enough. Cherry imparts all sorts of trivia, like the fact that two-thirds of all Gruyère is eaten in Switzerland or that scientists have detected up to 75 different scents in the cheese. After that, it's a familiar tale of everyday cheese-making: mixing the morning and evening milk, cooking in giant vats (the one on display holds 4800 litres), salt baths, pressing and storing. Like Emmentaler, Gruyère is AOC protected as it's made only in this part of Switzerland. And like Emmental, it takes 12 litres of milk to make one kilo. In fact, there seems to be very little difference between Gruyère and Emmental, apart from the former being blind, as in it has no eyes. Other than that it's a question of size: the average round of Gruyère is a mere 60 centimetres across and weighs only 35 kilograms; a lightweight in comparison.

Downstairs, you get to stare through a window at 7000 rounds, all maturing slowly while stacked from floor to ceiling. It looks like one of those scenes from a sci-fi film where the heroes find a warehouse, flick on the lights and are confronted with row upon row of clones stretching off into the distance. Kind of spooky, even though it's only cheese. Then a robot trolley glides into the aisle, sticks its arms out and turns over each of the cheese rounds in one stack; now it really does feel like another world.

Standard Gruyère comes in three varieties: mild, semi-salted and salty. None is my cup of tea but in the shop I try the Reserve, which makes it sound even more like a wine; the AOC label alone clearly wasn't enough. Having been aged for a minimum of one year, Reserve Gruyère is much less rubbery, with a grainy, crumbly texture and a much stronger flavour. Truly scrumptious. Until then the appeal of Swiss cheese had eluded me, but this was a revelation – and there were more to come.

THE REAL SWISS CHEESE

There are two big supermarket chains in Switzerland and between them they account for over 80 per cent of Swiss grocery shopping.[9] German discounters like Aldi or Lidl are nibbling at the edges, but most Swiss stick to what they know and trust (particularly if the competition is German). And what they know is Coop and Migros. Coop is the posher Swiss supermarket chain that differs from Migros, its cheaper, down-to-earth competition, in two big ways. First, Coop sells alcohol and tobacco, Migros doesn't. No really, it doesn't. I can't imagine a British supermarket surviving without ten aisles of wine, whisky and beer, not to mention the packets of cigarettes behind the till. However, it's not only about booze and fags, but brands. That's the second big difference: Migros shuns many multinationals, preferring to have own-brand products and local produce (the milk bottle labels even tell you which local area the milk comes from). Although Migros is slowly stocking more branded goods – it even sells Mars bars these days – in contrast, Coop is brand central: its shelves are brimming with Coke, Del Monte, Pringles, Persil and the like.

Branded produce aside, I was in Coop one day looking for something cheesey for a dinner party; in Switzerland, cheese is often served as a separate course between the main and dessert. I zigzagged through the aisles, stopping briefly to wonder at how many different types of muesli there were (28

– and I thought it was just Alpen), and found the cheese counter. And there they were, all those Swiss cheeses. Hard, soft, holey, solid, cows', goats', round and wedgy. It was mice paradise. The girl behind the counter proffered me a cube on a toothpick. I hesitated but gave in, more out of politeness than anything else, and popped it into my mouth.

Oh. My. God. (or *Oh. Mein. Gott,* now that I speak German). Gone were the Silly Putty texture and too-mild-to-be-noticed taste that I detest. Instead, my mouth was dazzled by this firm yet creamy cheese with a tangy, almost herby flavour. In my naïveté I thought I had found something special. Of course it was nothing new to our Swiss dinner guests, all of whom have been enjoying Appenzeller for centuries, though they politely let me relish my 'discovery'. It left me wondering why the only Swiss cheese we get abroad is Emmental or Gruyère.

Since that Damascene moment in Coop there have been many other Swiss cheeses to tempt me, each with a tale to tell: the wonderfully titled Tilsiter, named after a town in East Prussia where its Swiss expat creator lived before returning home in 1893;[10] the well-hard Sbrinz, a sort of Swiss Parmesan that's made in only 34 dairies around Lake Lucerne;[11] the silky Tête de Moine, which has its own special knife to shave it into delicate, curly rosettes. To the Swiss they're as normal as Emmental; but to me each was a revelation, though none of them danced on my taste buds like Appenzeller. That was as distinctive as the place it comes from.

SOMETHING FOR THE QUAINT-HEARTED

Don't be surprised if you've never heard of hilly, lush Appenzellerland; few people outside Switzerland have. But within the country, it's famous not merely for its unique cheese. This rural canton is the most traditional or, if you're a less charitable city dweller, the most backward and unsophisticated. Appenzell folk certainly have their own distinct architecture, dialect and costumes, which often make them the butt of many a Swiss joke. You still see men dressed in their embroidered scarlet waistcoats, black hats and breeches, with a silver earring dangling from one ear, 'as if time had stood still',[12] as the Appenzellerland tourist website so neatly puts it. This is where tradition is a way of life; never is that easier to see than on festival days such as Mother's Day. It's not a holiday but it still warrants celebrating.

Mother's Day in Switzerland is not the moveable feast it is in Britain, where it precedes and is linked to Easter so that it wanders around March like a lost lamb. Swiss Mother's Day is always on the second Sunday in May and it's a big deal. The trains are full of dutiful offspring heading home, carrying giant bouquets, pot plants, gaudily wrapped packages or pristine white cake boxes. It's all about presents, but oddly enough not about cards. In other countries card firms cash in on events like Mother's Day; in Switzerland they get nowhere, simply because the Swiss don't send many cards. Birthday, sympathy, get well, congratulations and even Christmas cards are all noticeable by their absence. Eight sent per year is the average for a Swiss person, compared to 45 for an American.[13] Perhaps the Swiss just prefer to say it with flowers, always the top choice for a Mother's Day gift.

The maternal festivities are in full swing when we arrive at Brülisau, a huddle of a hamlet at the base of Hoher Kasten mountain (see the map of eastern Switzerland on page 275). The whole place has gathered for a Mother's Day service at the church, with the village brass band playing on the steps and all the locals dressed up in their finery. For the women this means wearing a stiff, white lacy headdress that looks like one of those fan-shaped napkin holders. The most important detail is the ribbon at the back: married women wear red, widows black, while a white ribbon shows you're still available. No headdress at all means you're past your sell-by date. It all feels a bit like a medieval *Stepford Wives*, but it certainly looks dramatic when the whole female population is walking into church together.

Almost as spooky is the village of Oberriet, where every garden and field seems to have a scarecrow standing sentry, as if the villagers are expecting an invasion of birds, *à la* Alfred Hitchcock. And the scarecrows are a motley lot: one in a wedding dress, another in a business suit; a fat, roly-poly man near a minimalist, stick-and-straw curtain; even a giant crow, like something from the Hammer House of Horror. It turns out that the villagers have created 531 scarecrows to try to get into the *Guinness Book of Records*.[14] Perhaps they got bored of choosing which cow was beautiful enough to be Miss Oberriet and represent them at the Miss Rheintal competition. And I'm not joking. The straw men of Oberriet disappear as we go up into the heart of Appenzellerland, a verdant, undulating plateau set in a gentle dip surrounded by rocky mountains.

Despite the craggy horizon, there's a sense of openness that was missing in Emmental; nothing close to miles of flat prairie, but a feeling of space for nature to do its thing, though it doesn't feel empty or wild. As everywhere in rural Switzerland, farms dot the landscape with amazing regularity, each seemingly in easy yodelling distance of its neighbours. Each region of Switzerland has its own architecture, something the Swiss are quite proud of; compared to the mega-barns of Emmental, the Appenzell farmhouses are diminutive, ladylike affairs. The three-storey square houses are straight out of *Little House on the Prairie*, most with wooden shingle façades, some painted pale blue or yellow. Attached to each farmhouse at right angles, making a T-shape, is the barn, so that animals and owners are snuggled up together at night.

After all that rolling farmland and rustic traditions, Appenzell itself feels like a buzzing metropolis, though it's a town of barely 6000 people.

My previous visit to Appenzell (described in Chapter Four) was for the *Landsgemeinde*, or cantonal parliament, when the town was packed to the painted rafters. This time it's possible to see the buildings themselves. Walking down the pedestrianised main street is like being in a parallel Switzerland, one designed by Disney. The old wooden houses are painted a kaleidoscope of colours and decorated with intricate stencils. Dangling out above our heads is a succession of signs, most curly and golden, proclaiming the presence of a pharmacy, hotel or butcher. Window displays are filled with local handicrafts, such as pear bread and daintily embroidered cloth, among the standard Swiss souvenirs, like cows that yodel when you press their stomachs. And of course there's the cheese, looking temptingly tasty in its rounds and wedges. Every time a shop door opens, the pungent smell escapes and lingers in the air, like a cartoon trail of mist following us down the street. It's a Sunday and this is a Catholic canton, but some shops are open to make the most of the many tourists milling in the streets.

The irregular-shaped main square is noticeably emptier than in April. Now I can appreciate that almost every building has its wooden walls painted, the handsome façades displaying a rusty rainbow colour scheme, from sunflower yellow through lobster red to chocolate brown. We take a table under the linden trees and indulge in a spot of lunch from a menu as traditional as the location, with lots of treats for meat eaters and alcohol lovers. Beefsteak tartare served with Appenzell single malt whisky, anyone? Or maybe half a litre of *Hanfblüte* (hemp beer) to wash down that *Siedwurst*, a white veal sausage? Luckily, this is a cheese town so there's also plenty of choice for veggies, such as *Chäsmaggerone*, or macaroni cheese. Banish those traumatic memories of school dinners – this is nothing like the stodgy English dish. This is pasta and diced potatoes enveloped in a light, creamy-cheesy sauce, then sprinkled with crispy roasted onions and served with apple purée on the side.

After lunch, I pop into a cheese shop and buy a chunk of the local stuff to take home. Yes, I know I can buy Appenzeller in my local Coop, but there's nothing like getting it from the horse's mouth (or cow's udder). I'm convinced it tastes better.

Switzerland is not a great place for anyone who's lactose intolerant. Cheese is one of its most famous exports and a staple component of every Swiss diet. No winter passes by without at least one fondue, no *Apéro* is complete without a cheese platter. It's no surprise, then, to discover that there are 1.6 million cows in Switzerland;[15] they don't just look pretty in the fields, they produce milk and this is the land where milk makes money. And of course, they add to the sound of the countryside. A walk isn't Swiss until you've heard the sound of cowbells echoing up from the valley below.

There's more to Swiss cheese than meets the eye: only one truly has proper holes, none needs to have the texture of plastic, and there are far more varieties than the couple we see abroad. It's only when you come to Switzerland and taste the real deal that you realise that the Swiss export the plastic and keep the rest secret, not singing its praises, not telling the world how great it is. How very Swiss. But despite its success, Swiss cheese doesn't rest on its laurels. In Switzerland the three main brands[16] are continually being advertised in magazines, on television, in the cinema, in trams, pretty much everywhere in fact. And it clearly works. Swiss people eat an awful lot of Swiss cheese: an average of 15.9 kilograms per person each year.[17] Looking at consumption of all types of cheese, the Swiss manage an impressive 22 kilograms per head annually,[18] well above the EU average.[19] In comparison, the British are clearly not a nation of turophiles (cheese lovers to you and me), only eating about half the amount the Swiss tuck away.[20]

Successful advertising aside, there is a much stronger reason why the Swiss eat so much locally made cheese: they are fiercely protective of their country, its traditions and everything it produces. Any products, from fresh fruit to hand-carved wooden toys, that are Swiss in origin are always clearly marked to that effect. Farmers, manufacturers and retailers all know that's the quickest way to a sale. Swiss strawberries or cherries may be twice the price of Spanish imports, but when they're in season, the Swiss ones are the only ones in demand. It's the same with cheese. To the typical Swiss mind there's little sense in eating something French or British when you can buy something made just down the road.

And that really is the point. Switzerland is a small country with small cities, so that no one lives very far from the countryside, with all its rich produce and traditions. In his heart, every Swiss man (okay, and woman) is still a country boy, no matter if he was born and grew up in Zurich. Cow beauty contests and yodelling competitions may be ridiculed by some city folk, but they are an integral part of country life. And I suspect that even the Swiss dismissers secretly love the fact that such traditions still exist. They're what make Switzerland the way it is, different from any other country. And that's something every Swiss person is intensely proud of, and rightly so.

SWISS WATCHING TIP NO 8:
THE PERFECT GUEST

When it comes to eating with the Swiss, there are three crucial factors to being a good guest: the invitation, the present and the participation. Swiss people rarely welcome total outsiders into their homes, so when you are first invited for a meal it's more likely to be in a restaurant. A Swiss invitation means that the guest pays nothing, and it's not the done thing to suggest contributing something. Going Dutch in Switzerland is only an option when both parties have agreed to meet for the meal, rather than one inviting the other.

To Swiss people, this is all clear and logical; to outsiders, it can be a social minefield. Say it's your birthday and you'd like to celebrate by eating out with friends. In Britain, it's the norm for everyone to divide the bill so that you, as the birthday boy, don't pay anything even though you organised the meal. In Switzerland it's the exact opposite: you pay the whole bill. It's quite a shock for a Swiss person to be invited out for a British celebration, only to realise that not only does he have to pay for himself, he also has to pay for a share of the host's meal. It's an even bigger shock for a foreigner to invite his Swiss friends out and end up paying the lot. A Saturday night out can be a pricey affair if you don't phrase the suggestion correctly, and birthday celebrations can run to hundreds of francs.

Balancing this culture clash isn't always easy. For example, the first time my parents went to Liechtenstein to meet Gregor's family, all 18 of us were invited out for lunch by Hans, Gregor's father. My father wanted to split the bill with Hans as a way of thanking him for three days of hospitality, but we told him he wouldn't stand a chance. Hans had invited everyone, so he would pay and my father wouldn't even notice when it happened. Sure enough, the bill was paid as if it had never existed and my father knew nothing until it was too late.

If you do actually get invited to a Swiss home for a meal, don't forget to take a present. Nothing too hard about that, except that the present says everything about you, your host and the level of invitation. So going round for coffee or tea might warrant a little something from the patisserie or chocolate shop. Move up to an *Apéro* and you could take a bottle of wine (preferably Swiss) or some flowers. Either would also be fine for a dinner party, though you might upgrade the value, but if that dinner involves any sort of celebration, the world is your oyster. As hosts we have received all manner of gifts, such as a tea set, cinema tickets, espresso spoons, books, luxury mini food hampers, even a cuddly toy. All this is partly because the Swiss are generous when thanking you for opening up your home to them; it can also be a substitute for reciprocating that invitation. No one expects a thank-you note for the gifts; but as a host, you rarely receive a post-party thank-you either. After all, you have already been thanked with a present on the night.

The last part of being the perfect guest is remembering to be just that. Guests do not normally help in Swiss homes. Never set foot in the kitchen, never refill drinks, never clear the plates from the table. You can offer to help once, which will be politely declined, then you must sit back and relax, or at least appear to. A second offer, or helping unasked, implies that the hosts are not sufficiently organised and cannot cope on their own. Do that and there won't be a second invitation, even if you waited months (maybe years) for the first one. But perhaps, at some point in the future, your initial offer of help, given half-heartedly because by then you know the answer, will be accepted. Then you'll know that you are accepted. You are in. All you have to do is make sure your table manners are up to scratch, but that's a whole separate minefield.

NINE

WHERE THE CHOCOLATE COMES FROM

A national dish is so much a part of a country's image, both at home and abroad, that it becomes an integral factor in the stereotyping of every country. England has fish and chips, Spain its paella, while it's haggis in Scotland and a hamburger in the States. For Switzerland it's fondue, which is so popular with the Swiss that they don't just have the cheese-and-wine variety. There's also *fondue chinoise*, where thinly sliced beef is dropped into hot broth to cook and eaten with a variety of sauces; on high days and holidays, it makes a popular Swiss family meal. Or there's *fondue bour-guignonne*, which uses hot oil not broth to cook the meat. But while others love fondue, I fon-don't. Except for one, choco-late fondue, where pieces of fruit or cake are used for dipping. The ultimate Swiss dessert is the perfect combination of the national dish and the product for which the Swiss are possibly most famous. After all, milk chocolate is a Swiss invention, and for that we have Daniel Peter to thank. In my book he should be a saint, so I decided to make a pilgrimage to his home town.

WHERE MILK CHOCOLATE WAS BORN

Vevey isn't the sort of place you associate with a creation that has improved moods around the world for decades, or with being the headquarters of the world's biggest food company.[1] It's just a small town on the north shore of Lake Geneva, not far from Montreux (see the map of Romandie on page 184), with a huge market square and views of the French Alps. In fact, apart from being the worldwide HQ of Nestlé, Vevey does have one other claim to fame: the tiny cemetery of Corsier-sur-Vevey is the last resting place of Charlie Chaplin, whose statue graces the lakeshore promenade. The funny thing is that he isn't the only great Briton to be buried here. His neighbour is James Mason and literally across the road (but technically in the neighbouring village of Corseaux) is Graham Greene, making this a corner of Switzerland that will be forever England. I wonder if they all liked milk chocolate or just the sunny climate and lake views.

The biggest building in town isn't the prettiest but, considering the size and scope of Nestlé, it isn't a corporate monstrosity either. Founded in 1866 by German immigrant Heinrich Nestle (a name soon Frenchified into Henri Nestlé),[2] the company initially specialised in condensed milk and infant milk powder, a product that still causes it grief from campaigners. These days Nestlé owns so many brands it's practically a one-stop supermarket: Perrier, Mövenpick, Maggi, Felix and Buitoni to name a few. In the late 1980s it swallowed Rowntree, one of Britain's oldest confectioners, 60 years after Daniel Peter's chocolate company had suffered the same fate. That was perhaps rather apt, given that the invention of milk chocolate was the result of Peter and Nestlé being neighbours.

The son of a butcher, Peter had been a candle maker until he got sucked into the world of chocolate when he married the daughter of François-Louis Cailler, who already owned a chocolate factory locally. In those days chocolate wasn't the creamy, silky delight so loved today, but essentially cocoa paste mixed with sugar. And it wasn't cheap. Peter's brainwave was to add milk, making the chocolate more palatable and reducing costs. With no colonies Switzerland had to buy the necessary sugar and cocoa, but it had gallons of milk ready and waiting. Peter's first trials failed because ordinary milk is too watery, but luckily he had Nestlé next door with his thicker, condensed milk. A match made in heaven, or at least in Vevey in 1875.

The next few decades cemented Switzerland's reputation as the producer of the best chocolate in the world, helped by well-heeled tourists from abroad taking it home. Much like tourists today, though in far smaller quantities. Messrs Cailler and Peter, long since merged into one firm, were joined in Neuchâtel by Mr Suchard and in Bern by Mr Lindt[3] and Mr Tobler. Of all these brands, Tobler's is perhaps the most famous. There can't be a duty-free shop anywhere that doesn't sell his triangular creation, its shape inspired by a pyramid of dancers at the Folies Bergère.[4] Every single one of the seven billion triangles of Toblerone produced annually is still made in Bern,[5] even though the company now belongs to US food giant Kraft, known these days as Mondelēz.

Despite Vevey's place in chocolate's history, there isn't much of the old brown magic to see or taste. For that you have to go inland to Broc, the home of the oldest brand of Swiss chocolate still in production today, Cailler.[6] To have a chocolate factory stuck out in the middle of nowhere northeast of Gruyères might seem a little odd, until you realise it has everything a Victorian chocolatier needed; except the cocoa beans, of course. Running water to power the mills, a train line and crucially lots of Gruyères cows with milk on tap. The factory, which opened in 1898, is still the primary producer of Cailler chocolate, and it's well worth visiting.

Cailler is not a brand that's exported very much, so abroad it lacks the name recognition of Lindt or Suchard, but for those with a discerning palate it's apparently the best of the best. I have brought my family to this temple of chocolate heaven in the hope of seeing it being made. Sadly, the tour no longer includes any of the production process, thanks to health and safety concerns, but at least the whole place smells of chocolate. With the receptionist's promise of a 'wide disgustation' at the end, we set off on our non-factory tour.

A series of audiovisual displays guide us through the process of getting from cocoa beans to a bar of Cailler. Each year this one factory consumes four million kilograms of cocoa and 6.8 million kilograms of sugar, which gets mixed with 7.2 million litres of milk from 58 local farms. When you have a bite of Cailler you really are eating a piece of Switzerland. Interestingly enough, it is the only Swiss chocolate still made with fresh milk from local cows; the rest use the powdered variety. The milk, that is, not the cows.

For chocoholics there can be few better sights than a room of tables covered in massed ranks of chocolates. This is the 'disgustation', a buffet that puts most to shame, and we are momentarily stunned by the prospect. Two seconds later we descend on the first samples and savour each one. Various types of chocolate made by Cailler, from white bars to dark pralines, are here to taste, though after a few different sorts you do start to get a little queasy. Or maybe it was the fact that the final one was called Femina. It's one of Cailler's oldest brands of pralines (launched in 1902), but the name just doesn't do it for me. It sounds like something you expect to buy in a drugstore and certainly not something you'd want to put in your mouth. I skip the Femina in favour of Frigor, admittedly not much better on the name front and doing nothing to enhance chocolate's reputation as a sex substitute. Any man would be well advised never to give a woman the two brands together.

A NATION OF CHOCOHOLICS

Cailler is but one of many brands in Switzerland, the country with (almost) the highest chocolate consumption rate in the world. At 11 kilograms per head per year, the Swiss eat more than anyone except the Germans, who recently snuck into first place with 11.5 kilograms each.[7] In comparison, Brits only manage to devour eight kilograms per head while Belgians nibble on a paltry 4.3 kilograms, despite claiming to be a chocolate nation. Hidden within that headline – or waistline – Swiss figure are two interesting facts. Every year almost 35,000 tonnes[8] of chocolate are imported into Switzerland, which seems rather like taking coals to Newcastle; shockingly, imports now account for 40 per cent of all chocolate eaten in Switzerland. Secondly, that 11 kilograms is a sales figure (no one has checked how much the Swiss actually eat), so it includes the chocolate visitors buy to take home. Having seen a group of Japanese strip a supermarket of every last bar, I think a fair share is bought by tourists. Or indeed, as the website of Chocosuisse[9] puts it, 'those who drive over the border just to buy Swiss chocolate'.[10] All those Germans stocking up on Lindt for the winter. Perhaps that's why Swiss supermarkets carry such a huge range. My local Coop isn't that big and probably has few tourists as customers, but it stocks 84 different types. And that's not counting the likes of Twix and Mars; that's just normal 100-gram bars of the black, brown and white stuff.

Domestic consumption, however, only accounts for a third of Swiss chocolate, with the rest being sent abroad, where Germany narrowly beats Britain into second place[11] (as always) as the primary export market. The world loves Swiss chocolate. Nevertheless, as iconic as it is, chocolate is really quite a small industry in Switzerland. It employs just over 4500 people, has an annual turnover of 1.8 billion francs and, most surprisingly of all, accounts for only 1 per cent of the world's cocoa harvest.[12] In this case size counts for a lot, and small is more beautiful.

Although Swiss brands are some of the best known, do they taste better? I decide to conduct a taste test of six brands of chocolate, four Swiss and two British, to see if there's a clear difference. Choco-snobs maintain that only the dark stuff (with 70 per cent cocoa) is worth eating, but given that three-quarters of all the chocolate consumed in Switzerland is milk,[13] I stick to that. Alongside three Swiss brands (Cailler, Lindt and Frey) I include Coop's cheapest own label, Prix Garantie, and two British brands, Dairy Milk and Green & Black's. My 40 willing volunteers in Bern are mainly Swiss but about a third of them are expats, just to make things more interesting. Each chocolate is tasted blind (that is, without knowing the brand), then scored for flavour and texture. And the winner is . . .

Cailler, and by a clear margin. Obviously using real milk, not powdered, is a success because people really can taste the difference. Perhaps the more surprising result is that the Coop Prix Garantie chocolate comes second overall, the expats rating it as good as Cailler and the Swiss putting it on a par with Lindt. It's a quarter the price of its rivals, showing that not everything in Switzerland has to be expensive to be good. As for the Brits, they fare badly in comparison. Despite a few Dairy Milk fans (including two Swiss people), both British brands come last, even among the expats.

IT'S CIOCCOLATA IN TICINO

Cailler failed to give me a Willy Wonka moment by seeing inside a chocolate factory, but finding an alternative isn't that easy. Having closed its Neuchâtel factory, Suchard is now made in Germany, France and Austria, with milk coming from as far away as New Zealand;[14] the purple Milka cow is definitely not Swiss. Tobler and Lindt don't allow tours of their factories, for any one of a number of reasons. Just when it seems that all is lost, my golden ticket comes on the

Chocosuisse website. Tucked away in its pages is a list of five possible tours, though one is at Cailler and three others are only for groups, or on Wednesdays, or with advance written permission. That leaves one last hope, so I get on a train and venture to the deep south. The great names of Swiss chocolate may be French or German, but I am on a four-hour journey from Bern to Lugano. A surprise, but a pleasant one as I will get to sample both Swiss Italian life and some *cioccolata*. Ticino here I come!

In a country full of anachronisms and contradictions, Ticino is perhaps one of the greatest. This southernmost canton looks, feels and sounds 100 per cent Italian but is very much part of Switzerland. You can tell it's not Italy because the streets are clean, the trains run on time and the waiters speak German with some show of willingness. But spend a few hours here and you'll realise it's not totally Swiss. Your bus driver is likely to stop mid-route at a bar for a quick espresso; the newspapers businessmen read in the piazza cafés are *Corriere della Sera* not the *NZZ*; an early evening must is the see-and-be-seen *passegiata* or languid stroll through town; and every car driver thinks he really is Italian. This wouldn't be a problem but for the fact that most of the pedestrians are from northern Switzerland and expect the rules to be the same. In the rest of the country pedestrians have right of way on crossings, but in Ticino it's survival of the fastest – a culture clash that leads to many near-misses and a crash or two.

The German-speaking Swiss don't come for the thrill of crossing the road or for the food, which they can get in their local Italian, but for the scenery and sunshine. As a Swiss German visitor, not only do you get palm trees, blue skies, great ice cream and shimmering lakes, you can still use francs, survive without speaking Italian and not worry about pickpockets. Most guidebooks call Ticino, or Tessin as it's known by the rest of Switzerland, the Swiss Riviera but it's really the Swiss Jersey: a safe bet for Swiss in search of a sunny break without dodgy food or funny money. The big difference is that you can reach Ticino by train.

From Lake Lucerne the rails turn south through Canton Uri and the rocky mountains of the Gotthard massif, with the valley narrowing as the hillsides get steeper and the train climbs steadily. You duck in and out of tunnels, sometimes coming out facing the other way, the train having curled round inside the rock. Then one long tunnel and you're south of the Alps. The air seems clearer, the sun brighter and the houses more colourful, or maybe that's just because you can start speaking Italian. All of that takes about two hours from Zurich, thanks to the Gotthard tunnel, which was hailed as a modern marvel when opened in 1882. But in 2016 that 'modern' line was superseded – or actually undercut – by a deeper, longer, straighter tunnel: the Gotthard Base Tunnel.

At 57.1 kilometres it is the world's longest railway tunnel,[15] so in building it the Swiss showed the world that they can bore better than anyone. When the final breakthrough was made, back in 2010, the last 180 centimetres of rock was excavated live on Swiss television, accompanied by cheers, tears, fireworks and St Barbara, the patron saint of tunnellers. She also makes an appearance at every Swiss tunnel inauguration, so was back to witness the official opening ceremony on 1 June 2016, which was memorable for its normality, apart from the holey designer dress worn by Transport Minister Doris Leuthard ('Made of Swiss cheese?' was the most common comment on social media that day).

After seventeen years of construction and 12 billion francs, the new tunnel welcomed its first passenger trains whizzing through at 249 kilometres per hour on 11 December 2016. Journey times south to Milan have been cut drastically, but will shorten again in 2020 because the Swiss haven't stopped their boring behaviour. When it comes to building tunnels, the Swiss don't do things by halves, so north of Lugano they're constructing another one, the Ceneri Tunnel, a mere 15.4 kilometres long.[16] As for the original line, it's still there, winding its way up through the mountains at the heart of Switzerland. These days it has the romantic name of the Gotthard Panorama Express, although it's anything but fast.

Getting off the train in Lugano, you truly could be in Italy. Pencil-thin cypresses puncture the skyline, giant salamis hang outside the *macelleria* and the lakeside road is choked with horn-honking traffic. But to remind you which country you are in, there's a statue of Guglielmo Tell down by the water. And in nearby Caslano is a real Swiss chocolate factory. I follow my nose straight there.

For a moment, as I stand on the elevated walkway above the Alprose factory floor, I close my eyes and inhale the intoxicatingly rich aroma. I could stay there for hours, except that it's unbelievably noisy with so many machines clunking, hissing and banging away. Looking down through plexiglass screens I can see the whole process from gloopy brown liquid to neatly stacked boxes. The main moulding device relentlessly churns out 504 bars a minute, which are cooled then dispatched in batches to the wrappers. White-coated workers in gloves and hairnets test bars at random, picking out the duds, or package the finished product into boxes. It's all rhythmically hypnotic, but so much more like a clinical lab than I expected; definitely the unglamorous side of the chocolate industry. No chocolate waterfall and no Oompa-Loompas, though being encased in plexiglass does mean there's no chance of me being turned into a giant blueberry. But at least I get to see, and smell, chocolate being made. One last long sniff and I leave before I drool too much.

SWITZERLAND REALLY IS SMALL

Mission accomplished, I decide to take the longer route back to Bern, so completing a round trip of the whole country. That means a first change of train in Locarno, Lugano's great rival in the stakes to be Ticino's premier town. All the Swiss seem to like a spot of inter-city rivalry and the Ticinese are no different. Lugano is the financial centre, Locarno the cultural, with its annual open-air film festival; Lugano has an eponymous lake, whereas Locarno just has the top end of Lake Maggiore, most of which is Italian. The funny thing is neither is the cantonal capital; that's tiny Bellinzona to the north. My favourite is Locarno, mainly because it has the best local transport in Switzerland. Best not for its timekeeping or cleanliness but for its name: Ferrovie Autolinee Regionali Ticinesi. Never mind what it means,[17] all you need to know is that it's shortened to a four-letter acronym written in giant letters on the back of buses, on timetables and stations. In Ticino, a FART goes a very long way.

The best-known part of the local train network is the Centovalli, a slow, meandering single-track line that crosses into Italy. The carriage is a time warp of wood panelling, knotted-rope luggage racks and tapestry seats. It's so 1950s that I look round for Miss Marple and her knitting. The train soon leaves all signs of human habitation behind, apart from odd glimpses of a serpentine road and random stations in the middle of nowhere with no apparent reason to exist. Despite that the train is packed, with both locals and tourists out to enjoy the unspoilt scenery of the hundred valleys (hence the line's name in Italian). Tree-clad slopes amble past, the air has a pine-scented Glade hint to it, and crystal blue Italian streams gurgle along beneath the bridges. It's all rather idyllic until we change in Domodossola. This Italian town is part of the Swiss train network purely because it sits at the centre of a chunk of Italian territory that sticks up into Switzerland like an overgrown stalagmite. But it's soon very clear that it's not run by the Swiss.

Ninety minutes later, which for Swiss passengers is half a lifetime, the platform is still full of people waiting for the Italians to find a locomotive for the train to Bern. The conductor can merely shrug and say 'Italians!' with raised eyebrows, which is verging on emotional for a Swiss train conductor. The train finally departs, and what a difference a delay makes. Spurred on by a sense of communal suffering, people in the crowded carriage cast off their normal reserve and start chatting to one another.

The two gentlemen opposite me are 99 and 91, on their annual day-trip out together; the waiter with the tea trolley sings Charles Aznavour tunes; and the family across the aisle are trying to see the whole country in a day, having set out at 6 a.m. from Oberriet. The name sounds strangely familiar, and once they start telling me about the town's scarecrow-making exploits (which failed to make *The Guinness Book of Records*), I remember being there.[18] Months after briefly driving through Oberriet, meeting some of its inhabitants on the other side of the country shows me just how small Switzerland really is. Maybe if more Swiss trains were delayed, Swiss people would talk to each other more often and the whole country would open up just a little. What a revolutionary thought.

LAND OF THE MUESLI EATERS

With fondue and milk chocolate, the Swiss invented two of the world's more luxurious edible delights. As if to counteract all that decadence, they also created the most ridiculously healthy breakfast. So healthy that it looks distinctly unappetising, with the appearance and consistency of cold porridge. And that's, essentially, what muesli is, at least when it's made the Swiss way. The birdseed–sawdust mix that is Alpen has always had a bad rep in most of the English-speaking world, disparaged as being eaten by sandal-wearing hippies or fitness freaks, or more often dismissed as inedible. And, to be frank, it is. The Swiss realised this ages ago, so they soak it (preferably overnight) in milk, then mix it with yoghurt and add fresh fruit, usually apple and/or berries. The result looks strange but it is scrumptious. Truly.

It's so delicious that the Swiss can't help but eat it all day long. For them it's not only a breakfast staple, it's also a snack lunch, a light supper or a quick way to fill the odd gap. In Switzerland muesli, or *Birchermüesli* as it is generally known, is the Martini of foods, to be eaten anytime, anyplace, anywhere. It's the original Swiss fast food, not because it's quick to make (all that pre-soaking doesn't help) but because almost every bakery, café and supermarket sells it, ready prepared to take away and eat. Muesli was first made in 1900 by Maximilian Bircher-Benner,[19] a doctor from Aarau in northern Switzerland, as a healthy evening meal for his patients. The original recipe mixed oats with water, lemon juice, condensed milk and grated apple, which sounds less than appealing. The oats and grated apple are still prime ingredients, but thank goodness someone thought of replacing the rest with milk and yoghurt.

Not many Swiss German words have made it into the English language. Muesli is one, and is a good example of the Swiss German habit of ending words with -li. It's merely a way of making the noun a diminutive, but apparently there are an awful lot of small things in Switzerland. For example, a *Gipfeli* is a croissant, a *Wägeli* is a shopping trolley and, my favourite, a *Bitzeli* is a little bit. Even Tell's son Walter often gets a -li on the end of his name, just to show he's a small boy.

However, there's more to Swiss food than fondue and

muesli. Just as in any country, every region has its specialities, some of which are special for a reason: only the locals like them. But many are popular all across the country, so that as a visitor you don't have to trek to far-flung corners to enjoy a taste of Switzerland. For example, *Zopf*, the plaited milk-bread that's popular at weekends, originated in Canton Bern, while the veal, cream and mushroom *Züri Gschnätzlets*, as rich as it is unpronounceable, is clearly from Zurich. And Basel's most famous product is a hard spiced and iced biscuit, known as *Läckerli* (there's that -li again). Each is a source of much local pride but all are enjoyed everywhere, and there's possibly one reason for that: a woman named Betty Bossi.

COOKING WITH BETTY

She's the Delia Smith or Julia Child of Switzerland, and under her guidance the Swiss have not only mastered their own cuisine but, rather radically for many people, moved on to exotic creations like Thai curry or hummus. The thing is, Betty does not exist. She began life in 1956, the (brain)child of a marketing department from an oil and margarine producer.[20] Her name was created to sound comforting and be acceptable to all three main languages. What was initially a freebie newspaper given out in supermarkets has grown into a brand worth millions. Alongside the bestselling cookbooks are a magazine, a cookery school and kitchen equipment. And just in case you really can't cook, even with Betty's help, Coop now sells her ready meals. That in itself is quite a revolution. Ready meals are still a relatively new concept, with only half a chiller cabinet in Bern's largest supermarket. Nothing compared to the miles of them on offer in Britain, but a noticeable change in a country where most meals are, or at least were, prepared from scratch.

There are, however, three Swiss favourites that Ms Bossi

can't teach you to make, assuming you would even want to. First, Rivella, a soft drink made from milk serum. It's not quite as disgusting as it sounds, but is definitely an acquired taste; perhaps you have to grow up with it to like it, and most Swiss have done exactly that. It's been quenching their thirsts since 1952[21] and shows no sign of running out. Much more acceptable to a foreign palate is Aromat, an all-purpose seasoning made by Knorr. Despite its rather alarming colour (dayglo yellow), the Swiss sprinkle it on anything and everything, from boiled eggs and salad to cooked vegetables and meat. And as unnatural as it looks, its salty-herby-yeasty taste is quite addictive. Just as well, as it pops up on almost every table.

But both those are small fry against the cervelat. To you and me it may look like any other sausage, but to the Swiss it's the national sausage, revered and devoured in equal measure.

THE NATIONAL SAUSAGE

For the Swiss, the cervelat is a prerequisite at any barbecue and they consume 160 million every year.[22] Not bad going for a country of only eight million people. A *Pfadfinder* (boy scout or girl guide) summer week away, with cooking cervelat speared on sticks and grilled over an open fire, is a rite of passage for most Swiss children. The sausage itself is short, fat and pinky-brown, made from a mix of beef, pork, bacon, salt and herbs, all minced and stuffed into cow's intestines. Then it's smoked and parboiled before being sold to an eager public. The traditional way to prepare it is to cut both ends with a cross, so that when grilled they curl outwards, making it end up looking a little like a roasted pig.

In 2008 Switzerland had a cervelat crisis, with headlines bemoaning the imminent death of a national institution. It was all down to the intestine traditionally used for the skin being banned by the European Union, a decision which Switzerland had to honour under its bilateral agreements with the EU. Fears of mad cow disease led to the ban on the intestines from Brazilian zebu, the humpbacked cattle found mainly in India but also South America. Zebu intestines had long since replaced local (Swiss) varieties because they're much cheaper, despite coming a rather long way. With the national sausage threatened with extinction, a Swiss Cervelat Task Force was set up to find a second skin. Other animals' intestines apparently weren't good enough, being too wide, too expensive or too thin-skinned – no one wants a burst sausage – while synthetic skins prompt cries of horror. It sounds farcical but to many Swiss, for whom Switzerland without cervelat is unthinkable, it was a real issue. The Task Force had to save their skin somehow and the answer was a Paraguayan substitute. You can imagine the sighs of relief when the EU ban on zebu skins was lifted in 2012 and the Swiss could go back to their national sausage made the traditional way, with Brazilian intestines.

APPLE COUNTRY

The cervelat may have been under threat, but the national fruit has no such problem. Switzerland loves its apples. Perhaps it's a William Tell thing – an apple a day keeps the Austrians away – or maybe the Swiss just like them. Think of a way of using an apple and you can bet that the Swiss have thought of it already. Top of the list is *Apfelmus*, or apple purée, which is a standard dessert or served with *Chäsmaggerone*. This hearty macaroni cheese is a staple of almost every mountain-top restaurant, where it's known as *Älplermakkaroni* to give it that extra lift. Come September and Switzerland celebrates National Apple Day, with over a million apples given away in stations and supermarkets. Plus the ubiquitous *Apfelmus* is eclipsed by gallons of fresh-pressed cloudy apple juice lining the supermarket shelves and market stalls. And all year round the two most common varieties of fruit tart, popular for elevenses or a snack supper, are apple or plum.

It's just as well that the Swiss grow an awful lot of apples, given how many they eat (15.8 kilograms per person per year),[23] and every third apple is grown in the eastern canton of Thurgau. That's reason enough for the local tourist board to say that Thurgau is 'the orchard of Switzerland',[24] though Swiss Germans often call it *Mostindien*, from *Most* in Swiss German meaning apple juice and the canton being shaped like India, albeit a slightly deformed, pre-independence India. The big question is what sort of apple it was that Tell Senior shot off Walter's head. The most popular Swiss apple variety is Gala but these days the Tell apple could easily be a Granny Smith from New Zealand, which, despite a wealth of home-grown apples, you can see in Swiss shops. Crazy.

Antipodean apples aside, Swiss supermarkets seem much more in tune with the seasons. The changes in the fruit and veg displays are as marked as the weather outside, with local produce always to the fore. Plums, cherries, asparagus, apples, strawberries and lettuce all fill the shelves when in season. Especially lettuce, which seems to come in 20 different varieties at the height of summer and is one of the few things that's cheaper when Swiss grown. All because the Swiss are rather partial to a good salad.

SALAD DAYS AND NIGHTS

Many Swiss restaurants have a menu. That's not quite as daft as it sounds, since 'menu' doesn't mean a list of dishes with prices, as it does in English, but refers to a set menu for a fixed price. Ask for the menu and you'll end up with the dish of the day rather than a large piece of cardboard. The menu is particularly popular at lunchtime, so it usually changes daily, but is nearly always a starter and a main course. Nine times out of ten the starter will be a salad, or menu-salad as it's sometimes known. Go to a cheap eatery – and there are a few in Switzerland[25] – and the menu-salad will most likely be a small bowl filled with lettuce, a slice of tomato, some grated carrot and dressing from a bottle. Move up the food scale and you might get mixed leaves, toasted seeds and homemade dressing, but the concept is the same: keep it simple and quick to serve.

Even at home, the Swiss like nothing better than a small salad as a starter. This is more than a national food fetish, it's an important cultural marker. Salad in Switzerland is not just a predictable starter but a source of endless fascination at the dinner table. And it's all down to a lettuce leaf. Who would've thought that such a humble piece of greenery could be such a bone of contention? More than once during a lettuce debate I have reached for a knife and ended the matter in the most brutal way possible: shredding the leaves.

Cheap menu-salads aside, Swiss salads tend to have whole leaves. No ripping, no cutting, often no halving. Just big, round leaves covered in dressing. Aesthetically speaking, it's better than a mangled mess of green. Then you try to eat it, and aesthetics go out of the window as you tackle the unruly, slippery leaves while attempting to maintain some sense of decorum. After careful observation, I have deduced that there is a distinct lettuce etiquette, or lettiquette, involved in eating a Swiss salad. You have three choices – the elegant, the standard and the practical. To the Swiss, each is less acceptable than the previous one.

When done correctly, the elegant is a wonder to behold. First, you get a firm hold on a single leaf with your fork. Then, using your knife, carefully fold each side of the leaf into the middle, each time re-spearing the centre with your fork so that the whole thing doesn't spring open like a jack-in-the-box. Once all four sides are folded, you have a small, manageable parcel that can be eaten elegantly. No doubt this takes years of practice, rather like eating peas the proper way. The problem is keeping the already folded sides down while simultaneously trying to get the next in under the fork. It only seems possible without the slippery dressing, so my ongoing failure in lettuce origami leaves me only two options.

In a country where table manners are quite important, it's astonishing to watch someone eat a lettuce leaf the standard way. Just spear the centre of the leaf with your fork, shake off any excess dressing, and stuff it whole into your mouth. Simple as that. Of course, not everyone does this, but an alarmingly large percentage of the population, including refined ladies-who-lunch and suited businessmen, seem to have no problem cramming in public. All very well, unless you are sitting opposite them. At best it's enough to put you off your salad; at worst, when the leaf is bigger than the mouth, it looks like a scene from *Alien*, with the human losing the battle to breathe.

Then there's the third way, the practical, which is the choice of most foreigners when presented with a plate of ballooning leaves. For strict followers of Swiss lettiquette it's verging on blasphemy as it's so unrefined; for the uneducated it's the easiest option. The practical works on the same principle as tackling spaghetti: simply chop it up. With an Italian grandmother, I had no choice but to learn how to twirl my spaghetti round a fork; lacking a Swiss relative, my childhood was blighted by not being taught how to eat a whole lettuce leaf. So, as sacrilegious as it may seem, I am in the cut-then-eat camp. Less hassle, less mess and you stand a chance of finishing the salad before the pudding arrives.

The cultural differences in salad do not end there. My earliest lesson in Swiss salad was typical for many first-time visitors. Picture this: you order a salad and, as in many Swiss restaurants, are offered a choice of French or Italian dressing. You fancy a nice light vinaigrette, so you choose French and are then presented with leaves covered in a creamy white, runny dressing that looks like liquid mayonnaise. Essentially that's what it is, though with vinegar and mustard added. What the British call French dressing (oil, vinegar and other optional extras) is Italian dressing in Switzerland; what the Swiss call French doesn't really exist in Britain. As for blue cheese, ranch or salad cream, forget it – which you will once you have tasted this French dressing. So delicious that my family take bottles of it home with them after every trip.

But perhaps more important is knowing that a mixed salad is more mix than salad. It is certainly not some lettuce with tomatoes and cucumber, and possibly a slice of onion, thrown in. A Swiss mixed salad is four or five different salads arranged around a plate and covered in lettuce. Under the greenery you'll typically find sweetcorn in a mild curry dressing, pickled beetroot (grated not sliced), white cabbage in vinaigrette, grated carrots, cucumber in a yoghurt sauce and some kidney beans. It's like a mini-salad buffet on one plate.

As if that weren't enough, the typical Swiss way of eating a mixed salad is also a lesson in cultural norms. They don't mix and match the different mini-salads in one mouthful but take a little from each at a time. This doesn't just apply to salads; so many Swiss people, when presented with a plate of food, eat in a very similar way. They do not take a morsel of meat on their fork, add a bit of potato and a piece of cabbage (or carrot or whatever) then eat it altogether. Instead, they tend to eat everything separately, having some potato, then some meat, then some broccoli. This is so that each can be appreciated in turn and not be lost in the mix. No matter that you might discover a new flavour sensation by combining the foods on your plate; better to stick with what you know.

Fondue and muesli are the two foods that people most immediately associate with Switzerland, but it's chocolate that has become its iconic edible export. The fact that it's not a big country and lacks many natural resources (other than water and cows) makes it all the more remarkable that Switzerland became a pre-eminent chocolate producer. Its position as the crossroads of Europe helped secure the raw materials, and Swiss inventiveness provided the tools to create brown magic. But perhaps the crucial part is that with chocolate, as with so much else, the Swiss have always aimed for quality over quantity. Is there such a thing as bad Swiss chocolate? I have yet to find some. My taste test shows that the cheapest own label can compete with posh brands, but to buy that you really do have to visit Switzerland. Unlike Toblerone and Lindor, you can't get Prix Garantie chocolate abroad.

Ask a Swiss person about chocolate, or *Schoggi* in Swiss German, and they will say theirs is the best in the world. True, the Swiss say that about practically everything made in Switzerland, but perhaps with chocolate their unabashed pride in their own products is not misplaced. Swiss supermarkets are slowly joining the globalised world, so that now, unlike a few years ago, it's possible to buy cranberry juice, fajitas, red curry paste or salt-and-vinegar crisps. Swiss consumers are slowly waking up to the world of food beyond their borders. But in the chocolate aisle Switzerland still reigns supreme, with row upon row of Swiss brands and hardly a foreign interloper to be seen. After all, who would buy it when there's so much of the world's best chocolate on offer?

SWISS WATCHING TIP NO 9:
TABLE MANNERS

The importance of time in Swiss life is perhaps nowhere more notice-able than at meal times. Breakfast, lunch and supper, the Swiss eat early and seem quite surprised when everyone else doesn't. Lunch is the best example. On the dot of 12 most of the country stops. Offices close, as do shops and banks outside the city centres, children leave school, building sites fall silent, almost everything grinds to a halt, except public transport. Go into a Swiss restaurant at 12.15 and you'll think you've won the lottery if you get a table; go in at 1.45, and it'll be empty, but then so will the kitchen. Evenings are slightly more flexible, though at home most Swiss have finished eating by 7.30. This is partly because supper is usually smaller than lunch – often just salad, or bread and cheese, or a bowl of muesli – but also so that they can watch the evening news on Swiss television, which starts at 19.30 every day, Sundays and holidays included. In the bigger cities you can still find restaurants serving at the worryingly late hour of 10 p.m., and at the weekends McDonald's manages the ungodly time of 3 a.m.

So it's 7 p.m. and you're eating out with Swiss friends. Whether you have won the golden ticket of a home visit or are in a restaurant, there is a certain procedure to follow, starting from the moment the drinks arrive. Do not, under any circumstances, just raise your glass and say a general 'cheers' to everyone round the table. I used to think that this was enough; then I went to a Swiss dinner party and com-mitted my first major social faux pas. I raised my glass along with the others, said cheers and took a healthy gulp. Everyone stopped and stared at me as if I had just danced naked on the table. I soon learned that when Swiss people say cheers, it isn't a three-second communal affair. Like almost everything else in Switzerland, it's a deliberate procedure based on age-old traditions.

The host has to start by raising his glass, after which each person must clink glasses with every other person, ideally all holding their wine glass by the stem so that the 'ching' is clearer and more pleasing on the ear. Not only that but you must make direct eye contact as you clink, and say cheers followed by that person's first name. So, for example, at a dinner party of eight people, 28 separate moments of glass-clinking and well-wishing with names have to be completed before the first drop is drunk. To make things worse, some couples also indulge in a quick kiss after saying cheers with each other, prolonging things a little more. The whole procedure is only polite, but can seem interminable when you're gasping for water and barely able to say the final words for your tongue sticking to the roof of your mouth. Nevertheless, no one should take a single sip until everyone has finished toasting everyone else; woe betide anyone who sneaks a swift glug before the whole rigmarole is over. That's not a mistake I'll ever make again.

Then the food arrives. Do not let one morsel touch your lips, do not even lift a fork, until the host has led everyone is saying *En guete* (or *bon appétit* or *buon appetito*). At least this is done communally and not on a name-by-name basis, so it's not long before you can all tuck in. The Swiss find it unbelievable that there is no normal way of saying this in English. 'Enjoy your meal' sounds almost like a command and 'This looks delicious' verges on insincere, so we end up using the French rather than the awful English translation, 'Good appetite'. Even worse, we often say nothing at all, which would be unthinkable for the Swiss. They say it, at every meal in every situation. From about 11.30 a.m. onwards, Switzerland echoes to the sound of everyone wishing everyone else a good lunch. When your work colleague leaves the office, you say *En guete*; when your family sits down together, you all say *En guete*; when the stranger next to you on the bench starts his sandwich, you say *En guete*; when the waiter delivers the food, he says *En guete*, or at least he should. However, service in Switzerland isn't nearly as good as the food, which is perhaps why tipping isn't the norm, or maybe the service is poor because they know there's unlikely to be a tip at the end. Either way, good service stands out because it's rare.

Many Swiss waiters have perfected the art of looking straight through you. Not quite ignoring you, but not acknowledging your increasingly frantic efforts to attract their attention. What starts off as a smile or a half-raised finger progresses to a vocal *Entschuldigung* (sorry) or a definite wave. Then comes the stretched neck and exasperated sighs, but no matter how long it takes, no matter how frustrated you get, never resort to calling out *Fräulein* or *garçon*, or you'll wait for the rest of your life. The one advantage of this comes at the end of the meal. When the bill finally arrives, you can just put down the right money in cash and walk away, safe in the knowledge that no one will steal it and the waiter will not run after you demanding a 20 per cent tip. This is not America, after all.

TEN

CLIMB EVERY MOUNTAIN

National newspapers do not exist in Switzerland, thanks to the linguistic challenges involved. The people of Romandie are far more likely to read a French paper from Paris than a Swiss one written in German. But even within the German-speaking part, the fractured, parochial nature of Swiss society means that few people in Zurich would read *Der Bund*, which is published in Bern. Instead, every city and town has its own paper. But sometimes there's a news story that transcends all the divisions and in Switzerland that story often involves trains. Not just the big things like the opening of the new Gotthard Tunnel but also the small ones like punctuality. The truth is that Swiss Federal Railways (SBB; there is no English abbreviation) don't always manage to run every train on time, despite foreign rumours to the contrary. The exact figure is 88.8 per cent,[1] meaning that one in ten Swiss trains is late; in comparison the UK national figure is 89.1 per cent,[2] which rather incredibly would make British trains more punctual than Swiss ones. Almost any passenger in Britain would say that isn't the case, and indeed it isn't. It all comes down to the definition of 'on time', which is far stricter in Switzerland than in other European countries. Britain uses the European norm of on time meaning within five minutes late, though that is extended to ten minutes late for cross-country services. SBB however sets itself a three-minute target and achieves it almost 90 per cent of the time. The rest of the world can only look on in wonder.

Switzerland without its railways would be like America without its freeways, or Britain without its traffic jams. Almost unimaginable. Trains are as much part of the country as flower-decked chalets and bell-jangling cows, so much so that it sometimes feels like railways were invented in the Alps. Just the opposite, in fact.

THE START OF THE LINE

Switzerland was neither first nor particularly fast in building railways, but once it had embraced the train, the country was never the same again. A railway's ability to conquer mountains, by going either up or under them, had profound effects on all aspects of Swiss life. With journeys taking hours rather than days, valleys were no longer isolated and the country no longer cut in half by the mountains. People started leaving their home towns and moving around, something that is still quite unusual for many Swiss today, let alone 150 years ago. More importantly, this landlocked country could access the outside world more quickly than ever, providing the raw materials that Switzerland lacked and a means of exporting the finished goods. The downside was that some Swiss industries, such as textiles, couldn't compete with cheap imports and suffered. The bonus was that, connected to the once-distant ports, Switzerland became a more effective trading nation. Without the railways there might never have been a Swiss chocolate industry. What a thought!

The lasting effects of this can still be seen. Train lines reach into almost every corner of the country, so that a rail map of Switzerland looks like a lesson in the blood circulatory system. The main east–west and north–south arteries feed all the regional lines, which branch off into ever smaller local lines going down valleys and up hillsides. Dozens of private lines operate not against each other and SBB, but together to provide a unified, viable network. Like almost every part of Swiss society, the railways are a master class in communication and cooperation. And it clearly works. Annually, the Swiss travel an average of 2277 kilometres per person by rail,[3] by far the highest in the world, and well over twice as high as the British figure.

The funny thing is that this modern paragon of train usage is the exact opposite of how the railway system began in Switzerland. Unlike the British and Germans, who went full-steam ahead in the mid-nineteenth century, the Swiss were rather slow to embrace the new technology. It wasn't only that they were being unduly cautious, as is their wont, but also that plans couldn't be agreed because of cantonal quarrels over rights and permits to build the lines. As a result the first station in Switzerland opened in 1845, two years before the first line, a quirk of history made possible because it was the French who built the station in Basel as a terminus for their Alsace line. The Swiss cantons carried on squabbling and nine years later there was still only one short line, running the 30 kilometres between Baden and Zurich.[4]

No one back then would have dared to think that 150 years later the Swiss rail network would become one of the most used and most famous in the world; it looked like the train would never leave the station. But private companies took up the challenge and laid the lines, dug the tunnels and built the bridges that would conquer the Alps. Ironically enough, once the Swiss realised what an asset the railways were, they nationalised them. A referendum in 1898 approved the creation of the Swiss Federal Railways.[5] British Rail wouldn't be born for another 50 years, only to be abolished within another 50. Britain may have invented the railway, but it doesn't know how to run one. That's a role the Swiss have taken on with relish.

A less obvious effect of the railways was to help develop Switzerland as a tourist destination. For foreign visitors, the advent of the train meant they could reach the far-off mountainous country without spending a fortune in time or money. For the Swiss, trains not only helped them conquer their landscape, but provided a new source of income. For them, the railways became inextricably linked with tourism.

TRAINING THE TOURISTS

A trip to Switzerland became an achievable ideal for many middle-class Victorians in Britain. It was this explosion in British visitors that kick-started the Swiss tourist industry, not least because the tourists brought money, and still do. With over nine million foreign visitors arriving in Switzerland every year, tourism is a big earner and a big employer; nowhere is a Swiss current economic crisis more visible than in the empty beds and bars in mountain resorts. The one saving grace has been that the Swiss are the country's best customer, spending almost twice as much as foreign tourists. But back in the nineteenth century it wasn't only about the money. Hotels sprang up, paddle steamers were launched and locals became guides, all to satisfy Mr and Mrs Smith from Surrey. And with the construction of Europe's first cogwheel railway up Rigi, trains began to climb every mountain so that the Brits wouldn't have to. The Swiss Alps became a modern tourist attraction.

At 1797 metres high, Rigi is not the tallest, the steepest or even the most beautiful mountain, but it's been pulling in the crowds ever since visitors have been coming to Switzerland. Not for the mountain itself, but for the views. The 'Queen of the Mountains' sits like an island at the heart of Switzerland, surrounded on almost every side by the waters of Lakes Lucerne and Zug (see map of Lake Lucerne on page 30). Its 360° panorama includes the whole sweep of the Alps, from Säntis in the east to the Bernese Oberland out west. For tourists of past centuries watching the sunrise from the top of Rigi was the high point, in every sense, of a trip to Switzerland. Mark Twain wrote about it, Thomas Cook's first tour group walked up for it, and Queen Victoria had the luxury of being carried up in a sedan chair. These days finding human donkeys might be hard, but you can still walk the walk if you have four hours to spare. Better yet, catch the steamboat from Lucerne to Vitznau and ride up on a piece of history.

The little red train clambers up past the last few houses, on through the ranks of fir trees, then the flower-strewn meadows and finally over the rocky slopes at the top. This gentle half-hour ride has been wowing people since 21 May 1871, so I am by far from being the first, or the last, to drink in the views of the shimmering lakes with their mountain backdrop. And I'm certainly not the only one to overlook the revolutionary technology going on beneath my feet: a cog-wheel railway with a toothed track. It was this that made the conquest of Rigi possible, though the first railway didn't actually make it all the way to the summit. The technology wasn't lacking, but the political system in Switzerland was.

Sometimes the Swiss forget they are a nation continually in search of consensus and let cantonal pride overrule common sense. Rigi is a good example. It straddles the border between Cantons Lucerne and Schwyz, and each canton granted the concessionary rights to a different company. So that first line from Vitznau, in Canton Lucerne, could only go up as far as the border, some way short of the summit. On the other side of the mountain, a second line coming up from Goldau, in Canton Schwyz, wasn't completed until 1875, though the company did at least finish the top section two years earlier.[6] As daft as that sounds, that meant it could earn money from its Lucerne rivals by charging them to use the tracks from the border up to the summit. Not so daft, after all. The two lines merged in the 1990s, but even today both serve

242

the summit with their differently coloured trains: red for the Lucerne side, blue for Schwyz.

The Rigi railway started a Swiss craze for building one up anything that was big enough to hold it. In the following 40 years, mountains all over Switzerland succumbed to the might of iron and steam. These days it probably wouldn't be allowed on environmental grounds, but green was not a nineteenth-century colour, so up those lines went. Across Lake Lucerne from Rigi, craggy Pilatus hosts the world's steepest rack railway, opened in 1889 with a maximum gradient of 48 per cent;[7] over on Brienzer Rothorn is Switzerland's last steam mountain train, which has been puffing up the hill since 1892;[8] and topping them all is the ride up inside the Eiger to Europe's highest railway station, completed in 1912. If you build it, they will come. And come they did, and still do, in their thousands. Without the tourists, the mountain railways may never have been built, and would certainly not survive today. But without those railways fewer tourists might come to Switzerland, and those who did would spend much less money. A relationship benefiting both parties – and thank goodness for that. I'd hate to have to walk up all those mountains to get the best views. It's not as if I'm Swiss.

AN INTEGRATED NETWORK

Gravity-defying mountain trains might be the most famous part of the Swiss railway network, but they actually make up only 150 of the 5000 kilometres of lines nationally.[9] Trains are the workhorses of the Swiss economy, transporting not just tourists and commuters but cargo as well. An impressive 69 per cent of transalpine heavy goods vehicles travel by rail through Switzerland, twice as much as in neighbouring Austria.[10] Loading those mammoth trucks on to trains means less pollution, less traffic and less noise, so everyone wins. But the wonder of the Swiss railway system is not the cargo routes through the mountains, or the big-name rides, such as the Glacier Express, or even the intercity lines packed with the customers. The wonder of the Swiss transport network is the local services.

Decades after Dr Beeching cut such lines in Britain, the Swiss still regard them as an essential part of the national infrastructure, no matter if they aren't so well used. The crowded routes bring in the cash to subsidise the less-used ones so that the whole network survives. All very forward-thinking, anti-Darwinian and anti-capitalist to someone brought up on privatisation for profit. For the Swiss it's local services for local people, and occasionally the odd tourist, to ensure that no community is left off the transport map. To achieve that goal there are buses as well, designed to complement the railways, not replace them. A spidery network of 882 routes with over 2200 Postbuses, all of them bright yellow, carries 152 million passengers a year[11] to places the trains can't reach. But, this being Switzerland, the timetables are coordinated, so that passengers can change quickly from train to bus and back again. The Swiss make it all look so simple, as if that's the natural order of things. As if that's the only way public transport should be.

Such coordination is only possible because the Swiss plan the whole system as one. On the second Sunday in December, the new national timetable comes into effect and lasts for a whole year. Local, regional and national train services are all integrated, along with the bus network, so that connections are linked and waiting times reduced. You can find out an exact timetable for any trip anywhere in the country, even if it means using three or four different types of transport. Enter any two points into the SBB website or app and up comes a full itinerary, complete with connection times and platform numbers, no matter if that includes trains, boats, city trams, local buses or cable cars. What is more, you can buy one ticket to cover the whole journey, regardless of how many different operators are involved. Alongside SBB there are various regional companies, the Postbus, private mountain trains and local transport in every city. Numerous operators, one system. Not only is that more efficient, it's so much more customer friendly.

But that's not all. As well as the Swiss services from SBB and others, there are international ones run by railways from neighbouring countries. These all go through Switzerland, but can be used like any other train without reservations or restrictions. You might catch a German ICE from Bern to Interlaken or a French TGV between Zurich and Basel. It doesn't matter if they're going on to Paris or Innsbruck, or coming from Hamburg, while they're in Switzerland these international trains are integrated into the national time-tables. What's mundanely normal to the Swiss can still be rather exciting to others. For me the 20-minute ride from Bern to Thun is far more interesting in a German train, knowing that since it left Berlin seven hours previously it crossed most of Germany. This sense of wonder is helped by German trains being astoundingly long and having carriages with corridors and compartments. These may look modern but somehow they feel deliciously old-fashioned, like being on the Hogwarts Express or an extra in *The Lady Vanishes*.

PAYING THE PRICE FOR PERFECTION

The remarkable thing about Swiss trains is that, unlike *Star Wars* prequels and new John Grisham novels, they live up to their reputation: they are clean, comfortable, expensive and nearly always on time. As we know, a small percentage of Swiss trains are late, warranting loudspeaker apologies and often also the delaying of connecting services. Usually the only things that keep better time than the trains are the watches, most of which are Swiss, but even this rail network has bad-hair days. Luckily, they are as rare as a Swiss declaration of war. A while ago a power cut crippled the whole network for a day, an inconceivable catastrophe for a country used to reliable public transport. That evening's extended news carried pictures of crowded platforms and trains stuck on bridges, while interviews with bewildered commuters and harassed officials added to the air of incredulity. Watching it, you'd be forgiven for thinking the world had ended; in Swiss terms, it had. Of course, all affected customers got a refund.

The one uncomfortable thing about Swiss trains is the price, which is invariably high, though the Swiss always believe that you get what you pay for: quality costs, and in this case it's true. To offset this pain, for 185Fr anyone can buy an annual railcard that gives half-price fares across the entire country, including all trains, buses, boats and city transport. Three return trips between Basel and Zurich and it's paid for itself. No wonder over 2.5 million half-fare cards are currently in use,[12] and not only by people in Switzerland. For many regular visitors from abroad the card is a worthwhile investment and the best way to make Swiss trains more affordable.

At least normal Swiss tickets tend to have one price. Simple as that. No advance off-peak network saver anytime complications to get your head round. Buying a ticket two days or two minutes before your trip makes no difference, and you can catch any train at any time. No compulsory reservations[13] and no fines for being on the wrong train. But there are signs that this is slowly changing, and it's not always popular. The Federal Councillor responsible for transport once dared to suggest that commuters should pay more because they take trains at the busiest times of day. Cue howls of protest from all quarters. More successful was SBB's introduction of cheap tickets on the internet, where you book a specific train at a much lower price (and still use your half-fare card). This appeals to the Swiss love of forward planning as it's perfect for those who know they want to catch the 13:34 to Geneva. Of course, peak times are rarely offered and you have to catch the train you booked, so no rush-hour trains or last-minute change of plans.

For Swiss travellers there's a clear choice at a national level: pay the full price, have a half-fare card (and so logically pay half price) or invest in an annual pass that covers the whole country. Known as a GA, short for *Generalabonnement*,[14] it includes all forms of transport, from local buses to long-distance trains. Fancy a boat trip on Lake Geneva, then that's included, as are a day-trip to Ticino or exploring Zurich by tram. The main exceptions are most mountain trains and cable cars, which are merely half price with a GA.[15] That's because mountain services are there for pleasure, either to go up and enjoy the view (for tourists) or to bring you down after you have walked up (for the Swiss). There's no logical reason for them to be part of the GA as no one lives up there perma-nently. Conversely, every Swiss town and village is connected to the transport network in some way, even if it's only by cable car in the case of cliff-top Mürren in the Bernese Oberland, so it's covered by the GA.

All this travelling freedom comes at a price. A 2nd-class GA costs 3860Fr a year, or 6300Fr for 1st class,[16] though both are cheaper if you're over 65 or under 25, or if you buy two together as partners. That price hasn't stopped the Swiss becoming very attached to their GAs: over 5 per cent of the population has one.[17] They even inspire some very un-Swiss spontaneity of turning up at the station, getting on a train and going anywhere you fancy. And in terms of value for money it's actually a good deal: for that 3860Fr, or about £2800,[18] you get the whole country; for the same price you only get zones 1–7 in London.[19]

The GA is such a good idea that you can also buy one for your dog. It's not as ridiculous as it sounds since, unless it is under 30 centimetres high and can be carried as hand luggage, a dog has to have a ticket to travel on a train. Dogs must pay half the standard fare, or at least the owner must, and be accompanied; no Lassie adventures allowed. Since they need a ticket, dogs can also get a GA, which is a snip at 785Fr.[20] Unlike a human GA, the dog version is valid in any class; clearly dogs don't need to pay for the superior flooring in 1st.

Bikes also need tickets for trains, so can also have their own GA. See how Swiss logic works? At 240Fr a year[21] a bike GA is a great deal, especially considering that on most trains bikes get their own racks, or their own compartments on some long-distance ones. This typical example of Swiss thoughtfulness and efficiency stretches to the platform as well. Imagine the train is pulling in and you're standing with your bike ready to board, only to have to run like crazy when you realise the bike compartment is at the other end of the platform. That would never happen in Switzerland, because platforms have a blue poster showing the make-up of the trains that stop there. The bike compartment is clearly marked, as are the restaurant car and two different classes, so all you have to do is wait at the right spot on the platform.

That blue poster may seem insignificant in terms of running a railway, but for me it was a big revelation about Swiss trains. Cleanliness and punctuality were both givens, but knowing where a certain carriage would stop on a platform seemed like a miracle. After all, I was used to Waterloo, where you don't usually know which platform your train will leave from until a few minutes before. In Switzerland you never see a crowd of people standing in front of departure screens waiting to know which platform they have to run to. Even in big, busy stations like Zurich, the platform numbers for every train are set once a year and printed on the timetables. That

way everyone can wait in the right place and connecting services can be announced including the platform number. So
very Swiss.

IT'S A GROUP THING

SBB doesn't just plan its timetables well, it entices people off
the roads and into trains. Going to the Ed Sheeran concert in
Zurich or the cup final in Bern? Then your ticket includes the
train trip there, so no need to take the car. What a great idea
that is! Or how about paying 30Fr a year for a family card so
that your children travel for free when they are with you,
including on heart-stoppingly expensive routes like
Jungfraujoch (see below)? That's another winner, especially
if you use one of the cross-country double-decker trains,
which have a carriage set aside for families: room for buggies
downstairs and a playground upstairs, with all manner of
things to keep little angels happy; the Swiss like nothing better than attention to detail. Perhaps the best marketing success, or at least the one that appeals most to the Swiss, is the
group travel scheme.

The Swiss love being in a group. Think of any way of
spending time and there will undoubtedly be a club or group
for it somewhere in Switzerland; it must be something to do
with coconuts wanting to bunch together.[22] Or maybe it's
because the Swiss are so used to being organised that they
like their free time to be as well. Membership of a group is
almost a must in Swiss society and, as a foreigner wanting to
become a naturalised Swiss citizen, part of the process is
proving that you are integrated enough to have joined a club
of some sort. Time for me to improve my table tennis or get
singing lessons or maybe learn to blow something long and
hard, like an alphorn. The thing about groups is that they like

to travel together, or at least they do in Switzerland, where they get free seat reservations and discounts on the train tickets.[23] No wonder whole carriages can be full of a gaggle (or should that be woggle?) of scouts on an outing or pensioners going off for a mountain hike. Or school trips to a museum. Or a day out for the whole extended family. Or a work away-day to bond over sausages. You get the idea.

As a non-groupie, it was a surprise to see how the Swiss dynamic changes in a group and defies their national stereotype of being quiet, reserved and serious. They can be like that at first with strangers, but with each other they can be positively Italian in the way they all talk together without any idea of volume control. Share a carriage with almost any Swiss group and you're certain to have a headache by the end, or want to strangle the woman with the chicken laugh, or both. Perhaps that's why SBB separates them out, usually putting groups in the last carriage of a train. It's practical but it also saves lives. If the group sitting behind you is unusually quiet for most of the journey, they're probably playing cards. And that means only one game.

PLAYING THE SWISS AT THEIR OWN GAME

Jass is similar to bridge, though with completely different cards, and is a national obsession, for young and old alike. Played not just on trains, it can also be seen in the corner of a bar, after dinner in a restaurant or online. There are even mass *Jass* evenings, where twenty pairs compete in a round-robin tournament.

Picture this: 6.45 p.m. on Saturday on SF1, the main Swiss channel. Perfect time for a family drama, pop talent show or even ballroom dancing competition. Any of those might happen in Britain, but Switzerland gets to watch *Jass*. It's a simple affair: views of the cards in play, snooker-style commentary, musical interludes, and that's about it. Not quite *Play Your Cards Right* (no points making prizes and no Brucie), but it's been popular ever since it started in 1967. That's way before *Late Night Poker* turned cards into a spectator sport in Britain, making *Samschtig-Jass* the grandmother of TV card games. It's certainly much cosier than poker, as the programme takes place in real restaurants and bars around the country. But for novices like me, there's nothing cosy about trying to understand what's going on.

First, you need to know that it's pronounced 'yass', since *j*s in German are *y*s. Then you have to get to grips with the cards. Gone are the familiar black-and-red cards of a regular deck, replaced by four suits (bells, roses, shields and acorns) that look like they were designed when the Borgias were in power. The 36 cards are all so vibrantly painted in yellow, red, blue and green that the mix of colours and strange shapes still flummoxes me. I have to stare at each card to work out what it is. How many little acorns are attached to that branch? Is that pipe-smoking *Bauer* (equivalent to a Jack) really holding a rose? What happened to all the cards under the number 6? Throw in extras like the game progressing anti-clockwise, trumping whenever you fancy, some cards (such the 9 of trumps, known as Nell) being worth more than they should be and the world's most complicated scoring system, and you see why only the Swiss are experts. Maybe *Jass* is like cricket – a game you have to grow up with to stand any chance of understanding what on earth is happening. At least it keeps the Swiss happy.

TO INTERLAKEN AND BEYOND

Just about the only trains where the Swiss don't play *Jass* are the ones in the mountains. You might think that's because they're admiring the views, but while most Swiss are immensely proud of their scenery they're also rather blasé about it; for them, it's merely a backdrop to their lives. No, it has more to do with the lack of room on mountain trains, which are built for strength not comfort. It seems to be a standard requirement for Swiss mountain trains to have uncomfortable seats with minimal leg room; it's like being on an easyJet plane, but without the glamour. The higher you go, the more uncomfortable they get, so by the time you arrive in Europe's highest railway station at Jungfraujoch, you really do need to stretch your legs. That's after having stretched your wallet to get there. A return trip costs 210Fr, or roughly £155. It takes 120 minutes each way, or about 65p a minute, which is cheaper than most telephone helplines and far more enjoyable. You do at least get a lot of mountain for your money, with the journey ending at 3454 metres above sea level, over three times as high as Mt Snowdon. Of course only the very foolish or very rich (or both) pay the full price, but even then it's worth it. This trip of a lifetime needs three different stages to scale the heights and begins in Interlaken, Switzerland's biggest resort.

Take away the 7419 beds,[24] and all the associated restaurants, bars and souvenir shops, and there wouldn't be much left of Interlaken. Its whole existence is dependent on the tourist trade and has been ever since the 1860s, when the first British tour groups started arriving. And they've been coming ever since. Walk down the main street in August and it will feel like a mini United Nations. This is still a favourite spot for Brits, but they are outnumbered these days by guests from China and the Gulf States. They all come not because the resort itself is particularly charming, but because it is perfectly located at the centre of the Bernese Oberland. From Interlaken you can catch a paddle steamer on the two lakes that sandwich the town and gave it its name, or hop on a train to take you up to an Alpine wonderland. With all that on your

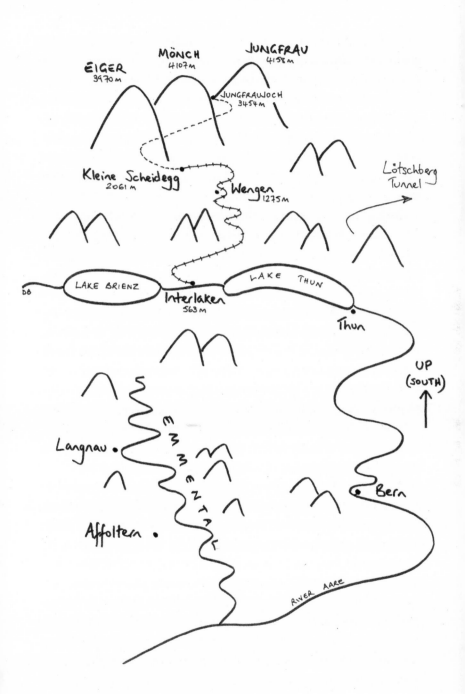

doorstep, it's possible to forgive the town planners who allowed buildings like the Hotel Metropole right in the centre. If there were awards for Switzerland's worst eyesore, this 18-storey concrete monstrosity would get my vote. In itself it's no worse than some blocks in the Geneva or Zurich suburbs. What makes it so objectionable is how badly it scars an otherwise low-rise town and its mountain backdrop. You're better off staying there, purely because once you're inside, you don't have to look at the exterior.

There are two reasons the Swiss come to Interlaken. One is to change trains. It is the Clapham Junction of Switzerland, though distinctly more scenic and with fewer platforms. Mainline trains from Basel, Zurich or even Frankfurt all terminate here; they can go no further because that requires a narrower gauge and smaller trains. Every half hour a 14-carriage train pulls in and disgorges its hundreds of passengers, most of whom then have to attempt the Interlaken Dash. With the timetables finessed to the last second, you have about five minutes to change platforms via the subway and catch one of the waiting mountain trains, first making sure you get the right one. On a Sunday morning at the height of summer, this can be rather chaotic with all those Swiss walkers joining the tourists in the fight for places. The tourists usually lose.

The other reason is one of Switzerland's best tearooms. In a country that loves its coffee-and-cake breaks, there can be few better places to have one than Café Schuh. It's been delighting guests with its gâteaux since 1818, and shows no sign of losing its touch. True, the décor was modern when the Berlin Wall was still standing, and the live piano music can verge on being too schmaltzy-waltzy, but the cakes are divine. The summer terrace overlooks Interlaken's vast village green, the Höhematte, a favoured landing spot for paragliders. If you see someone on a mountain train with a rucksack the size of a mini, then it's a paraglider lugging his chute up so he can jump off and waft back down. Watching them as they leap into thin air is almost as exciting as seeing them drop down to earth beside Café Schuh.

If you have indulged in a little too much chocolate mousse cake, you could always work it off by running up a mountain. No really, some people do exactly that, though possibly not straight after a visit to the café. Thousands have completed the Jungfrau Marathon, which is the normal 26-mile race except that it has a height increase of over 1600 metres. Quite a challenge, but one which around 4000 people take up annually, with the winner in 2017 managing it in under three hours.[25] Impressive stuff, but better to let the trains take the strain.

UP ON THE ROOF OF EUROPE

The first carries me away from the plain where Interlaken sits, and along the floor of the deep, U-shaped valley that slices right through the heart of the mountains. Being in this glacial valley is like seeing a physical geography textbook brought to life: sheer cliffs 1000 metres high, the wide, flat valley bottom, bridal-veil waterfalls, the river far too small to have carved such an grandiose sight. This is the Lauterbrunnen Valley, one of the most dramatic in Switzerland. For Tolkein it was the inspiration for Rivendell, the idyllic home of the elves, but it's not a place I'd like to live. It spends too much time in the shade and fog, especially in winter when the sun struggles to reach the valley floor. Far better to be up on one of the suntrap cliff tops, which is where the next train goes.

With the BOB and the WAB trains[26] (Swiss rail companies really do love their initials) on adjacent platforms, changing is a more comfortable experience than in Interlaken. The same can't be said about the seats. Still, with such great scenery to look at, you soon forget your numb bum and cramped feet. It's surprising how quickly the valley floor is left behind, so that the farmhouses and cars all look like tiny Matchbox models. Just before reaching the cliff top (and, as a result, car-free) Wengen, there's the best view of the whole valley framed by towering mountains on both sides. A few metres before this panorama appears from behind the trees, beside the track there's a little sign with a picture of a camera, all so you don't miss the photo opportunity. So thoughtful. It is but the first of many great views, so that by the time you reach the halfway point of Kleine Scheidegg, you might need to insert a second memory card.

If you thought that being up a mountain was going to be a solitary, peaceful affair, you were wrong. Kleine Scheidegg is like Piccadilly Circus. It's where tourists must change trains for the final leg up to the top, and where the Swiss walkers get the train back down, but it's also a popular destination in its own right. And all because it sits beneath the North Face of the Eiger. Having a plate of *Älplermakkaroni* while staring up at that forbiddingly steep and dark wall of rock is a lunchtime experience like no other. The Swiss German for the North Face is *Nordwand*, or sometimes *Mordwand*, a rather morbid reference to how many climbers' lives it has claimed (*Mord* means murder in German). And people say the Swiss have no sense of humour. The first successful ascent was in 1938 by a team including Heinrich Harrer, who went on to find fame by being played by Brad Pitt in *Seven Years in Tibet*. These days the quest is not to conquer the North Face (been there, done that) but to break the speed record for an ascent. The Jungfrau Marathon, which has its finish line at Kleine Scheidegg, might sound odd, but it's even weirder to want to race up the Face. The current record holder without using ropes is Ueli Steck, from Langnau im Emmental, who sprinted up in 2 hours, 22 minutes and 50 seconds;[27] sadly he died in 2017 attempting a record climb on Mt Everest.

The Eiger is the first and most famous of a mountainous trio; its neighbour is Mönch, and then comes the tallest of the three, Jungfrau. Together they dominate the Bernese Oberland skyline, clearly visible even from Bern city centre. In English – Ogre, Monk and Virgin – they seem much less imposing or challenging; maybe that's why we tend not to translate mountain names. Mont Blanc sounds far better than White Mountain. Sitting in the dip between Mönch and Jungfrau is my destination, Jungfraujoch, and getting there means taking a third train up inside the Eiger. Other than a lot of rock there's not much to see during the 25-minute ride, though one short stop lets you go and peer out through giant windows cut into the North Face. It's the feat of engineering rather than the scenery that is the attraction, but all that changes when you reach Jungfraujoch. The air is thin, the sun is blinding and the wind can be icy, but you feel on top of the world, looking down on the Aletsch Glacier, the longest in the Alps. With all the snowy peaks and that river of ice it's like being back in the Ice Age, though not all of Jungfraujoch's half million annual visitors come prepared for the cold; just as well I brought a fleece and a hat, even though it's August.

OFF THE RAILS AND ON THE ROADS

Despite all the spectacular mountain trips, the successful marketing ploys and record train usage, the Swiss also love their cars. There are 4.5 million private vehicles on Swiss roads,[28] giving Switzerland more cars per head than either Britain or France.[29] The strange thing is that the roads don't seem that crowded, at least not compared to the M25, so where are all the Swiss cars? Surely not sitting in garages? Certainly not in driveways, because few buildings have those. In summer, though, it's easy to spot where the Swiss cars are – all queuing to get through the Gotthard Road Tunnel. Radio and television news have regular reports on the length of the lines heading south on Fridays and returning north on Sundays. It's far worse at the beginning and end of the school holidays, when 20-kilometre queues and five-hour waits are not uncommon. And you thought the A303 to the West Country was bad.

Even during peak queue season there are no live traffic cams on Swiss breakfast television, mainly because there is no breakfast television. No perky double act on the sofa, no pointless outside broadcasts or endlessly repeating news stories. Instead, the Swiss get to watch the weather around the country, via a series of ever-rotating camera feeds, with music playing in the background. That might sound as exciting as watching snow melt, but it serves a useful purpose. Most of the pictures come live from mountain tops, not for the panoramic views but so that you can see where the weather is good before you set out for a day's walking or skiing. For each weather station there's not only the live feed but a mini local forecast for the day. So if Rigi looks dodgy, you can go up Brienzer Rothorn instead. It's strangely compulsive viewing, not to mention eminently practical, as there's no point in setting off to go up a mountain, only to be swathed in cloud when you get to the top.

The pleasant thing about driving in Switzerland is that everyone seems so polite. Road rage is not a Swiss concept, mainly because rage is so very un-Swiss. In almost any situation, be that at work or in the car, most Swiss would prefer to avoid a confrontation and try not to provoke one. You rarely see drivers arguing over a parking space, shouting out the window or honking furiously; except in Ticino, but there the rules are different. Speeding is easier to witness – where there are drivers, there are speeders – but it doesn't seem as endemic as elsewhere. That's partly due to the Swiss being naturally careful, but more likely down to the hefty fines. It's a novel concept, where what you pay is based on how far over the limit you were and also on how much you earn, but it seems to work because fines can run into the thousands. One man landed a 300,000Fr bill for driving his Ferrari at 50 kilometres an hour over the limit through a village in eastern Switzerland.[30] Some reports suggested he was German, though that may have been a Swiss rumour designed to maintain their reputation as law-abiding citizens and the Germans as the bad guys.

In comparison, the charge for driving on Swiss motorways is a bargain. All vehicles using the motorways must display an annual pass, or *vignette*, costing 40Fr. It takes the form of a coloured sticker in the windscreen; so much more elegant than having ugly toll booths, which also slow down the traffic and take up too much space, all of which make booths an illogical concept for the Swiss. Of course, all the Swiss dutifully go to the post office and buy their stickers every year. It sounds very regulated because, like many aspects of Swiss life, it is, though no more so than tax discs, speed cameras and congestion charges.

Perhaps the nicest part of owning a car in Switzerland is that you own the number plate. Replace your current car with a new one and the number plate, which is not dated, goes with you. A Swiss number plate is for life, not just for one car. Unless you move cantons, when you might have to change plates to avoid be classed as a 'foreigner'. That's because every number plate starts with two capital letters denoting the canton of origin. Often it's the first two letters of the canton's name, for instance SO plates come from Canton Solothurn, but this changes if there's any chance of confusion. The neighbouring cantons of Valais and Vaud clearly couldn't both be VA, so the former is VS. And the latter? Well, if you own a car in Vaud, you have VD your whole life. Then you might want to move.

To outsiders Switzerland's transport network is one of the modern wonders of the world; to the Swiss it's merely a means of getting from *A* to *B*. Or at least that's how it seems; in fact the Swiss love their transport system in general, and their trains in particular. But, as with so many things, while they know that theirs is better, they are too modest to show it. The only time you really see how much it means is when something new comes along. New trams are shown off like babies by proud parents, new buses are always newsworthy, and as for new tunnels, they invariably get a party. The completion of the motorway tunnel under Zurich prompted weekend-long festivities, with thousands walking, cycling, skateboarding and jogging down underground. And the opening of the 34-kilometre Lötschberg train tunnel under the Bernese Alps was an event in itself, where bands played and tickets to be the first to ride through the tunnel sold out well before the day. The tracks were even blessed (by Catholic and Protestant churchmen, just to be safe) and that was in addition to having been protected by St Barbara.

Their railways may be superior, but the Swiss are so used to punctuality, quality and service that they take them for granted. And they are just like any other nation when it comes to train travel: they read, they listen to music, they doze, they chat and they text – mobile reception is good even inside the tunnels. And most of them don't look out of the windows at the passing natural splendour. But for tourists, and still-unjaded foreigners like me, Swiss trains are more than a means to an end; they are an attraction in themselves. You don't have to be an anorak to enjoy sleek trains that run on time; and you don't have to be a tourist to get excited at climbing up inside the Eiger. You just have to be human.

SWISS WATCHING TIP NO 10:
MOBILE ETIQUETTE

Much of Swiss life is governed by rules, both explicit and unspoken, and travelling is no exception. Here are the most golden.

Rule number one: Don't queue if you don't have to. For an otherwise polite society, the Swiss can't queue, so this rule is assiduously followed by almost everyone. At bus stops, train platforms and cable-car stations it's a free-for-all. Scrum down, elbows out and every man, woman and child for themselves. Getting off a tram can be a battle against the tide of humanity getting in, even when there's enough time and space for all. But when places are limited, such as in cable cars, the only ones waiting in an orderly fashion are the tourists, who'll probably end up not getting in. In such situations the best option is to indulge in the 'Swiss sidestep'. You start at the back and edge your way round the side of the queue, sidling in slowly among the unsuspecting tourists until you're near the front and sure of a spot. Most Swiss have this sidestep down to a fine art so that it's used everywhere, not just when waiting for transport: at market stalls, restaurant buffets, Carnival crowds, pretty much anywhere with more than two people waiting. No wonder busy post offices, banks and railway counters have ticketed queuing systems.

Rule number two: Be seen and not heard. It's quite possible to go a whole day without being too disturbed by public noise. Few cars have music so loud that the air around them throbs as they sit at traffic lights, ghetto blasters are rarely heard in trains, most shops are music free, and whistle-while-you-walk is seemingly not a Swiss trait. This isn't because the Swiss are puritanical killjoys but because they respect each other's privacy and need for peace. The main exception is mobile phones, which are a national obsession and transform a reserved Swiss person into someone who shares a conversation with everyone. Swiss trains used to have a silent carriage, where mobiles were banned, but SBB abolished them in 2nd class in 2009. Enforcing it proved too hard for the conductors; evidently the Swiss, for once, chose to break the rules. As an example of the breakdown in public order it's hardly a riot, though in Swiss terms it was a minor revolution.

Rule number three: Know where to park. Street parking is colour coded with lines painted around the spaces. Stick to white and you'll be alright, though blue will sometimes do. Some streets have one parking meter, and each space is numbered with a corresponding button on the meter. It took me a while to work that one out the first time, especially as there's no ticket to display. And if you see a space with CAR painted on it, do not park there as, despite evidence to the contrary, it is not a space for cars. Ignore the writing on the floor and look at the size of the space, which is huge because car in French, and Swiss German, means coach.

Rule number four: Ring the bell. On many forms of Swiss public transport, such as trams and buses, you have to ring the bell to let the driver know you want to get off at the next stop, but the doors won't open automatically unless you push the button on the pole beside them. So a second push is needed, except, of course, if the button you originally pushed to ring the bell is the same as the one to open the doors. Got that? This actually becomes second nature, so much so that when I am back in Britain, I forget that there's no need to push the button beside the door, and if you do the bell rings again. Ringing the bell for a second time usually prompts a sarcastic remark from the driver, and I can only smile. I'm clearly so used to Swiss buses and trams that my finger cannot resist pushing the button again. It's like being a visitor in your own homeland.

Rule number five: Learn to cross the road. In Switzerland this isn't as fraught as in Cairo or Bangkok – your life as a pedestrian is rarely in danger – but it isn't as simple as it looks. It's all to do with lights. When traffic lights are present, as a pedestrian you should wait for the green man before you cross, even if there is no traffic. This is to set a good example to children as much as for safety. Even if no kids are visible, one may be watching from a nearby window and you, as the responsible adult pedestrian, have to do the right thing. There's also the small matter of being fined if you get caught crossing on red, though I've never known that happen.

If, however, there are no traffic lights, you can use a zebra crossing when you want and the cars must stop for you – pedestrians have right of way. Swiss people seem to step out into the path of oncoming cars, safe in the knowledge that the vehicles will stop; which, of course they do, not least because their drivers know they risk a fine if they don't. So at any junction, it's always possible to tell which pedestrians are Swiss and which tourists: the Swiss ones dutifully wait at traffic lights beside an empty road until the red light stops the non-existent traffic and the green man flashes up; but at lightless crossings they plunge headlong out across the road, no matter what is coming, though most wisely wait for trams to rumble past. Of course, it's tourists who cause the system to break down. As pedestrians they do it all backwards, not waiting for the green man on empty roads but hesitating to cross busy ones; and as drivers they are faced with countless Swiss pedestrians seemingly all wanting to commit suicide under their wheels. Perhaps such confusion is down to a Swiss zebra crossing having yellow stripes, not white. It's still called a zebra crossing but it must be named after very jaundiced zebras; wasp crossing would be better.

As a non-Swiss local I try to have the best of both worlds. I stride onto lightless crossings, stopping the traffic like a successful, modern-day Canute, but also wilfully ignore the red man if the road is empty. This has worked. So far, at least.

ELEVEN

SEEKING HEIDI

Driving south-westwards from Bern on the A12 motorway, one moment the exit signs are all *Ausfahrt* to Düdingen and St Wolfgang, then it's *Sortie* to Granges-Paccot and Givisiez. It's the same on the local trains, where the nice lady switches her announcements from *Nächster Halt* to *Prochain arrêt* without warning. The countryside outside the window still has the same, lumpy-under-the-eiderdown quality, and red-and-white Swiss flags still flutter in people's gardens, but it feels different once you read the signs and billboards. They are proof that you have crossed a linguistic Grand Canyon, known locally as the *Röstigraben*, literally the 'fried-potato trench' (see the map of Romandie on page 184). The odd name refers to the fact that the German-speaking Swiss love their *Rösti* (grated fried potato eaten with anything) and the French speakers don't. Of course the trench is invisible, but you soon know when you've gone over it. And it's one of the many things that make Switzerland what it is, perhaps one of the most important.

For many countries, particularly in Europe, language is one of the prime factors defining their national identity. Italy is Italy, and Poland Poland, primarily because all the people speak the same language (at least historically). Language also plays a big role in the Swiss national identity, but in a very different way. Instead of having one they have four, and it's this multilingualism that makes Switzerland special. Without Ticino and Romandie the Swiss would just be a small German-speaking country. Another Austria, and there's nothing they'd hate more than that. But equally, if they weren't part of Switzerland, Ticino and Romandie would merely be distant, neglected provinces of a large, centralised state. Far better to be a little fish in a little pond than a speck of algae in a large lake.

This unusual situation suits everyone. Swiss Germans may complain that the work ethic is lacking in the other parts, and that its inhabitants are less focused, less organised and simply less Swiss. But they secretly envy the way the French and Italian regions enjoy life more, have a sense of humour and drink wine at lunch. The Swiss French are more pro-European and less nationalistic, as referenda results consistently show,[1] and moan about Swiss German arrogance, but they have a voice in national affairs that wouldn't be the case in France. As for the Ticinese, they may not have a seat in the Federal Council very often but they'd rather feel ignored in Bern than ruled by Rome.

SPEAKING IN TONGUES

There's no escaping the fact that Switzerland is a multilingual country. Catch the intercity train from Basel to Zurich, both German-speaking cities, and you're exposed to a flurry of languages. The polite lady announcer says everything in triplicate just to make sure everyone on the train understands. She welcomes you on board, wishes you a pleasant journey, tells you that refreshing drinks and appetising snacks can be found in the bistro car in the middle of the train, and that staff are available for any questions or further information. All so informative, and so long-winded when said in German, then French[2] and then English that you're almost halfway to Zurich by the time she's finished her spiel. Such multilingual announcements are the norm in Switzerland, but what's interesting is the presence of English. No sign of

Italian[3] or Romansh, though the former at least makes it on to the written notices dotted around the trains and stations. When signs telling you not to cross the tracks are presented in German, French, Italian and English (they are big signs), there's no doubting the meaning. Of course they really only need to be in English, as no Swiss person would ever be daft or daring enough to cross anywhere except at a designated point.

It's not only the safety signs that come in a choice of languages. Food packaging, for example, has to accommodate everything in German, French and Italian. All the ingredients plus various nutrition, health, allergy and product information are given trilingually; it makes me wonder what the English producers do with all that space on a cornflake box or yoghurt pot. Even those stark health warnings on cigarette packets get the trilingual treatment, with the basic 'Smoking Kills' warning becoming *Rauchen ist tödlich*, *Fumer tue* and *Il fumo uccide*. You certainly get the deadly message. By the time you've read all that you'll probably have lost the will to live, let alone to have a smoke.

For Switzerland is indeed a nation of polyglots, with many Swiss able to switch easily between languages. Starting in primary school Swiss children have to learn another national language; typically children in the German- and French-speaking parts learn each other's language, while Italian-speaking kids have to learn both the others. In many schools this is all alongside English, which begins at much the same age. Canton Zurich caused a bit of a storm a few years ago by deciding that English would take preference over French in its schools, as it was far more useful to children in the outside world. The problem is that though they may learn another national language at school, most Swiss need only their own one on a daily basis, unless they move to another part of the country or work for the government.

An added twist to the linguistic conundrum is that the German-speaking Swiss don't actually speak German, or at least not the German you find in Germany. They speak Swiss German or *Schweizerdeutsch*,[4] an umbrella word for the various dialects found across Switzerland. It's largely a spoken language that wasn't seen in written form until quite recently. Books, newspapers and magazines are all pretty much still published in *Hochdeutsch* – High German (or 'written German' as they call it in Switzerland). Even on television there's a distinct variation in usage of the two forms: the main national news is given in High German, but the weather and local news are in Swiss German. In general most Swiss Germans would far rather speak their dialect than the more formal version from the north. And the difference?

To the Swiss they are like chalk and cheese, with their German clearly being the latter, but to outsiders they sound remarkably similar. Swiss German is more singsong and at the same time more guttural – almost as if a Swedish tourist is speaking High German but keeps having to clear his throat mid-sentence. Swiss German also throws in a French word or two, as if to say it's as Swiss as the country. So *poulet, trottoir* and *velo*[5] are all used in preference to the High German words. This French–German mix reaches its high point with the very Swiss way of saying thank you: *merci vielmal.*

However, French and Italian Swiss schoolchildren learn High German not dialect, which doesn't sit very well with their Swiss German compatriots. Of course, it doesn't help that most French speakers seem to forget every word of German once they've left school. In the French-speaking cantons the locals can be as bloody-minded as the French themselves about only speaking their own language, but if they do deign to switch, it's far more likely to be into English than German. In a way, the encroachment of English into everyday life, where it can be the sole common language, has deepened Switzerland's linguistic divide. Instead of being as multilingual as expected, some Swiss now speak their mother tongue (be that German, French or Italian) and English. And quite a few can only manage the former – rather like citizens of most other countries.

For the Swiss Germans, their dialects are a defining feature of their nationality, proudly and vociferously defended. How strange, then, that one of the most celebrated Swiss icons of all time doesn't speak the language of her country. She is a much-loved personification of Switzerland, but since she existed originally only in written form, she was created in High German. She's as Swiss as red penknives. She is Heidi.

TEN OF THE BEST

At Zurich airport the satellite terminal is linked to the main one by a connecting shuttle train. The yodelling starts as the train leaves, followed by jangling cowbells and deep-throated alphorns, all from the loudspeaker system. And then she appears, as if by magic, larger than life outside the window. She turns her head of golden, braided hair towards us, blows a kiss and vanishes. It's all an illusion, of course, her motion mere animation resulting from our moving past her series of pictures on the walls of the tunnel. But it's clever and kind of cute, and brings home just how much of a Swiss icon Heidi is. No one comes close to having such cult status, but perhaps that's because she's fictional. It's far easier for the Swiss to adore someone who never existed.

Celebrity isn't a big deal in Switzerland, probably exactly the reason so many stars come here to live, though the tax laws might help as well. Swiss magazines are more likely to have Prince William or Angelina Jolie on the cover than any-one Swiss. And chat shows? They don't really exist; the idea of watching one celebrity interview another is rather alien to most Swiss viewers. As with almost all of Swiss life, it's about privacy and modesty. Keep a low profile, even if you're stink-ing rich, and both of those can be achieved. Roger Federer is the big exception, Switzerland's one world star, but even he manages to have a homespun solidity about him. How many other stars put their baby pictures on Facebook instead of selling them to *Hello!* magazine? It is Switzerland that is famous, not its people. But who would the Swiss choose if they had to? Who are their big cheeses?

In 2010 *Der Bund* newspaper listed the ten most important Swiss people ever, and the choices say so much about the Swiss themselves. There are no monarchs or presidents in the list, as the Swiss have never really had any, and no one born after 1906, as if it's too soon to judge anyone so recent. Instead, this Swiss list is made up of:

✤ Two wartime army leaders, as befits a militaristic nation obsessed with self-defence: Henri Guisan (Second World War) and Jürg Jenatsch (Thirty Years' War).
✤ Two who were born abroad, mirroring the 25 per cent of the population who are not Swiss: Albert Einstein and Jean Calvin.
✤ Two men of words, just as Switzerland itself is a grand talking shop: Jean-Jacques Rousseau and Henry Dunant, though he at least acted on his words.[6]
✤ Two pioneers, fitting for a nation of innovators: Albert Hoffman (the LSD man[7]) and Alfred Escher, who founded Credit Suisse and funded the early railways.

And the last two? They are perhaps the most intriguing of all. No sign of William Tell, or General Dufour, or even such

Swiss notables as Le Corbusier, Carl Jung or Max Frisch. No, the last two are both women. And both fictional. I'm not quite sure what it says about the role of women in Swiss history that the two most famous examples never actually existed, but Heidi and Helvetia both make the list. Two very different pictures of Swiss femininity: one all sweetness and innocence, the other Athena-like in her stature and armour. The real Swiss woman must be someone between the two. Or perhaps she starts out as Heidi and grows up into Helvetia.

In some ways a naïve little girl is a fitting choice for a country that doesn't crave figureheads. She's certainly no Uncle Sam or John Bull. But can a fictional character really represent a nation? For the Swiss, and many more foreigners, Heidi is Switzerland personified. She is the national identity. She is someone I have to meet, though perhaps where I least expect.

WHEN RONALD MET HEIDI

It's Heidi Week at McDonald's, and for the first time since I stopped eating dead cows many years ago, I am strangely drawn to the golden arches. Going over to the dark side will be easy enough; in Bern, as in most European cities these days, it's not far to a House of Ronald – there are three within spitting-fat distance of each other.

I struggle to envisage what awaits me. Japanese Week means teriyaki burgers, and for Mexican Week a bit of salsa is thrown in between the buns. But Heidi Week? What can they possibly do to a burger for that? Dress it up in gingham? Make the burger box yodel when you open it, like those little round toys that moo when you turn them upside down? Trouble is, my expectations of Heidi Week are severely limited by my lack of knowledge about the girl herself. She's the original Swiss Miss, but as hard as I try I can't remember much of her story. Then a distant memory emerges from my mental fog: Saturday mornings in the summer holidays, and somewhere between *Champion the Wonder Horse* and *Flash Gordon* was a grainy, jumpy Heidi with dodgy dubbing and schmaltzy music.

At that moment I am 10 again, lying on the sitting-room floor with my sister, head on hands, watching television: the impossibly cute Heidi, the gruff grandfather, the silent Peter (probably just as well given the dubbing) and the goats. There were lots of those. Maybe that's it: maybe they're doling out goatburgers. And why not? We already have beef, chicken and veggie varieties, so why not goat? Then again, they don't sound too appetising – all gristly from bounding along mountain slopes. Even if I ate red meat, when it came to a goatburger I don't think I'd be loving it.

The jangle of a tram bell brings me back to Bern and I dash across the cobbled street. A helpful poster tells me it's only 15 seconds to the next McDonald's, but I'm there in 10, so eager am I to see the expected pigtails and cowbells, goatburgers and gingham. But what do I get? A shiny American takeaway that could be anywhere, dishing out monstrous towers of cholesterol – beefburgers with *Rösti* and Emmental cheese layered between the meat and buns. Not a yodel to be heard, not one square inch of gingham. And definitely no goats.

It seems that Heidi has been hijacked by the outside world. She is no longer that sweet girl of my youth and, unlike Red Riding Hood, has been eaten by the Big Bad Wolf. As the airport encounter showed, the Swiss themselves have realised her potential, using her to sell Switzerland and its products. It's a canny marketing ploy, but one which depends on Heidi representing the essence of all things Swiss. Time to see if that's true.

AT HOME WITH JOHANNA

After that close encounter with a Heidi-burger I get another Heidi surprise in Migros. Rows of little Heidis stare back at me from the chiller cabinet. She is a brand – for anything and everything that could have a dairy connection. Milk, yoghurt, cheese, cream, all of it plastered with a picture of a cherubic girl and 'Heidi' in big red script. The only problem with it is that there really aren't many cows in the story. It's all goats. Clearly a marketing version of poetic licence.

It seems that Heidi is everywhere in Switzerland. She may be a national icon, both at home and abroad, but she is the ultimate advertising campaign for anything and everything Swiss. It really is time I met this little Swiss girl, time in fact to find out more about Heidi and, in doing so, more about the Swiss national identity. Clearly I can't actually meet her, except on the label of a yoghurt pot, so I will have to settle for reading her story and meeting her maker.

In the realm of one-name women, Heidi is up there with Cleopatra and Cher on the name-recognition front, but what do I actually know about her? Not even her surname, it seems. In the Swiss Interest section of Stauffacher English Bookshop is a shelf of local authors, where Heidi can be found easily enough under S for Spyri. The cover picture shows a suitably wholesome blonde-haired girl striding up a grassy hill, her red dress and white apron adding a nice patriotic Swiss touch. A quick flick through the helpful intro reveals that Johanna Spyri wrote almost 50 stories, but there are few details of her life. The creator of the most famous Swiss person in literature and she remains something of a mystery. My best bet is to start with Spyri's end and go to Zurich, where she lived much of her life and died.

On the train there I settle back and immerse myself in an English translation of a Swiss book written in German. Given that it's a children's book with fairly large print, the pages go past almost as quickly as the towns. Here is Heidi's tale, part one: Having been deposited with her surly grandfather by an unwelcoming aunt, orphan Heidi wins the old man's heart with her innocence, befriends Peter the goatherd and his blind grandmother, frolics through endless meadows, feeds those goats and even finds time to grow a little (she's only five when the book starts). By the time I reach Zurich, I feel quite exhausted on her behalf.

Switzerland's second largest cemetery doesn't seem like the obvious place to look for a fictional incarnation of Swiss nationhood, but finding Heidi means finding her author. It might seem strange to begin with Johanna Spyri's death, but her grave is my most concrete starting point, if I can locate it. Inside the gates of Sihlfeld Cemetery is a plan posted on a notice board, but there's no clue where Johanna is buried. Having expected a slice of Swiss efficiency to help me find the grave, the prospect of searching the whole cemetery is less than appealing.

Salvation comes in the shape of a porter's lodge and its promise of help makes me smile, possibly not the best thing to do when entering a cemetery. Perhaps that's why the lady in the lodge looks at me so sternly; more likely is that it's 11.57 and her lunch starts at 12. Determined to get the most from my three minutes, I confront the formidable opposition behind the counter. This woman could have been an Olympic shotput medallist, though her severe demeanour is a little undermined by the Tropical Sunset on her head. Her hair is two shades the other side of puce, but perhaps you need a bit of colour in that job. And Frau Tropischer Sonnenuntergang is actually very friendly and helpful, giving me far more than three minutes and a list of famous people buried in Sihlfeld. Apart from Frau Spyri I recognise only one other name; no doubt they're all famous in Zurich, or maybe even Switzerland, but this Englishman has never heard of them.

Directions in hand, I set off to find grave number PG 81210/D, otherwise known as Johanna Spyri. Sihlfeld is hemmed in on all sides by houses, but it still has a remarkable sense of space. Miss Tropical Sunset told me that it was full, as in there's no room for any new graves, which seems hard to believe. Walking down the pristine gravel paths I begin to doubt that it is a cemetery at all. Wide avenues lined with trees and expanses of green grass make it feel more like a public garden, helped by the fact that four men are raking the already flawless paths and lawns. It's all so very Swiss, more sculpture park than place of mourning; I rather like this verdant oasis of death in the middle of a busy city. It doesn't feel depressing, but calming and uplifting. A place for truly quiet contemplation.

Graves seem to be an afterthought, peeking out from between bushes and flowers, and those that can be seen are stylish, modern and look as if each has a personal carer. Immaculate is the best word for them. Most just have names and dates engraved on them; no cloying sentimentality, no trite euphemisms for death, nothing but the barest facts in true Swiss style. Many are family affairs, even if that means an extended family; one covers 146 years of lives and six different surnames, each linked to the last like in that mental challenge where you go from cold to warm by changing one letter at a time. This family managed Gloor–Pfenninger to Oppiker–Schweitzer in six moves, giving a whole new meaning to six degrees of separation, especially seeing as they all ended up together in the end.

Compared to these family reunions, the Spyri lot is rather empty. Set against the back wall of the cemetery, with ivy trailing all around, is a simple white stone embossed with a large cross. Along with Johanna Spyri's name and dates (12.6.1827 to 7.7.1901) is a quote from Psalm 39 in German.[8] Her stone is flanked by matching white crosses for Diethelm Bernhard and Johann Bernhard, who both died in 1884. Her son died aged 28 from tuberculosis and her husband followed soon after, unable to cope with the loss. Twin crosses, twin dates, and twice the pain for Johanna. All rather sad.

Before leaving, I take a detour to visit the grave of the other recognisable name on Miss Tropical Sunset's list of not-so-famous people: Henry Dunant, founder of the Red Cross.[9] His grave is a much grander affair, almost the grandest in the whole place. A square stone pergola covers a white statue of two men, one lying wounded, the other propping him up as he tends to him. Both are naked to the waist, giving the statue a forlorn Pietà-esque quality, albeit with homoerotic over-tones. Faded red roses, burnt-out tealights and garlands of folded paper birds adorn the grave, while a mournful hint of incense lingers in the damp air. On the back wall is M Dunant himself, in the form of a relief of his bearded face. Like a giant cameo brooch, it's so life-like that it's almost like a death mask, and a shiver ripples down my spine. Even in death, Henry Dunant makes an impression.

At the cemetery's side entrance is a large white sign detailing all the things not allowed – No Jogging, No Beachwear, No Cycling, No Dogs, No Littering – before ending with Keep Quiet. I can relate to most of them, this is a cemetery after all, but No Beachwear? This is not Barcelona or Brighton. Zurich is perhaps 500 kilometres from the nearest beach, so it seems highly unlikely that any of its residents will be wandering round in bikinis or Bermudas, least of all in a cemetery. They may be far from the sea, but the Swiss still like to have as many rules as possible covering any eventuality; in this case it's probably because you can swim in Lake Zurich, though that's quite a way from this cemetery.

On the other side of the city is the house where Johanna lived. A stone plaque on the wall of Zeltweg 9 tells me this is the right place – it says, Johanna Spyri lived here from 1886 until her death. The list of bells shows that Number 9 is still mainly residential but a sign on Number 11 attracts my attention – the Johanna Spyri-Stiftung. Right name, wrong building, but it's only next door, so how different can it be? Climbing up the stone staircase, it's like going back a century or so. Lovely, curly wrought-iron banisters guide me up to a stained-glass door, as colourful as it is delicate. Inside, it's a riot of moulded ceilings, parquet floors, stucco detail on the doors – and, in among all the period detail, a humming modern office.

Julia, the receptionist, tells me that the building, known as the Escherhäusern, was built in the 1850s as Zurich's first purpose-built apartment block for rich residents. Johanna Spyri moved in after the deaths of her husband and son, but apparently didn't live here much; it was merely her *pied-à-terre* for when she was in town, which wasn't often. Her name lives on in the Schweizerisches Institut für Kinder- und Jugendmedien,[10] as the Stiftung is formally known, an organisation that promotes children's education and literature. How fitting.

A DAY IN THE COUNTRY

Having found where Johanna died, my next stop is the village of Hirzel, up above Lake Zurich, where she was born. Predictably enough its one sight is a Spyri Museum, though it has rather eclectic opening hours: Wednesdays, Saturdays and Sundays, 2 p.m.–5 p.m. Not exactly rolling out the welcome mat. With that in mind, Gregor and I have timed our trip to arrive a few minutes after 2 p.m. on a

Sunday. And I'm well prepared – I now know more about Hirzel than is healthy, having spent far too long clicking through the village website.[11] It was a virtual mine of data, to say the least. Who knew (or needed to know) that of Hirzel's 2168 inhabitants, 23 per cent are aged under 19 and 27 per cent are Catholic? Or that 298 foreigners live there? Amazingly, it has seven restaurants and two cafés, which must cater to all the Heidi tourists who turn up on days other than a Sunday and have nowhere to go. After discovering that the library is closed on Tuesdays and Fridays and only open 9–10.30 am on Wednesdays and Thursdays, I tore myself away from the computer. Almost every Swiss municipality has just such a website, but who else in the world looks at them?

We glide along the western edge of Lake Zurich in a near-empty local train, not quite hugging the shoreline (there are too many houses in the way for that) but close enough to see the sunlight dancing on the water. Lake Zurich is a long, thin sliver, less than 4 kilometres across at its widest point, so it's easy to see the far shore, known as the Gold Coast, one of the most expensive places in Switzerland, which is probably why Tina Turner lives there. Its residents fight a constant battle with the authorities over the flight paths to Zurich airport; it just wouldn't do to have their high life ruined by an incoming jet, unless of course it happened to be one of their private ones.

At Horgen we change to one of those ubiquitous yellow Postbuses, which, of course, is already there waiting for the connecting passengers. Our driver greets us all as he gets in and we're off, up into the hills. Unlike the train the bus is full, and soon it's standing room only. Not only that but the average age seems to be 77 – and our presence must lower it a fair deal. Either we've stumbled on a pensioners' outing to Hirzel or the old folks in these parts don't drive very much. I only wish I could remember the percentage of over-65s living in Hirzel.[12]

Although we climb up 311 metres, it's not the most spectacular ride but it is pleasantly Swiss: undulating green fields dotted with brown cows, occasional rustic farmhouses in among all the new ones, tiny villages that are gone before you've read the sign, and periodic glimpses of the brooding mountains. And rarely any flat land bigger than Hyde Park. As we leave the bus in Hirzel, I see a sign informing me that our driver today is W. Christen and he wishes us a *gute Fahrt*. For English speakers, the typically Swiss politeness of it is slightly undermined by the German for a good journey.

The Spyri Museum is housed in an old schoolhouse straight out of a Grimm fairytale: a fine half-timbered building, its wood stained blood-red, its roof a typical A-frame. In the tiny garden stands a stone statue of Heidi, Peter and prerequisite goat; we're definitely in the right place, and at the right time. It's 2:03 and the door is already open; what's more, we are not the first visitors – four others are inside already. Perhaps they are all Swiss.

Downstairs, the rough stone walls host black-and-white photos of Johanna and her family, all of them looking as severe as only Victorians can. None of them resembles someone you'd like to meet on a dark night, let alone have read you a bedtime story. Johanna Louise Heusser was the fourth of six children, her father a doctor, her mother the preacher's daughter. She pretty much stayed put until, aged 25, she met one Johann Spyri. It must have been a tad confusing, a Johanna with a Johann, especially given that her father was also called Johann, but that didn't stop her marrying the Zurich lawyer and moving to the big smoke. However, she never really took to city life and depression took hold, particularly after the birth of her son. Solace came from her writing and visits to the countryside around Maienfeld. Her greatest success came with *Heidi* in 1880, only to be followed a few years later by the deaths of her son and husband. She wasn't exactly a merry widow, but she gave time and money to charitable causes and carried on writing until her death in 1901. It's rather grim reading, with Heidi the only glimmer of joy in her life, and going up the steep staircase my heart is as heavy as my feet.

The all-wooden first floor features Spyri's most famous character, and the friendly lady in charge chats about our heroine, whom she views as an early feminist. She confirms that, although *Heidi* has been translated into over 50 languages, it isn't available in Swiss German. Peering into the glass cases I make a startling discovery. The original Heidi book, called *Heidi's Years of Wandering and Learning*, was first published in Germany, not Switzerland, and was actually only half the story. It was so successful that a sequel, *Heidi Uses What She Has Learned*, came out the following year; the *Heidi* we know today is these two books together. More revealingly, the first volume was published anonymously. Maybe it was a case of, like her contemporary George Eliot, having to hide her gender to achieve success. Even today that can still be an issue: Joanne Rowling became JK in order to make her book appeal more to boys. Or perhaps Johanna sought refuge in anonymity. Either way, the charade was over by book two, when Johanna Spyri's name finally appeared on the cover.

All manner of memorabilia is on display: books in a host of languages, videos, records, clothes and food packaging. It seems that it isn't only McDonald's and Migros who have used our young heroine over the years; she's been put upon to sell tea, wine, salad, sausages and of course yet more dairy products. There might have been fewer companies falling over themselves to use her if she'd kept to her real name and not shortened it to Heidi; somehow Adelheid lacks that romantic ring, sounding far too Teutonic to be cute. All the same, I wonder what Johanna would make of her little girl's image being prostituted around the world in the name of profit.

Museum done, we stroll through the village, which straggles out along a downhill road and will never win any awards. Not every Swiss village lives up to the picture-postcard hype. Some, like this one, are pleasant but plain ordinary. There's a typically bare Protestant church, with a modern Catholic counterpart nearby, a post office, a butcher, a baker (no candlestickmaker) and two of those aforementioned restaurants. The other five must be hidden away in the backstreets. Spyri's childhood home is one of the grander old buildings, mainly because it was also her father's surgery. Down at the main road is one of the ubiquitous *Wanderweg* signs, but here it seems a little superfluous to be told that it's a four-and-half-hour walk back to Zurich. As tempting as that is, when the bus trundles into view exactly on time, we hop on.

WELCOME TO HEIDILAND

'I can't believe I'm finally standing in Heidi's house; it's like a dream come true.' Not my words but ones written by an enthusiastic American tourist in the visitors' book at the Heidihaus in Maienfeld, over in the far east of Switzerland near the Austrian border. This pretty town is the setting for the book, and it milks the Heidi connection for all it's worth – and given the number of tourists here, it's clearly worth quite a lot. Not for nothing is this area of Graubünden known as 'Heidiland' in tourist-board marketing speak. The whole place looks like it has just stepped out of the book, its stark grey

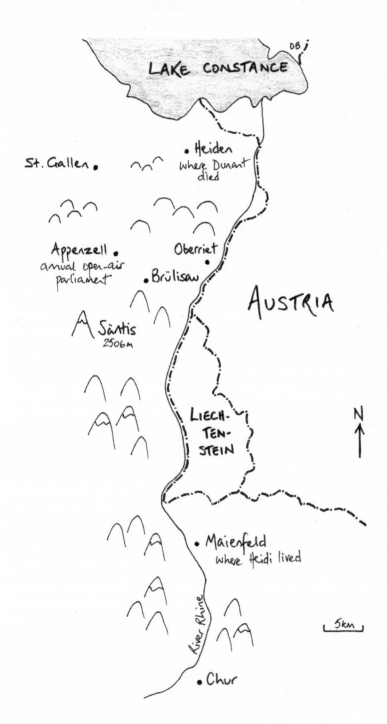

LAKE CONSTANCE   DB

St. Gallen •   • Heiden
                              where Dunant
                                  died

Appenzell •   • Oberriet
annual open-air
parliament   • Brülisau   AUSTRIA

    Säntis
    2506m

                      LIECH-   N
                      TEN-   ↑
                      STEIN

                      • Maienfeld
                      where Heidi lived

                                                    5km

    River Rhine

    • Chur

mountains towering over heavily wooded slopes and lush Alpine pastures that roll down to the flatter plain along the banks of the Rhine. The big difference between here and central Switzerland is that these mountains aren't the pointy triangles dusted with snow that fit with images of the Swiss Alps. Instead, their jagged profiles make a ragged skyline, their sides too steep for all but the stickiest snow, their presence threatening rather than inviting.

Gregor and I are visiting his parents in Liechtenstein, a tiny principality sandwiched between Switzerland and Austria that doesn't have many claims to fame, apart from being the world's sixth smallest country.[13] Its 37,000 citizens are ruled by a prince in a castle, but it doesn't have its own currency; Swiss francs are used. Its main products are false teeth, nails (of the hammer variety rather than the stick-on type) and banking of a secretive nature. For sure, it's a sweet country for a day-trip but, more importantly for us, it happens to be close to Maienfeld. We take the scenic route past the mountains, travelling through practically the whole of Liechtenstein (it really is that small) before re-crossing the border, marked only by a flag and a sign.

Maienfeld is a small place, its centre little more than a cluster of handsome stone buildings around a church with a pickled-onion-topped spire. Although it's probably never the busiest place, Maienfeld is particularly dead today as it's Easter Monday. Holiday or not, the Heidihaus is open. It's clearly far too sensible to close when there's tourist money to be taken – and too canny to let anyone leave Maienfeld without visiting it. There's hardly a corner in town that doesn't sport a signpost touting the route to The Original Heidihaus and, as with most Swiss signage, giving the estimated walking time.

It's a mere 45 minutes up the gentle slopes towards those forbidding mountains. The old town, little more than one street deep, is quickly replaced by newer houses, and almost as quickly by fields of grass-munching cows. If Hollywood wanted a better backdrop for Shirley Temple to be cute and wholesome, they'd have trouble finding one. Somehow I doubt her 1937 version of *Heidi* came anywhere near this bucolic scenery, given how inaccurate it was in other respects. After all, it's largely because of her that most people think of Heidi as having cherubic blonde hair, rather than the plainer, browner hair in the book. Plus the fact that the Shirley Heidi sings and dances, something I'm sure Johanna Spyri never envisaged.

In case your childhood was blighted by not reading the Heidi story, here's part two of her tale. Just when she's settled in with Gramps and the goats, along comes her aunt to whisk her off to Frankfurt as a companion to Clara, a rich sick girl. It's a disaster. Not only is she in a German big city but Clara's governess is a dragon with the delicious name of Fräulein Rottenmeier. Before long Heidi's wasting away, pining for her daily infusion of goats' milk and mountain air, but the tale ends happily, of course, with Heidi back in her beloved Swiss mountains. When Clara comes for a visit that goats' milk and fresh air soon cure her, and she's off out of her wheelchair, gambolling through the meadows. Tears of joy all round.

You may have noticed that my initial enjoyment of the book disappeared at about the same time as Heidi went to Frankfurt. True, the first part was a little schmaltzy, but there was an endearing quality about Heidi's innocence, love and belief in others. However, throw in a German baddy and our heroine's descent into surliness and you can almost lose the will to read on. By the time Clara is cured on a diet of bread, goats' milk, love, faith and fresh air (with not a fresh vegetable in sight, let alone five a day), it was a trial to finish the book. Perhaps I am just too full of twenty-first-century cynicism to appreciate a Victorian morality tale.

If the second half of *Heidi* was a let-down, that's nothing compared to the Heidihaus. There was I expecting a rustic wooden chalet, and what do I get instead? A house that is Buckingham Palace in comparison: three storeys, with a stone ground floor, glass windows and a neat garden. Inside, things get worse. A full kitchen, Dutch oven, indoor loo and Heidi even has her own bedroom, one clearly furnished for Barbie. My disappointment, however, is more than compensated for by the gushes of delight to be found in the visitors' book. Few seem to realise that it's all a mirage, a Disney-Heidi built to sate tourist appetites for anything relating to the girl. It seems so different from the other Spyri places on my Heidi quest: her grave in Sihlfeld, her house in Zurich, her museum in Hirzel – all of these were typically understated, typically Swiss. No razzamatazz, no exploiting their connection, no surrendering to the tourist dollar (or yen and euro); just modest and discreet, like so many Swiss people themselves.

In the Heidi shop her name is used even more blatantly to sell anything tourists might (not) want. It's hard to remember the little girl's innocence when you see her plastered on a bottle of wine or a bag of coffee beans. Such mercenary use of her image feels all the more uncomfortable given how much it contradicts her persona in the book. She, after all, gets sick just from moving to the big, bad capitalist city in Germany, where she has to eat foreign oddities like fish and vegetables and can't run and play. Give her a chunk of bread, a field of goats and a view of the mountains, and she's the happiest girl in the world. Then again, given how much the Swiss love making money, maybe Heidi hasn't sold her soul at all; maybe she just grew up into a normal Swiss woman, albeit one who, here in Maienfeld, displays her wealth far too conspicuously to be truly Swiss.

My Heidi quest is over. Heidiland slips past the train windows, its sharp-toothed mountains giving way to the softer, greener fuzziness of tree-covered hills. The little girl who represents Switzerland to the outside world is alive and well, popping up all over her own country. But some believe that her country isn't actually Switzerland.

HOW SWISS IS HEIDI?

Many months after my trip to Heidiland a revelation shocked the nation: Heidi is German! She might be the personification of Switzerland, but the original Swiss miss may not be quite as Swiss as we all thought. It's almost tantamount to blasphemy to suggest such a thing, but it's a question that made front-page news in her homeland: one paper had the headline '*Unser Heidi hat einen deutschen Vater!*' or 'Our Heidi has a German father'. Notice the 'our' – the Swiss are very possessive of their heroine, so you can imagine how much it niggles to have her parentage questioned. It's on a par with saying that Robin Hood was French, or Tom Sawyer Canadian. So how could such a thing happen?

A German studies scholar found a story about a little girl who lives with her grandfather, gets sent away to a foreign land, suffers terrible homesickness, but lives happily ever after once she is back in the mountains. And her name was . . . Adelaide (which can also be written as Adelheid, often shortened to Heidi). This version was written by a German author, Hermann Adam von Kamp, in 1830, half a century before Johanna Spyri wrote her *Heidi*, the one we know and love. Did Johanna plagiarise a forgotten work? It was an outrage comparable with suggesting that Shakespeare copied Marlowe, and the penknives came out immediately.

The scholar behind the discovery was cast as Switzerland's public enemy number one, but remained adamant that Heidi was a second-hand version of a German original. She might have had a Swiss mother, but her father was clearly Herr von Kamp. This is possibly an argument that will never end as, with both authors long since dead, there's no one to ask. Maybe it's just a matter of faith, like believing that Jesus never had children. And when it comes to belief in their own country and its icons, the Swiss are second to none. So for them, there is no doubt: Heidi is, was and always will be Swiss through and through. That belief is shared by millions around the world.

More than 50 million copies later, the public still loves Heidi as much as ever, particularly in America and Japan. Not bad going for someone who's over 130 years old. Heidi was the Harry Potter of her time, not least in terms of how ruthlessly she has been merchandised right up until today.

And the parallels between the two authors are striking. Johanna Spyri was once the most celebrated children's author alive, the JK Rowling of her day. Both found fame and fortune from writing, though in very different quantities, and helped children's charities as a result. They even share a similar first name, one that initially remained hidden. But Johanna never found the happiness that JK seems to have, was never at peace with the world around her. It can't be a coincidence that Heidi gets sick when she goes to the big city, just as happened to her creator, or that she has a happy ending in the mountains she loved. Before she died Johanna burned her diaries and letters, so we'll probably never really know the real her. Perhaps that's why it's Heidi, not her creator, who is perennially seen as the epitome of Swiss womanhood. Or perhaps because it's easier to believe in a picture that never changes. The Switzerland of Johanna Spyri may be long gone, but the spirit of her creation lives on, as a romanticised image of everything that is essentially Swiss.

MEET THE MÜLLERS

To reveal the real Swiss identity, maybe we must look not at historical figures or fictional heroines, but at the people themselves. After all, they are why Switzerland exists and why it is the way it is. To do that, we have to do what the Swiss would do and use statistics. So it's time to meet the Müllers, the archetypal Swiss family.[14]

Stefan and Nicole are in their late 30s and have two children, Laura and Luca, after eight years of marriage. They live in a rented four-room flat[15] and get on with their neighbours, as long as they always say hello and are considerate of everyone's peace and privacy. Nicole only works part-time, as bringing up the kids is more important than her career; instead, she spends 53 hours a week cooking, cleaning, washing and shopping. That's twice as much as Stefan, who works full-time in the largest sector of the economy, the service sector. He drives to work and racks up 40 hours' overtime a year. The Müllers watch television for 2½ hours a day, but always find time to read the local paper.

At the weekends they go cycling, or better yet hiking. Both are free family fun, and they'd rather save for their annual holiday in Italy, France or Spain. The children go to football training, ballet or horse riding, and will live at home until they are 23. Both will be expected to get good grades at school, but Laura will have sex before she is 14, Luca when he's 17. Their parents have already settled down to having it twice a week, lasting 19 minutes each time, including foreplay.

They always shop in Migros or Coop, with yoghurt their most purchased item. Per person, they eat 250 grams of vegetables, 120 grams of potatoes, 160 grams of meat and 390 millilitres of milk every day. Family finances are carefully watched, as Stefan and Nicole worry what would happen if he lost his job. And of course, they have to think about their own old age and pay the dentist. Straight white teeth are as important as good grades for the children.

The three words the Müllers choose to describe themselves are cautious, friendly and punctual; they are highly unlikely to see themselves as open, spontaneous or disorganised. They might be just the average family, but the Müllers are patriotic and proud to be Swiss.[16] And in that respect, they are typical Swiss people.

Defining the national identity is hard enough for any country, but for Switzerland it's a challenge up there with climbing the Eiger. As a country it lacks many of the elements that usually bind a nation together: a common language, state religion, monarchy, an overriding ideology or revolutionary ideals. But that's not to say that Switzerland is not a nation; it's just not one in the stereotypical sense. It is maybe the best example of national self-determination. It is a country because it wants to be one, or, as the Swiss say, a *Willensnation*. Despite the different languages, Lugano, Lausanne and Lucerne are all Swiss, simply because that's what their inhabitants want. In some ways this makes Switzerland as fictional as Heidi, a place that exists because its people believe in it. Like heaven, only more mountainous and with better public transport.

Nevertheless, being an atypical nation doesn't mean that it has no identity, more that it's harder to identify. Perhaps that's where Heidi comes in. Despite being far too uncomplicated and carefree to be truly Swiss, the fictional Heidi is in fact the perfect personification of the Swiss nation: loving and giving to her nearest and dearest but wary of foreign complications, a determined heart beneath that picture of innocence, and devoted to her homeland above all else. Most of all she's an illusion the Swiss still believe in, just like the country itself.

SWISS SURVIVAL TIP NO 11: MASTERING SWINGLISH

Contrary to official statements, there are in fact five national languages in Switzerland. Alongside German, French, Italian and Romansh, there is also Swinglish, the product of Swiss meets English. It may be less developed than its linguistic cousins Franglais and Spanglish but, within its home country, it's widely spoken and widely (mis)understood. Before we get to grips with Swinglish, it should be noted that it is entirely different from the liberal sprinkling of English words that appear in normal Swiss speech, such as ticket, sandwich, quickie, management, online, sofa, hobby, snack and so on.

Swinglish has two levels, Basic and Advanced, though paradoxically the former is actually harder for outsiders to understand. The reason for this is twofold: the English words are hugely outnumbered by the Swiss ones and, more disconcertingly, they sometimes have completely different meanings from their original English root. For example, a mobile phone is known as a *Handy* in Swinglish – an appropriate enough word but with a totally different meaning in English, where it's not even a noun. At this level, most Swinglish words are there for one of two reasons. First, it is cool. Using an English word is so much trendier than a dull old Swiss one, especially when trying to sell something. Secondly, it overcomes the language barrier. It's much easier to use one English word, such as *Sale*, which can be understood by everyone (even if sale means 'salt' in Italian and 'dirty' in French), than translating it into four separate words; it saves space for one thing. Swinglish is thus at once both hip and helpful.

A good everyday example is the word *Drink*, which in Swinglish roughly means semi-skimmed milk; in any Swiss supermarket there is *Milch* (or *lait* or *latte*), the real deal with all its fat intact, and then *Drink*. To a native English speaker, using the word *Drink* in relation to milk or juice (as in the dreaded 'fruit juice drink') usually means it's been watered down and/or sweetened up. For Swinglish speakers, it merely means milk that is not whole, but using an English word makes it appear trendy, and so more marketable, and avoids translating 'semi-skimmed milk' in triplicate.

The trouble for foreigners is that when the Swiss speak English, some forget that many of the words they're using are actually Basic Swinglish. This is fine when misspelt, such as (k)now-how often losing its k, or when the meaning is self-explanatory, for example anti-baby-pill. But just as American and British English have different meaning for pants, purse and rubber, so too can Swinglish and English produce moments of mutual misunderstanding. A few examples, with the Swinglish meanings given:

Hit – a special offer; it comes after, and is joined to, the word it is qualifying, producing some unfortunate results: Price Hit becomes *Preishit*, and Dish of the Day is *Tageshit*. Not too appetising for English speakers.

Mobbing – bullying, usually within the workplace.

Old-timer – a vintage car, but also buses and trams, though never men.

Pudding – a specific dessert rather like a blancmange.

Smoking – a dinner jacket.

Tip-top – very good, but usually written tipptopp.

Trainer – a tracksuit.

Wellness – a spa, though normally used as an adjective, as in wellness weekend or wellness hotel.

Advanced Swinglish is far easier for outsiders to understand, for the simple reason that sentences are constructed in English rather than Swiss. Advanced Swinglish speakers usually speak good English but their Swinglish roots reveal themselves every so often. It's not always a question of vocabulary, as most Advanced speakers have learnt to drop (or translate) many Basic words. At this level it's a matter of 'mid-translation'; that is, translating from their mother tongue but not quite reaching English. For example, the Swiss German *Hoi zäme!*

becomes the Swinglish 'Hello together!' (the literal translation) rather than 'Hello everyone!'.

The most noticeable quirk of Advanced Swinglish is its grammar. Many nouns develop a plural where none existed before (*informations*, *behaviours*) while other plurals pop up with odd spellings (*babys*, *partys*). Verbs present more of a challenge. Swinglish speakers do an awful lot of things reflexively — dressing, hurrying, shaving, imagining, remembering and sitting down are all things you do to yourself. The problem lies in the mid-translation of the reflexive pronoun. In Swinglish, 'we meet us', 'I shame me' and 'we see us' are all often heard. Then there's the use of the continuous tense, which most Swinglish speakers do with relish, possibly because it doesn't exist in Swiss. 'Are you speaking German?', said in perfect Swinglish, is a question designed to confuse everyone involved.

Perhaps the trickiest part of Advanced Swinglish to master is the pronunciation. It seems just like English, but small variations make all the difference. I found that out the hard way when I started work in Stauffacher English Bookshop:

Swiss customer: I need a book on cheeses.
Me: Okay, I'll show you what we have.

In the Cookery section, I get out our three books on cheese.

Customer, shaking her head: Not cheese. CHEE-SES.

At this point, I am wondering if cheese has a plural. Was it like sheep, with none? Or more like fish, plural when more than one type is involved? Or was this a Swinglish plural, like informations? Not wanting to get into a discussion on that, I try again, going with her plural in the hope that it helps.

Me: So you are looking for something about cheeses?
Customer: Yes. Books on holey cheeses.

Me, smiling: Ah, a book on Swiss cheeses!

Customer, looking at me as if I am simple: There is no Swiss cheeses.

Me, now wondering about a singular verb with a plural noun: We do have
some books on Swiss cheeses.

Customer, very irritated: Cheeses was not Swiss. He was the Son of
God.

Me, finally catching up: Oh you mean, Jesus.

Customer: Yes, this is what I have been saying. A book on cheeses.

The problem, apart from me being rather slow that day, lies in the
Swinglish speaker finding it hard to differentiate between J and CH in
English. In Swiss German, a J is a Y (so that Jesus is pronounced
Yay-sus), whereas a CH is similar to the one at the end of loch. The
English pronunciations sound the same to a Swinglish ear. This was
made even clearer to me when I met a Canadian expat in Zurich a while
ago. He listened to my tale of encountering the Swiss Jesus and
came up to me afterwards to shake my hand.

'At last, someone has recognised the hell I'm living in every day,' he
said, cryptically. Before I could ask anything, he added, 'My name is
Jerry.'

As if being called Cherry by all his work colleagues wasn't bad
enough, it turned out he came from Vancouver. I'll leave you to mull
that one over.

That's it, until we are seeing us next time in Switzerland.

CONCLUSION

The Swiss are rich but like to hide it, reserved yet determined to introduce themselves to everyone, innovative but resistant to change, liberal enough to sanction gay partnerships but conservative enough to ban new minarets. And they invented a breakfast cereal that they eat for supper. Privacy is treasured but intrusive state control is tolerated; democracy is king, yet the majority don't usually vote; honesty is a way of life but a difficult past is reluctantly talked about; and conformity is the norm, yet red shoes are bizarrely popular.

It's perhaps no surprise that the Swiss are contradictory, given how divided their country is. Since its earliest days Switzerland has faced geographic, linguistic, religious and political divisions that would have destroyed other countries at birth. Those divisions have been bridged, though not without bloodshed, but Switzerland remains as paradoxical as its people. While modern technology drives the economy, some fields are still harvested with scythes (all the hilly landscape's fault); it's a neutral nation and yet exports weapons to many other countries; it has no coastline but won sailing's America's Cup and has a merchant shipping fleet equal in size to Mexico's. As for those national stereotypes, well, not all the cheese has holes, cuckoo clocks aren't Swiss and the trains don't always run exactly on time.

This book started at the foot of the Matterhorn and finished above the Eiger. Those two famous peaks may both look like mountains, but they are as different as two people from Zurich and Basel. It has been said that a Swiss person only feels Swiss once he leaves the country; until that point his heart belongs to Geneva, Schwyz, Ticino or any of the 23 other cantons. But no matter what language they speak, where they live or who they pray to, what all Swiss have in common is a will to remain Swiss. They trust each other not to falter in the face of all their contradictions, but to harness them for the greater good. It doesn't always work – just look at their bloody past – and it isn't always easy, as their uncertainties about the future show. The secret of Swiss success is making the whole far more than the sum of its parts, but at what price?

For the collective to succeed, the individual must be sacrificed on the altar of conformity. Switzerland is, like its cheese, a country of round holes; square pegs need not apply. It also has no heritage of monarchs and presidents, as from the very beginning it's been a cooperative entity. I think that's why there are so few Swiss celebrities: it's not in the Swiss nature to stand out in a crowd; if you do, you might get cut down to size. Egoism is not popular in Switzerland, as ex-Federal Councillor Mr Blocher found out. This lack of figureheads is so Swiss that the Swiss themselves don't even notice. Switzerland has always been a collective enterprise and that's just how they like it: deciding for themselves, with no one telling them what to do.

Perhaps that strong sense of self-determination is why the Swiss are satisfied with the lot they have chosen – even to the degree of seeming self-satisfied. True, their national self-esteem took a few dents recently (Nazi gold, the Swissair collapse, the banking secrecy traumas), so that it's no longer the norm to see their country as the envy of the world (unless you're an SVP supporter), but Swiss national pride and self-confidence have certainly been on the up in the past few years, with some British politicians even saying that the UK should be more like Switzerland. They were obviously thinking about the Swiss relationship with the EU, rather than abandoning nuclear weapons, reducing taxes, improving public transport and giving far more power to the people.

While most Swiss like living in their orderly, controlled environment, some find it simply too restrictive. It can't be a coincidence that so many Swiss go abroad as a way of finding fame, or even finding themselves: César Ritz, Ursula Andress and Le Corbusier, for example. They escaped the prison, as Swiss writer Friedrich Dürrenmatt might have put it. He once said that his country was a prison where the prisoners themselves are the guards. It's a little harsh – Switzerland may be a desert island but it's no Alcatraz – though the Swiss do go to extraordinary lengths to protect themselves, their money and their country from the outside world. Perhaps it's more fortress than prison.

Then again, a better analogy is a bee hive. All those industrious bees look very similar but they each has its own role in achieving a common goal: to protect the queen. In this case she is Helvetia, that elegant, beautiful and well-armed woman who graces the coins and lends her name to the stamps. She is the reason the Swiss all work as one, even if that means compromising their sense of self as a result. Of course, a wonderful by-product is honey, or in Swiss terms, chocolate. If one thing is worth a bit of collective mentality, it's that.

To truly understand the Swiss, one elderly Swiss man told me, all you have to do is read William Tell. He's right in that the Tell story sums up the Swiss character very well, but isn't it odd that a fictional tale written by a German is the basis of a nation? Then again, it's the myth of Switzerland, be that Tell or Heidi or the wartime experience, that is as important as the reality. In essence, Switzerland is a marketing exercise on a national scale, using every possible means to be successful. The German-speaking majority quite readily adopt clichés such as fondue and chocolate, both invented in the French part, because they add to the country's sales image, an image based on being somewhere clean, neat, precise and efficient. Living up to that can be hard, but it works because the Swiss themselves believe in it. And they put community before individual to achieve it.

To describe this common desire to pull together, the Swiss rarely use the motto inscribed in the dome of the Federal Parliament: *unus pro omnibus omnes pro uno*, or one for all, all for one. All very uplifting, but this is the twenty-first century so what's needed is a trendy new word. English is the new Latin, so the word is Swissness. Just as they once created a Latin name for their country to overcome their differences, the Swiss now use an English, or actually Swinglish, word for their collective sense of nationhood. While Swissness may mean nothing to outsiders, it encapsulates the country's sense of self like nothing else. Using a made-up foreign word to express a national desire may sound contradictory, but this is Switzerland. This is the landlocked island, and there's no bigger contradiction in terms than that.

The Alpine republic is by no means a perfect country; it can sometimes feel like an exclusive club where outsiders are reluctantly welcomed and rules are forever set in stone. But its virtues – the scenery, the quality of life, the sense of community – more than outweigh its faults. There is no paradise on earth, but the land of milk and money comes close.

A PERSONAL POSTSCRIPT

Half-past seven on a cold, dark Saturday morning in November and I'm sitting outside an exam room in Bern. And I'm rather nervous, to say the least. Not only is this the first exam I have taken since leaving university but it's also the first step on the road to me becoming Swiss. Yes, after more than 12 years of living here, I've decided it's time to take the plunge and apply for citizenship. That's not an easy decision because it's not an easy process in Switzerland. Like everything here it takes time and money but, like everything here, it's worth it in the end. Every country has rules for outsiders wanting to join the club, which is only right. Prospective citizens should have to prove that they can speak the language, know something about their new home and can abide by the rules. But even most Swiss would probably agree that they make it that much harder to join their club. In the race to become a citizen, the Swiss hurdles are higher and more numerous but they all have to be overcome. And I am merely at the starting blocks.

TAKING THE TESTS

Before I can even fill in the application form, Canton Bern requires that I take two tests. Step one is a language test, which in Bern can be in German or French. I chose the former, because although my French is passable, I couldn't pass an exam in it. To pass you have to achieve certain levels in written and oral tests; fail one and you fail the whole thing. And, this being Switzerland, you need a stamped piece of paper to show you have reached the required levels. It's not enough to have a long, detailed conversation in German with the naturalisation office; they have to know that you're able to have that conversation so you have to prove your ability by taking an official test so you have the certificate to show that you can have that conversation. Unless of course you happen to have taken a recognised language test at a recognised language school, so already have the certificate to prove it. I hadn't so I had to take the official test at one of the three designated test centres. Hence my nervous wait outside the exam room in November, trying to remember which verbs take the dative.

The exam was a test of two halves. First, the hour-long written part, which involved the likes of writing a description of your flat and correcting grammatical mistakes in a piece of text. All par for the course. My downfall was the vocabulary test, mainly because I don't have a garden and I'm not Imelda Marcos. My knowledge of garden implements in German is a tad limited, as I've never had to use a rake here, let alone learn the word for it (it's *der Rechen*, by the way). As for Imelda, she probably knew the words for every single part of a shoe in many languages. But I don't. For me a shoe is a shoe is *ein Schuh*.

Next up, the oral exam, which was marginally more pleasant than going to the dentist. Thirty minutes of chatting to the examiner about my life and my job, plus some role playing where I had to order a meal in a restaurant. Now that's something I've had a lot of practice at in German, French and Italian. Much harder was listening to a phone conversation while answering questions about what was being said. I find that difficult in real life let alone in a test.

Reader, I passed. Even allowing for the garden rake incident, I did it – and have the certificate to prove it. On to Step two.

A month later, it's colder and darker but I'm back outside the same exam room, this time to test my knowledge of

Switzerland, alongside 31 other would-be citizens. Naturally, I'm hoping that having researched and written this book I can pass, but it may not be as easy as that. The problem is there is no way of knowing what they will ask. In Britain there is a nationwide government exam, with a course book and practice tests so that you stand a good chance of preparing properly. In Switzerland, next to nothing.

Only two cantons (Bern and Aargau) currently have an official written test – the rest are usually oral interviews – and practice tests are hard to come by. Canton Bern has two available online. Two. As for reading material, there isn't much more than two thin booklets. One an annual guide to the confederation from the Federal Government, the other published by the Evangelical Church of Switzerland to help refugees and immigrants. It's better than it sounds. Other than that, the only option is to sign up for the (expensive) citizenship course approved by the canton.

I skipped the course and went straight to the exam. Ninety minutes for 48 multiple choice questions on topics such as geography, history, politics, taxation, education and healthcare (there are sample questions in the Appendix at the end of this book). Some were surprisingly easy, such as naming the fruit William Tell shot off his son's head, though alarmingly one option was a cherry; he would've needed to be an expert marksman to see a cherry let alone hit it with an arrow. Or knowing the date of Swiss National Day, or recognising a picture of Roger Federer. Others were more taxing, relating to social security, the economy and pension plans. Even so, most of us were finished well within the allotted time so could leave with a sigh of relief.

Reader, I passed again – and have a second certificate to prove it. Now I could actually fill out the application form to start the official naturalisation process. Everything up until this moment was just foreplay.

BECOMING SWISS

The process of becoming Swiss is like most things in Switzerland: the rules will depend on where you live. While there are federal regulations, the cantons and municipalities can decide for themselves what else is required, how long it takes and how much it will cost. That's because you actually have to be accepted by your municipality (and by extension your canton) before you can become a Swiss citizen. In other words, I have to be Bernese before I can be Swiss.

At federal level the basic rules were streamlined for 2018, cutting two years off the minimum residency time and standardising the necessary language levels. For a normal naturalisation you must:[1]

✤ have lived in Switzerland for ten years, with three of them being within the last five years;
✤ have a residency permit C (the highest possible for a foreigner);
✤ be successfully integrated in Switzerland;
✤ be able to speak one of the national languages to a certified level (A2 for written, B1 for spoken);
✤ prove you have no criminal record, no debts and no outstanding taxes due;
✤ respect the values of the Swiss Constitution and not endanger Switzerland's internal or external security;
✤ participate in economic life, or be in education or training, and not be in receipt of any benefits;
✤ be familiar with a Swiss lifestyle and know about Swiss geography, history, politics and society;
✤ participate in the social and cultural life of Switzerland;
✤ maintain contact with Swiss nationals.

These fairly broad brushstrokes apply nationally, but it is up to each canton and municipality to decide how to implement them. As we have seen, cantons Bern and Aargau have a written exam to test the knowledge of Switzerland, whereas others don't. Up until these new rules (i.e. until December 2017), most cantons also did not have written language tests but merely an oral one instead. Written tests or not, municipalities require that you also pass a naturalisation interview, which involves being grilled by one or more officials on why you want to be Swiss, what you know about your local area and who your friends are (aside from your character references who have to be Swiss and local). Visits to your home used to be the norm, as anyone who's seen the wonderful Swiss film from the 1970s, *Die Schweizermacher*, can testify. Today such visits are far less common, though some places do not rule them out.

Small details can vary, for example Canton Bern requires that as well as not currently receiving any benefits, if you have received any in the past decade, you must pay them all back before you can apply.[2] Local residency requirements within the ten-year minimum can differ hugely: most cantons require five years' residency, with at least three in the municipality where you are applying, but it's only two years in Zurich or Geneva and at least eight in St Gallen.[3] Move to another canton, or in some cases to another town in the same canton, and you might well have to start again from zero. No wonder people don't move house very often.

And of course the costs and timings are as variable as everything else. The fixed federal fee is 100 francs for an adult, but on top of that come the cantonal and municipal fees, which generally add over 2,500 francs.[4] That's not including paying for each certificate needed for proof of residency, lack of criminal record, taxes, debts, etc. As for timings, most cantons estimate it takes about 18 months to two years for the whole process.

For foreigners born here, e.g. any *Secondos*, nearly all these rules still apply. The big difference is that the ten-year residency requirement is easier to reach as from age 8 to 18 the years lived here count double.[5] You also don't have to take a language exam if you can show that a national language is your mother tongue or you had at least five years' schooling here. Other than that, it's the same including proving that you're integrated and paying all the fees. A vote in 2017 made it slightly easier for third-generation immigrants (i.e. children of *Secondos* whose grandparents settled here) to become Swiss, though they still have to fulfil basic criteria.

If you're married to a Swiss national, it's much simpler as you can use facilitated naturalisation. For starters, minimum residency is five years, though you must also have 'lived in a stable marriage with your spouse for at least three years'[6] – bad news for on–off couples in tempestuous relationships. Then your language levels are tested but not your knowledge of Switzerland.[7] Oh, and it's cheaper: usually a mere 900 francs. Sadly this simpler, cheaper version is not available to same-sex couples in a civil partnership. They have to follow all the standard naturalisation rules, except for being able to apply after only five years' residency.

Once you have ticked all the boxes, filled in the forms, provided the certificates, paid your dues, passed the interview and proved you are worthy, then comes the final part. The vote. Yes, this is Switzerland so your fate is decided by a vote. It is citizenship by direct democracy, which is very Swiss.

CHOOSING THE CITIZENS

In theory it sounds perfectly reasonable. Before you can be approved by the canton or country, you first have to be accepted by your local community. And what better – or more

Swiss – way to show that acceptance than a vote by your friends and neighbours (and strangers) in said community. Citizenship by popular acceptance. How this actually happens depends on where you live.

One thing that is no longer allowed is a secret ballot, which was ruled unconstitutional in 2003 by the Federal Supreme Court after it was shown that one municipality in Canton Lucerne unfairly rejected applicants from the Balkans.[8] Some smaller municipalities still have public votes at general assemblies, while in others it's the local parliament that decides, but most choose to use a naturalisation committee to approve applications. In some places, applicants' names also appear in the local paper so that everyone is informed. Rather like the way planning permission works in some countries.

In practice the system works well enough, although it is far from perfect. Any process that allows prejudice to creep in is open to abuse, and voting on citizenship is no exception. Cases of unfair dismissal regularly make the headlines, such as these two in 2017. Dutch-born Nancy Holten had lived in Switzerland since she was eight, spoke fluent Swiss German and fulfilled all the relevant criteria. But voters in her municipality rejected her application. Twice. As a strict vegan she'd annoyed people by campaigning against cow bells and Sunday roasts. She appealed to the canton, which overruled the vote and she became Swiss.[9]

Or the case of Funda Yilmaz, a 25-year-old engineer born and raised in Switzerland but with Turkish parents. She was rejected by the local parliament after failing her interview. For example, she couldn't name the village shop (like most Swiss people she went to Migros or Coop), she didn't know where to recycle oil and when asked to name a traditional Swiss sport said 'skiing' (instead of *Schwingen* or *Hornussen*). She appealed, the decision was reversed and she is now Swiss.[10]

What it boils down to is that you can pass the tests, speak the language, fulfil all the preconditions and might still be rejected because you don't fit in. It doesn't help that there are no standardised national tests, unlike in Britain, so acceptance could be decided by emotional reactions rather than empirical results. This unquantifiable element of politics over procedure is possibly one reason why naturalisation rates in Switzerland are relatively low. That alongside the time, cost and complexity of the process for applicants.

In 2016 only 42,974 foreigners became Swiss,[11] which given the vast numbers of foreigners living here isn't that many. In absolute terms, it's twice as many as 20 years ago but in relation to the numbers of foreigners living here, it's 2 per cent, or below the EU average of 2.4 per cent.[12] Data from the Federal Statistics Office shows that almost one million foreigners in Switzerland are eligible for naturalisation, as they've lived here for more than ten years,[13] not forgetting all the *Secondos* born here.

A glimpse at the figures for Canton Bern is revealing, considering it's the second largest canton in terms of population. In 2014 Bern introduced stricter naturalisation rules, including written tests and obligatory repayment of any benefits received. As a result, naturalisation numbers halved compared to just three years before, and dropped 80 per cent compared to eight years earlier. The goal had been achieved: make it harder for foreigners to become Swiss and fewer will succeed.

Having the municipalities and cantons in charge of the process means that naturalisation can be a lottery based on where you live. Given that I am only just setting off down the long and winding road to citizenship in Bern, I asked two fellow Brits in other parts of the country about their experiences.

A TALE OF TWO BRITS

At the most recent count, there were 41,471 Brits living in Switzerland.[14] Many are married to Swiss nationals, while some were born in Switzerland, but the rest are simply here on a residency visa. That used to be straightforward, thanks to free movement of people under the bilateral treaties between Switzerland and the EU (and so by default with the UK). The Brexit vote changed all that. Brits in Switzerland soon realised that their visas would be directly affected by the outcome of the Brexit negotiations, even though they were unlikely to be covered by any final agreement as they live outside the EU. With no concrete information to rely on, and the Brexit negotiations an ongoing mess, more than a few British permanent residents decided to settle their status and apply to become Swiss. My friends Jackie and Paula were two of them.

Jackie moved to Switzerland 17 years ago, settling in the French-speaking part because of her (British) husband's job. She learnt the language, made Swiss friends, found work and created a life for herself, so the natural next step was to become Swiss. That began in November 2016 with no written exams or a formal language test, just two short interviews with immigration officials and the police. Then the deluge of obligatory paperwork, plus a motivational statement on why she wanted to become Swiss. A year later came the crucial interview with the naturalisation committee. 'It was more interrogation than interview,' she told me after she had been grilled for over an hour. 'But,' she joked, 'at least I didn't have to do what someone in a nearby village had to do. Her "interview" was in a local restaurant and she had to make a fondue for the panel.' In hindsight, that might've been better as Jackie failed her interview. Swiss politics was her undoing, especially not being able to name the members of the cantonal government, though few Swiss citizens would be able to manage that either. She decided not to appeal but instead take a citizenship course and try again next year.

Over in Canton Zurich, Paula married her Swiss husband eight years ago, meaning that she could apply for facilitated naturalisation, a decision she made the day after the Brexit vote. In May 2017 she sent in her application, along with all the necessary documentation, but there were no formal tests. Her one interview was at the police station in September, with questions ranging from Swiss geography and sports to her hobbies and interest in politics. She wasn't required to provide official proof of her language skills, though she had no problem with the interview in High German. As she pointed out: 'My American friend's German was so poor, the interview was conducted in English.' As I write this, Paula is hoping for final approval, which involves waiting for 30 days to see if anyone objects to her becoming Swiss.

Both women applied before the new federal naturalisation rules came into force in 2018, hence the lack of official language tests in each case. That aside, together they show that there is no such thing as a normal naturalisation procedure in Switzerland. At the very least there are 26 variations, thanks to cantonal differences, but more likely there are many hundreds of possible permutations, given that there are over 2,200 municipalities in Switzerland. The new federal rules create the basic structure but local politics is what really determines the naturalisation process in each community.

Paula's experience is a far cry from how foreign women used to get citizenship via marriage. I once met an elderly British woman who told me her new Swiss passport was ready and waiting for her on her wedding day back in the sixties. That's because when a foreign woman married a Swiss man she automatically became Swiss, whereas a Swiss woman marrying a foreigner automatically lost her Swiss nationality.[15] These unbelievably sexist laws weren't finally changed until

1992.[16] Now equality rules and all Swiss citizens can be dual nationals with any other country (assuming the other country allows that), at least for the moment. A new popular initiative from the SVP is seeking to ban dual nationality, forcing everyone to be Swiss and Swiss alone.

FACING THE FUTURE

For the past decade or so I have been an expat, an immigrant, an outsider, a foreigner. Now I have started the process of changing that and becoming Swiss. But, even once I have that famous red passport, for some Swiss I will still be a foreigner, one referred to as a *Papierli-Schweizer*, or a person who's only Swiss on paper. Luckily I won't be alone in that. Almost 850,000 Swiss citizens were not born that way, i.e. they became Swiss through naturalisation.[17] That's a lot of people in the same boat as me. Many of them will have faced the same questions I'm now asking myself. Questions about home and belonging.

The twenty-first century has transformed expat life. I don't have to read three-day-old English papers, wait for letters to come in the post, or watch badly dubbed television programmes. Thanks to modern technology I can watch BBC1, read *The Guardian* online, text my friends and talk to my family on Skype. Living in Switzerland is actually not that different from living in Britain, except that the trains run on time, there's less litter in the streets and the chocolate is better.

The funny thing is that when I do go back to Britain, it no longer feels quite the same, like I'm back home but not really. That's when I feel that I have slowly become more Swiss. I haven't changed so much that I no longer talk to strangers about the weather or have forgotten how to form an orderly queue, but little things are enough to trigger a sensation of not being 100 per cent British any more: smiling when the cash machine gives you only small notes, spending ages trying to find the @ sign on an English-language keyboard, and feeling relieved that Harrison Ford has his real voice on television. Or just being amazed at very ordinary moments, such as shopping on a Sunday, walking down escalators easily because everyone else is standing on the right, and hearing people whistle in public. Pretty much how it must feel to be one of the 35,000 Swiss expats living in Britain[18] or the 940,000 Swiss who visit every year.[19]

The biggest change is, of course, that punctuality has become a way of life. I am now so used to Swiss public transport that anything else feels distinctly inferior. It's a sure sign of my inner Swissness that I relish landing at Zurich or Geneva airport. Not just because I am home, but because I love that little info screen at the luggage carousel, the one that tells you when the next trains are leaving. Such a great example of attention to detail. So simple, so helpful, so Swiss.

It's clear that Switzerland is definitely my home now. I wouldn't want to live anywhere else and can't imagine why I would leave. It's not perfect but it suits me perfectly, not least because it's endlessly fascinating to live here as an outsider on the inside. But as an outsider trying to become an insider, I have to face the fact that it's no longer just up to me. My (soon-to-be) fellow Swiss will decide if I can join their ranks, meaning my future is not entirely in my hands anymore but perhaps I can get an inkling of that future by looking at the recent past, at the Swiss reactions to this book.

When the first edition was published, I asked myself: would the Swiss want to read a book about them written by an Englishman? The answer was immediately yes! *Swiss Watching* became the bestselling English book of the year (and has carried on selling). It wasn't only expats who were buying it – the Swiss themselves lapped it up. Within a few weeks I was getting emails from happy readers all over

Switzerland and beyond. It seems that the Swiss, like any other nation, love to discover how others see them, especially if that 'other' is living amongst them.

That so many people took the time to email me was surprising. But that was nothing compared to the physical, rather than virtual, response. Positive feedback jumped out at me, no matter where I was: on the tram in Bern, walking down a Geneva street, in a Zurich supermarket, on a mountain path. At first I wasn't sure about this new-found openness from Swiss strangers; I couldn't help but question what lay behind this uncharacteristic spontaneity. Maybe they thought they knew me a little after reading my book? Or having heard me on national radio or seen one of the many articles in the newspapers, they saw me as more approachable? Whatever the reasons, at a time when politics in Switzerland can seem ever more anti-foreigner, it's refreshing and heartening that so many Swiss want to interact with this foreigner on a personal level.

But it is true that you can't please all the people all the time. Some people didn't like the book because I'm a foreigner, others because I'm gay. Some didn't like it because I'm a foreigner writing about Switzerland (kind of missing the point) and, for the really special ones, it was because I was a gay foreigner writing about Switzerland. But for every negative there were 99 positives, not least helping the Swiss laugh more in public: one person said, 'my sudden outbreaks of laughter earned strange looks from people around me; (they must have been Swiss as well).' And perhaps the most fascinating aspect was people agreeing with what I'd written but then stating that they were the exception. It happened at almost every event around Switzerland where I spoke or read – and still does, whether I'm in Lausanne, Lucerne or Lugano. That makes me smile every time.

Perhaps the most common question has been: did I now feel that Switzerland was my home? As an expat, that's always a hard one to answer. No matter how far you go and how long you stay away, the place where you grew up will always be a part of you. But equally, the longer you live in another country, especially one you love, the more it begins to feel like the right place to be. It's often said that home is where the heart is, and my heart belongs to Switzerland. Now I need to wait and see if Switzerland will accept my heart. Watch this space . . .

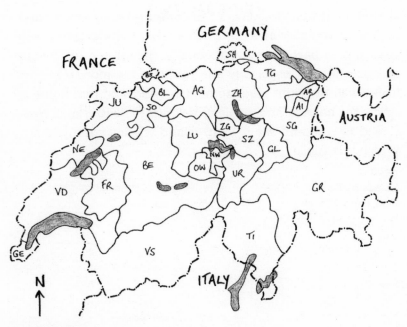

L= LIECHTENSTEIN

ALL BORDERS HAVE BEEN SIMPLIFIED

AG-AARGAU
AI-APPENZELL INNERRHODEN
AR-APPENZELL AUSSERRHODEN
BE-BERN
BL-BASEL-LAND
BS-BASEL-STADT
FR-FRIBOURG
GE-GENEVA
GL-GLARUS
GR-GRAUBÜNDEN
JU-JURA
LU-LUCERNE
NE-NEUCHÂTEL

NW-NIDWALDEN
OW-OBWALDEN
SG-ST GALLEN
SH-SCHAFFHAUSEN
SO-SOLOTHURN
SZ-SCHWYZ
TG-THURGAU
TI-TICINO
UR-URI
VD-VAUD
VS-VALAIS
ZG-ZUG
ZH-ZURICH

APPENDIX I

Switzerland and its 26 cantons in alphabetical order:

Switzerland
Standard abbreviation: CH　　Date of foundation: 1291
Capital: Bern　　Area: 41,285 km²
Population: 8,419,550　　Foreigners: 25%
Population density per km²: 203.9
Religion:
Catholic 37.3%　　Protestant 24.9%
No religion 23.9%　　Muslim 5.1%
National languages:
German 63%　　French 22.7%
Italian 8.1%　　Romansh 0.5%

Aargau
Standard abbreviation: AG　　Date of entry: 1803
Capital: Aarau　　Area: 1404 km²
Population: 663,462　　Foreigners: 24.7%
Population density per km²: 475.6
Religion:　　Catholic and Protestant
Language:　　German

Appenzell Ausserrhoden
Standard abbreviation: AR　　Date of entry: 1513*
Capital: Herisau　　Area: 243 km²
Population: 54,954　　Foreigners: 16.2%
Population density per km²: 226.3
Religion:　　Protestant
Language:　　German

Appenzell Innerrhoden
Standard abbreviation: AI　　Date of entry: 1513*
Capital: Appenzell　　Area: 172 km²
Population: 16,003　　Foreigners: 11.1%
Population density per km²: 92.8
Religion:　　Catholic
Language:　　German

*The two half-cantons of Appenzell split in 1597

Basel-Land

Standard abbreviation: BL
Capital: Liestal
Population: 285,624
Population density per km²: 551.7
Religion:
Language:

Date of entry: 1501*
Area: 517 km²
Foreigners: 22.3%

Protestant
German

Basel-Stadt

Standard abbreviation: BS
Capital: Basel
Population: 193,070
Population density per km²: 5,225.2
Religion:
Language:

Date of entry: 1501*
Area: 37 km²
Foreigners: 35.8%

Protestant
German

*The two half-cantons of Basel split in 1833

Bern

Standard abbreviation: BE
Capital: Bern
Population: 1,026,513
Population density per km²: 175.8
Religion:
Languages:

Date of entry: 1353
Area: 5959 km²
Foreigners: 16.1%

Protestant
German and French

Fribourg

Standard abbreviation: FR
Capital: Fribourg
Population: 311,914
Population density per km²: 195.8
Religion:
Languages:

Date of entry: 1481
Area: 1671 km²
Foreigners: 22.4%

Catholic
French and German

Geneva

Standard abbreviation: GE
Capital: Geneva
Population: 489,524
Population density per km²: 1,991.4
Religion:
Language:

Date of entry: 1815
Area: 282 km²
Foreigners: 40.2%

Protestant
French

Glarus

Standard abbreviation: GL
Capital: Glarus
Population: 40,147
Population density per km²: 59
Religion:
Language:

Date of entry: 1352
Area: 685 km²
Foreigners: 23.7%

Protestant
German

Graubünden

Standard abbreviation: GR
Capital: Chur
Population: 197,550
Population density per km²: 27.8
Religion:
Languages:

Date of entry: 1803
Area: 7105 km²
Foreigners: 18.5%

Catholic and Protestant
German, Italian and Romansh

Jura

Standard abbreviation: JU
Capital: Delémont
Population: 73,122
Population density per km²: 87.2
Religion:
Language:

Date of entry: 1979
Area: 838 km²
Foreigners: 14.6%

Catholic
French

Lucerne

Standard abbreviation: LU
Capital: Lucerne
Population: 403,397
Population density per km²: 282.3
Religion:
Language:

Date of entry: 1332
Area: 1493 km²
Foreigners: 18.4%

Catholic
German

Neuchâtel

Standard abbreviation: NE
Capital: Neuchâtel
Population: 178,567
Population density per km²: 249.1
Religion:
Language:

Date of entry: 1815
Area: 803 km²
Foreigners: 25.6%

Protestant
French

Nidwalden

Standard abbreviation: NW   Date of entry: 1291*
Capital: Stans   Area: 276 km²
Population: 42,556   Foreigners: 14.2%
Population density per km²: 176.3
Religion: Catholic
Language: German

Obwalden

Standard abbreviation: OW   Date of entry: 1291*
Capital: Sarnen   Area: 490 km²
Population: 37,378   Foreigners: 14.7%
Population density per km²: 77.8
Religion: Catholic
Language: German

*The two half-cantons (together known as Unterwalden) have always
  been separate

Schaffhausen

Standard abbreviation: SH   Date of entry: 1501
Capital: Schaffhausen   Area: 298 km²
Population: 80,769   Foreigners: 25.9%
Population density per km²: 270.9
Religion: Protestant
Language: German

Schwyz

Standard abbreviation: SZ   Date of entry: 1291
Capital: Schwyz   Area: 908 km²
Population: 155,863   Foreigners: 20.7%
Population density per km²: 183.1
Religion: Catholic
Language: German

Solothurn

Standard abbreviation: SO   Date of entry: 1481
Capital: Solothurn   Area: 791 km²
Population: 269,441   Foreigners: 22%
Population density per km²: 340.9
Religion: Catholic
Language: German

St Gallen

Standard abbreviation: SG   Date of entry: 1803
Capital: St Gallen   Area: 2026 km²
Population: 502,552   Foreigners: 23.8%
Population density per km²: 257.6
Religion: Catholic
Language: German

Thurgau

Standard abbreviation: TG   Date of entry: 1803
Capital: Frauenfeld   Area: 991 km²
Population: 270,709   Foreigners: 24.5%
Population density per km²: 313.6
Religion: Protestant
Language: German

Ticino

Standard abbreviation: TI   Date of entry: 1803
Capital: Bellinzona   Area: 2812 km²
Population: 354,375   Foreigners: 28.1%
Population density per km²: 129.3
Religion: Catholic
Language: Italian

Uri

Standard abbreviation: UR   Date of entry: 1291
Capital: Altdorf   Area: 1077 km²
Population: 36,145   Foreigners: 11.9%
Population density per km²: 34.2
Religion: Catholic
Language: German

Valais

Standard abbreviation: VS   Date of entry: 1815
Capital: Sion   Area: 5224 km²
Population: 339,176   Foreigners: 23.2%
Population density per km²: 65.1
Religion: Catholic
Languages: French and German

Vaud

Standard abbreviation: VD   Date of entry: 1803
Capital: Lausanne   Area: 3212 km²
Population: 784,822   Foreigners: 33.6%
Population density per km²: 278.2
Religion: Protestant
Language: French

Zug

Standard abbreviation: ZG   Date of entry: 1352
Capital: Zug   Area: 239 km²
Population: 123,948   Foreigners: 27.5%
Population density per km²: 598.3
Religion: Catholic
Language: German

Zurich

Standard abbreviation: ZH   Date of entry: 1351
Capital: Zurich   Area: 1729 km²
Population: 1,487,969   Foreigners: 26.6%
Population density per km²: 895.9
Religion: Protestant
Language: German

All data from Federal Statistical Office, 2018.

APPENDIX II

CAN YOU PASS THE SWISSNESS TEST?

These sample questions were taken from official citizenship tests in Bern and Aargau, the only cantons that currently have a written exam. Other cantons ask similar questions but in an interview without multiple choice answers. All the answers can be found somewhere in *Swiss Watching*, but we also give them at the end of the test. To pass you need to get at least 15 out of 24 correct.

Section One: Geography and history

1. How many cantons (including half-cantons) are there in Switzerland?
   - A. 21
   - B. 22
   - C. 26
   - D. 28

2. What made Henri Dunant famous?
   - A. He founded the Red Cross
   - B. He founded the Nobel Prize
   - C. He was the first Federal Councillor from Geneva
   - D. He was the first man to climb Mont Blanc

3. When did women get the right to vote at federal level?
   - A. 1971
   - B. 1945
   - C. 1979
   - D. 1919

4. In which three cantons are French and German the two official languages?
   - A. Fribourg, Geneva and Valais
   - B. Lucerne, Graubünden and Bern
   - C. Neuchâtel, Solothurn and Basel
   - D. Bern, Fribourg and Valais

5. What was the name of the Swiss Reformer in the sixteenth century?
   A. Jan Hus
   B. Heinrich Pestalozzi
   C. Ulrich Zwingli
   D. Henri Dufour

6. Which canton has the largest area?
   A. Vaud
   B. Graubünden
   C. Zurich
   D. Valais

7. Which international organisation did Switzerland join in 2002?
   A. United Nations
   B. NATO
   C. European Union
   D. OECD

8. What is the largest lake entirely within Switzerland?
   A. Lake Thun
   B. Lake Lucerne
   C. Lake Neuchâtel
   D. Lake Geneva

Section Two: Democracy and federalism

9. Who elects the Federal Supreme Court?
   A. The Federal Council
   B. The voters
   C. The Swiss Federal Assembly
   D. The Council of States

10. If I want all of Switzerland to have a minimum wage, what do I have to do first?
    A. Collect 100,000 signatures in 100 days to launch a popular initiative
    B. Collect 50,000 signatures in 18 months to launch a popular initiative
    C. Launch a referendum then collect 50,000 signatures in 100 days
    D. Collect 100,000 signatures in 18 months to launch a popular initiative

11. How many members does the Federal Council have?
    A. 7
    B. 5 plus the president
    C. 8
    D. 9

12. Swiss municipalities are responsible for?
    A. Foreign affairs
    B. Planning permission
    C. The military
    D. The motorways

13. What does 'federalism' mean in Switzerland?
    A. All duties of the state are carried out by the cantons and mutually agreed by them
    B. The cantons promote and support each other
    C. Municipalities, cantons and the state all have the same duties
    D. Cantons are sovereign except where their sovereignty is limited by the constitution

14. What is a double majority in a referendum or initiative?
    A. When both houses of parliament vote in favour
    B. When the Yes vote has to be twice the No vote
    C. When there needs to be a majority in both the popular vote and the cantonal vote
    D. When the people and parliament both vote in favour

15. How often is the Swiss Federal Parliament elected?
    A. Every 4 years   C. Every 2 years
    B. Every 6 years   D. Every 7 years

16. Which of these statements about the Swiss President is *not* true?
    A. He/she is elected for a one-year term
    B. He/she is elected by both houses of parliament together
    C. He/she has to be a member of the Federal Council
    D. He/she is elected for a four-year term

Section Three: Health and employment

17. Which sector of the economy has the largest percentage of foreign workers?
    A. Construction   C. Hospitality
    B. Agriculture   D. Manufacturing

18. Which insurance is automatically deducted from a worker's wages?
    A. Health insurance
    B. Unemployment insurance
    C. Theft insurance
    D. Car insurance

19. Which of these is a public holiday in every canton?
    A. Good Friday   C. St Berchtold's Day
    B. All Saints' Day   D. Christmas Day

20. What is the emergency telephone number for an ambulance?
    A. 114   C. 144
    B. 444   D. 411

21. When was the last General Strike in Switzerland?
    A. 1918   C. 1968
    B. 1850   D. 1945

22. How can you reduce your health insurance premium?
    A. Take a policy with a higher *Franchise*
    B. Take a policy with a lower *Franchise*
    C. Opt for having only private treatment
    D. Buy it at the same time as travel insurance

23. Which federal department covers health and social security?
    A. Finance
    B. Justice and Police
    C. Home Affairs
    D. Economic Affairs and Education

24 What are the three main elements in the Swiss pension system?
    A. Employee pension scheme, private pension, tax deductions for
       the over-70s
    B. Health insurance, state pension contribution, private pension
    C. State pension contribution, invalidity insurance, health
       insurance
    D. State pension contribution, employee pension scheme, private
       pension

17:C, 18:B, 19:D, 20:C, 21:A, 22:A, 23:C, 24:D
9:C, 10:D, 11:A, 12:B, 13:D, 14:C, 15:A, 16:D
1:C, 2:A, 3:A, 4:D, 5:C, 6:B, 7:A, 8:C
Answers

NOTES

Chapter One: The landlocked island

1 Italian and French speakers usually manage more than just a name, or don't use a name at all.
2 English used to have you and thou, which roughly correlated to *Sie/vous* and *du/tu*.
3 Saline de Bex: *Salzmonopol*.
4 Federal Statistical Office: German 63% of the population, French 22.7%, Italian 8.1% and Romansh 0.5%.
5 Liechtenstein also shares a short border with Switzerland and is not an EU member.
6 swissinfo.org.
7 The top three are Great Britain, Iceland and Ireland.
8 In 1999.
9 blick.ch report, 9.8.2009.
10 Part of the Monte Rosa massif, the mountain is shared between Italy and Switzerland.
11 Dufour Peak is 4634m, Lake Maggiore 193m above sea level.
12 glacierexpress.ch.
13 *Ibid.*
14 meteoschweiz.ch.
15 Swiss Federal Office of Energy.
16 meteoschweiz.ch. Highest in Grono (GR) on 11.8.2003; lowest in La Brévine (NE) on 12.1.1987.
17 meteoschweiz.ch.
18 In German, Romandie is known as *Westschweiz* or *Welschland*.
19 ecopop.ch.
20 ONS: 450 people per square kilometre.
21 worldbank.org: 505 people per square kilometre.
22 Federal Statistical Office: *Sprachen*.
23 *Ibid.*
24 bloomberg,com article, March 2007.
25 In 1803.
26 For a complete list see the appendix.
27 *Mercer Quality of Living Survey 2017*: Zurich 2nd, Geneva 8th, Basel 10th.

Chapter Two: Stepping back through time
1 *Weg der Schweiz.*
2 *Ibid.*
3 swissworld.org: National Day.
4 wandern.ch.
5 *Ibid.*: road total 71,400km.
6 statista.com: including Pyeongchang 2018.
7 gardasvizzera.va.
8 *Ibid.*
9 swissinfo.ch.
10 *Coop Zeitung* Nr 28, 7.7.2004.
11 swissinfo.ch report, 26.7.2004.
12 perrier.com.
13 swissinfo.ch.

Chapter Three: In the land of cocks and crosses
1 feiertagskalender.ch.
2 foodreference.com.
3 Federal Statistical Office: *Wahlen 2015.*
4 swissrecycling.ch; *The Guardian.*
5 *PET-Recycling Schweiz.*
6 *Daily Telegraph*, 12.4.2017.
7 petcore.org: Recycled products.
8 *Mercer Cost of Living Survey 2017.*
9 Federal Statistical Office.
10 *Ibid.*
11 *Ibid.* (Swiss population: 36% Catholic, 31% Protestant).
12 *Ibid.*
13 *Ibid.*
14 Federal Statistical Office; UK figure 4.8% (ONS)
15 Federal Statistical Office.
16 srf.ch.
17 Kanton Bern Staatskanzlei: Kirchensteuergesetz, Art 11.2.

Chapter Four: Ask the audience
1 Except when it clashes with Easter; then it moves a week.
2 Appenzell Innerrhoden official website.
3 NZZ Online report, 26.4.2009.
4 Appenzell Innerrhoden official website.
5 Federal Chancellery: *Volksinitiativen.*
6 *The Swiss Confederation: A Brief Guide.*

NOTES

7   Kanton Bern Staatskanzlei.
8   Chancellerie d'Etat du canton de Fribourg.
9   Kanton Aargau Wahlbüro.
10 20 full votes plus 6 half-votes makes a total of 23, so a majority has to be 12.
11 swissworld.org.
12 Federal Statistical Office, 1 January 2018.
13 In 2013 a popular initiative to change Federal Council elections to a popular vote failed: 76% of voters rejected the proposal (srf.ch).
14 NZZ Online report, 13.12.2007.
15 Das Schweizer Parlament website.
16 Times Online report 2.5.2007, quoting from *Quirkology* by Richard Wiseman.
17 Credit Suisse *Worry Barometer 2017*.
18 Federal Statistical Office.
19 *Ibid.*
20 State Secretariat for Migration.
21 UK Border Agency.
22 escotoday.com.
23 Federal Statistical Office: *Erwerbstätige nach Nationalität 2016*.
24 Front page story in *The Independent* on 7.9.2007.
25 Federal Statistical Office: *Wahlen 2007*.
26 Federal Chancellery: Volksabstimmung 29.11.2009, 57.5% and 22.5 cantons yes.
27 20min.ch.
28 Federal Chancellery, Volksabstimmung 5.6.2005, 58.0% yes.
29 Federal Chancellery, Volksabstimmung 6.12.1992, 50.3% yes.
30 Federal Statistical Office: *Verurteilte Personen*.
31 Office for National Statistics.
32 Statistisches Bundesamt.
33 State Secretariat for Migration: as of 2018; before that it was 12 years.
34 Der Bundesausländerbeauftragte.
35 UK Home Office.
36 Federal Chancellery, Volksabstimmung 28.11.2010, 52.3% yes.
37 Federal Chancellery, Volksabstimmung 14.2.2012, 50.3% yes.
38 Federal Chancellery, Volksabstimmung 28.2.2016, 58.9% no.
39 Gettysburg Address, 19.11.1863.
40 Federal Chancellery: *Nationalratswahlen 2015*.
41 smartvote.ch.
42 *The Swiss Confederation: A Brief Guide.*
43 *Ibid.*

Chapter Five: Wealthy, healthy and wise?

1 Swiss National Bank, 2016 figures.
2 *Switzerland in its Diversity.*
3 Except for immigrants living in Switzerland for less than five years.
4 *Blick am Abend* interview with Hans-Peter Portmann, 2.2.2010.
5 switzerlandcasinos.ch.
6 Federal Statistical Office: 303,000 Germans resident in Switzerland in 2016, up 160,000 since 2004.
7 Some restrictions may apply to nationals of EU countries in Eastern Europe.
8 Bergier Commission report.
9 As quoted in *Living and Working in Switzerland* by David Hampshire.
10 Federal Statistical Office.
11 OECD Health Data. Per capita figures for 2016: USA $9,892; Switzerland $7,919; UK $4,192
12 comparis.ch: 2018 figures.
13 As of December 2009.
14 dignitas.ch.
15 Swiss National Bank.
16 *Ibid* (Old series was 74mm, new series is 70mm).
17 *Ibid.*
18 Swiss Money Museum.
19 1 franc = 100 *rappen,* also known as *centimes* and *centesimi* in the French and Italian speaking parts.
20 Swiss Money Museum, quoting *Schweizerische Numismatische Rundschau.*
21 swissmint.ch: *Paul Burkhard und der Fünfliber.*
22 Federal Statistical Office.
23 IMF World Economic Outlook Database.
24 swissbanking.org.
25 Federal Statistical Office.
26 World Health Organisation 2015.
27 IMF World Economic Outlook Database.

Chapter Six: War and peace

1 Swiss Identity Survey as part of Credit Suisse *Worry Barometer.*
2 Federal Department for Foreign Affairs website: *International Geneva.*
3 swissinfo.ch.
4 Federal Chancellery, Volksabstimmung 3.3.2002, 54.6% yes.

5 *Ibid*: Volksabstimmung 16.3.1986, 24.3% yes.
6 icrc.org.
7 The same Dufour as the civil war general, Swiss flag promoter and highest peak in Switzerland.
8 icrc.org.
9 *Ibid., The Nazi genocide and other persecutions*, adopted 27.4.2006.
10 ICRC Annual report 2016.
11 IMF World Economic Outlook Database.
12 *Switzerland in its Diversity*.
13 Schweizer Armee website: *Zivildienst*.
14 *Frankfurter Allgemeine Zeitung*.
15 *The Swiss Confederation: A Brief Guide*.
16 Schweizer Armee website: *Finanzielle Entschädigung*.
17 *Switzerland in its Diversity*.
18 srf.ch: highest is Finland.
19 Small Arms Survey.
20 watson.ch.
21 20 Minuten: report 10.11.2017.
22 SECO Staatssekretariat für Wirtschaft.
23 nationmaster.com, quoting SIPRI Stockholm International Peace Research Institute.
24 blick.ch, 11.12.2008.
25 Federal Chancellery, Volksabstimmung 26.11.1989, 35.6% yes.
26 swissinfo.ch.

Chapter Seven: Made in Switzerland

1 victorinox.ch.
2 swissinfo.ch: report 4.1.2007.
3 Virtual Absinthe Museum.
4 Federal Chancellery, Volksabstimmung 5.7.1908, 63.5% yes.
5 Virtual Absinthe Museum.
6 *A History of Mathematical Notations* by Florian Cajori.
7 BBC News online report 30.4.2008.
8 Nestlé Research.
9 Oxo's History.
10 Unilever Food Solutions: Knorr History.
11 Foundation Dr J.E. Brandenberger.
12 *Ibid*.
13 *Ibid*.
14 kristofcreative.com/great_ideas/invention-of-aluminum-foil.shtml.
15 Broxo (Swiss Healthcare Solutions).

16 Düring AG.
17 Die Offizielle Schweizer Hitparade.
18 *Ibid.*
19 BBC News Online report, 24.7.2000.
20 *Coop Zeitung* survey, 29.7.2008.
21 Federation of the Swiss Watch Industry report 2017.
22 *Ibid.*
23 Federation of the Swiss Watch Industry: History.
24 *Ibid.*
25 unesco.org.
26 *Ibid.*
27 Federation of the Swiss Watch Industry.
28 guebelin.ch.
29 Federal Statistical Office: *Vornamen-Hitparade.*
30 *Ibid.*
31 vornamen.ch/namensrecht-schweiz.htm.
32 babycenter.ch.
33 biel-bienne.ch.
34 *Blick am Abend* report, 7.5.2009. Swiss brands: Emmentaler, Gruyère, M-Budget, Migros, Nespresso, Ovolmatine, Ragusa, Rivella, Swatch, Thomy, Toblerone, Zweifel. Non-Swiss brands: Coca-Cola, Google, Ikea, Kellogg's, Lego, Nivea, Nutella.
35 Superbrands.co.uk.

Chapter Eight: The hole truth

1 *Emmerdale* is an English television soap opera set in a fictional Yorkshire village of the same name.
2 SBB timetable.
3 Stade de Suisse.
4 Jörg Abderhalden website.
5 Emmentaler official website.
6 *Ibid.*
7 *Ibid.*
8 Swiss Cheese Marketing.
9 bilanz.ch.
10 Tilsiter official website.
11 Sbrinz official website.
12 appenzell.ch/en/.
13 *Der Bund.*
14 *St Galler Tagblatt.*
15 Federal Statistical Office.

16 Appenzeller, Emmentaler, Gruyère.

17 swissmilk.ch.

18 schweizerkaese.ch.

19 International Dairy Federation: EU average 18.3kg.

20 *Ibid*.: UK consumption 12.1kg.

Chapter Nine: Where the chocolate comes from

1 telegraph.co.uk article, 27.9.2009.

2 nestle.com.

3 lindt.com; Lindt was bought by Zurich-based Sprüngli in 1899.

4 Interview on WRS radio with Daniel Meyer.

5 *Ibid*.

6 *Chocology* booklet, published by Chocosuisse.

7 Chocosuisse (2016 figures).

8 *Ibid*.

9 The Association of Swiss Chocolate Manufacturers.

10 *Ibid*.

11 *Ibid*.

12 *Ibid*.

13 *Ibid*.

14 Die Welt von Suchard exhibition, Neuchâtel.

15 alptransit.ch.

16 *Ibid*.

17 Ticino Regional Railway and Bus Services.

18 See Chapter Eight: The hole truth.

19 *NZZ Folio* article.

20 bettybossi.ch.

21 rivella.ch.

22 NZZ online article.

23 swissfruit.ch.

24 Thurgau official website.

25 Coop and Migros both have cheap, cheerful cafeteria-style restaurants.

Chapter Ten: Climb every mountain

1 sbb.ch.

2 Office of Rail and Road.

3 srf.ch.

4 swissinfo.org.

5 Federal Chancellery, Volksabstimmung 20.2.1898, 67.9% yes.

6 rigi.ch.

7 pilatus.ch.

8 brienz-rothorn-bahn.ch.

9 swissworld.org.

10 Federal Statistical Office.

11 postbus.ch: Facts & Figures.

12 SBB Annual Report.

13 On some tourist trains, e.g. the Glacier Express, reservations are obligatory.

14 Also AG in French or Italian, short for *abonnement générale* or *abbonamento generale*.

15 The train up Rigi is included in the GA, unusually for a mountain train.

16 sbb.ch.

17 SBB Annual Report.

18 January 2018 rate £1=1.35Fr.

19 £2616 from tfl.gov.uk.

20 sbb.ch.

21 *Ibid.*

22 See Chapter One for more on coconuts.

23 sbb.ch: for groups of 10 or more, 20% discount on the tickets and every 10th person travels free

24 interlaken.ch: Facts & Figures.

25 jungfrau-marathon.ch.

26 BOB = Berner Oberland-Bahn; WAB = Wengernalpbahn.

27 blick.ch.

28 Federal Statistical Office.

29 Eurostat.

30 BBC news report, 7.1.2010.

Chapter Eleven: Seeking Heidi

1 In the minaret vote of November 2009, only 3½ cantons voted no – Geneva, Neuchâtel, Vaud and Basel-Stadt; in the failed EEA vote of 1992, all the French-speaking cantons were heavily in favour.

2 In Romandie, the French announcement comes first.

3 Trains to Ticino and Italy have Italian announcements.

4 Also spelt *Schwyzerdütsch* or *Schwiizertüütsch* depending on dialect.

5 Chicken, pavement and bicycle respectively, or *Huhn*, *Fussweg* and *Fahrrad* in High German.

6 Note that four of the ten are French speakers (Calvin, Dunant, Guisan, Rousseau), just above the average for the country as a whole. No Italian Swiss in the list.

7 See Chapter Seven for more on LSD.

8 English translation: 'But now, Lord, what do I look for? My hope is in you.'

9 For more on Dunant see Chapter Six.

10 Translates as Swiss Institute for Children's and Youth Media.

11 hirzel.ch.

12 18%, according to hirzel.ch.

13 *UN Demographic Yearbook.*

14 Data from beobachter.ch report *Typisch Schweiz.*

15 Property in Switzerland is always marketed using the number of rooms. The kitchen and bathroom usually don't count as 'rooms', so that a two-room flat is effectively a one-bedroom flat. But you can get half-rooms, meaning that the kitchen or hall is bigger than normal, e.g. I live in a 4½-room flat.

16 Swiss Identity Survey as part of Credit Suisse *Worry Barometer 2017*: 90% proud or very proud.

A PERSONAL POSTSCRIPT

1 State Secretariat for Migration.

2 Kanton Bern Polizei- und Militärdirektion.

3 State Secretariat for Migration.

4 ch.ch The Swiss Authorities Online.

5 State Secretariat for Migration.

6 *Ibid.*

7 *Ibid.*

8 nzz.ch.

9 swissinfo.ch.

10 aargauerzeitung.ch.

11 Federal Statistical Office.

12 Eurostat.

13 Federal Statistical Office.

14 *Ibid.*

15 Federal Commission for Women's Issues.

16 *Ibid.*

17 Federal Statistical Office.

18 Federal Department of Foreign Affairs.

19 Visit Britain.

FURTHER READING

Andrew Beattie, *The Alps: A Cultural History*, Signal Books, 2006

Angela Bennett, *The Geneva Convention: The Hidden Origins of the Red Cross*, Sutton, 2006*

Diccon Bewes, *Around Switzerland in 80 Maps*, Helvetiq, 2015

Diccon Bewes, *Slow Train to Switzerland*, Nicholas Brealey, 2013

Paul Bilton, *Xenophobe's Guide to the Swiss*, Oval Books, 2008

Betty Bossi, *The Swiss Cookbook*, Betty Bossi Verlag, 2009

Tom Bower, *Blood Money*, Pan, 1997*

R. James Breidling, *Swiss Made*, Profile Books, 2013

Xavier Casile, *So Sweet Zerland*, Good Heidi Productions, 2008*

Clive H. Church & Randolph C. Head, *A Concise History of Switzerland*, Cambridge University Press, 2013

Angelo Codevilla, *Between the Alps and a Hard Place*, Regnery, 2000

Dianne Dicks (ed.), *Ticking along with the Swiss*, Bergli Books, 1995

Gérard Geiger (ed.), *1291–1991: The Swiss Economy*, SQP Publications, 1991*

Mavis Guinard, *Made in Switzerland: Petit Guide de la Suisse insolite*, Metropolis, 2007

Stephen Halbrook, *Target Switzerland*, De Capo Press, 2003

Stephen Halbrook, *The Swiss and the Nazis*, Casemate, 2005

David Hampshire, *Living and Working in Switzerland*, Survival Books, 2015

Derek Jackson, *Swiss Army Knives: A Collector's Companion*, Compendium Publishing, 2007

Hanspeter Kriesi & Alexander Trechsel, *The Politics of Switzerland*, Cambridge University Press, 2008

Joëlle Kuntz, *Switzerland: How an Alpine Pass became a Country*, Historiator Editions, 2008

Sergio Lievano & Nicole Egger, *Hoi: Your Swiss German Survival Guide*, Bergli Books, 2005

Sergio Lievano & Wolfgang Koydl, *Switzerland: A Cartoon Survival Guide*, Bergli Books, 2017

Kendall Maycock, *Culture Smart! Switzerland*, Bergli Books, 2004

John McPhee, *La Place de la Concorde Suisse*, Noonday Press, 1994

Jean Henri Merle d'Aubigné, *For God and his People: Ulrich Zwingli*, BJU Press, 2000*

Grégoire Nappey, *Swiss History in a Nutshell*, Bergli Books, 2010

Clare O'Dea, *The Naked Swiss*, Bergli Books, 2016

Margaret Oertig-Davidson, *Beyond Chocolate: Understanding Swiss Culture*, Bergli Books, 2002

Max Oettli, *Culture Shock! Switzerland*, Marshall Cavendish, 2009
Stephen O'Shea, *The Alps*, W.W. Norton, 2017
Andie Pilot, *Helvetic Kitchen*, Bergli Books, 2017
Jim Ring, *How the English Made the Alps*, John Murray, 2001*
Padraig Rooney, *The Gilded Chalet*, Nicholas Brealey, 2015
Jonathan Steinberg, *Why Switzerland?* Cambridge University Press, 2015
Sue Style, *A Taste of Switzerland*, Bergli Books, 1996
Mark Twain, *A Tramp Abroad*, Penguin, 1998
Isabel Vincent, *Hitler's Silent Partners*, William Morrow, 1997*
Richard Wildblood, *What Makes Switzerland Unique?*, The Book Guild, 1990*
Switzerland in its Diversity, Hallwag Kümmerly+Frey, 2009

A few books set in Switzerland
Anita Brookner, *Hotel du Lac*
Vicki Cooper, *The Bears Are Coming Back*
Graham Greene, *Dr Fischer of Geneva*
Richard Harvell, *The Bells*
Thomas Mann, *The Magic Mountain*
Christopher Reich, *Rules of Deception*
Joel Ross, *White Flag Down*
Mary Shelley, *Frankenstein*
Rose Tremain, *The Gustav Sonata*

Some Swiss authors available in English
Nicolas Bouvier, *The Way of the World*
Selina Chönz, *A Bell for Ursli; Florina and the Wild Bird*
Friedrich Dürrenmatt, *Inspector Barlach Mysteries; The Physicist*
Max Frisch, *Homo Faber*
Jeremias Gotthelf, *The Black Spider*
Franz Hohler, *At Home*
Zoë Jenny, *The Pollen Room; The Sky Is Changing*
Pascal Mercier, *Night Train to Lisbon*
Johanna Spyri, *Heidi*
Beat Sterchi, *The Cow*
Claude Sulzer, *The Perfect Waiter*
Martin Suter, *A Deal with the Devil; Small World*
Robert Walser, *The Assistant; Institute Benjamenta; The Walk*
Johann Wyss, *Swiss Family Robinson*

* Denotes currently out of print

ACKNOWLEDGEMENTS

Many authors say that their books are their babies. This one was conceived at the Geneva Writers' Conference but its birth was thanks to the publisher of the first edition, Nick Brealey, who took a leap of faith for which I am forever grateful. To Nick (a different one), Ben and Louise at Nicholas Brealey Publishing, now an imprint of John Murray Press, thanks for everything.

I probably committed more than one social *faux pas* so sorry to all my Swiss friends for that. Answering my many questions about your lives and your country helped immensely. That goes doubly for all my former colleagues at Stauffacher Bookshop.

A special mention for Markus, who has shown how good a friend a Swiss man can be; without him this book would have been far less interesting. And Jane and Marcela, who make my life as an expat in Bern so much better.

Not forgetting, in no particular order, Julie Lennard, Sebastien Desprez, Christina Warren, Kate Coleman, Martin Girven, Kate Dietrich, David Rose, Karen Davies, Peter Schibli, Beat Stoller, James Woodall, Tom Derungs, Catherine Nelson-Pollard, Martin Tschirren, Matt Wake, Zelda McKillop, Hermann Bachmann, Patricia Yates, Patrick Jost, Beth Zurbuchen, Hugh Brune, Anna Galvani, Jonathan Spirig, K. Starr Schoell, Elsbeth Baxter, Vicki Cooper, Daniel Geiser, Robin Bognuda, Beatrice Meier, Dimitri Burkhard, Marcelline Kuonen, John Sivell, Christa Schuppli, Michael Gaedeke, Simon Denoth, Eric Mueller, the Scheibelhofer family and all my ever-supportive friends in the book group. Each of you knows how you helped me create this book.

Thanks also to my sister Sara, my brother Andrew and particularly my parents, for instilling a love of travel in me from a very early age. And Gregor, whose love and support have been there from the beginning of this journey. This is for you all.

CREDITS

Unless marked with *, all photographs © Diccon Bewes.

Photos on front cover, clockwise from top left:
The Eiger
Heidi House (with Gregor) above St Moritz. Built in 1792, it was used
    in 1977–78 TV production of *Heidi*, then moved here in 1979
Paddlesteamer *Uri* on Lake Lucerne
Swiss flag on Lake Brienz
Bernina Express
Bundesplatz fountains, Bern
Mountain train*
A cow in Canton St Gallen
WAB train (in front of the Eiger) at Kleine Scheidegg
Model planes at Swiss Miniatur, Ticino
Toblerone*
Alpine scene*
Zytglogge clock tower, Bern
Schloss Oberhofen at Lake Thun
Farmhouse above Wildhaus
Alpine valley*
Train on Brisio viaduct*
Schreckhorn, Berner Oberland
Clock*
Bundeshaus, Bern
Holländerturm (Dutch Tower) in Waisenhausplatz, Bern
Madonna del Sasso monastery above Locarno
Cable car up to Stockhorn

Photos on back cover and spine
Lake Lucerne
Alpine cow

SELECT INDEX

Note: entries marked with an asterisk refer to a map

ALSO BY DICCON BEWES

Slow Train to Switzerland
One Tour, Two Trips, 150 Years – and a World of Change Apart

'Charming'
The Spectator

It was the tour that changed the way we travel. In the summer of 1863 seven people left London on a train that would take them on a thrilling adventure across the Alps. They were the Junior United Alpine Club and members of Thomas Cook's first Conducted Tour of Switzerland. For them it was an exciting novelty; for us it was the birth of mass tourism, and it started with the Swiss. 150 years later Diccon Bewes set off on the same three-week trip. She went in search of adventure, he went in search of her, and found far more than he expected.

'Fans of Bill Bryson will find him a kindred spirit'
The Lady

ISBN 978-1-857-88651-1